PERSPECTIVES ON *THE PASSION OF THE CHRIST*

❖

PERSPECTIVES ON
THE PASSION OF THE CHRIST

❖

RELIGIOUS THINKERS AND WRITERS EXPLORE THE ISSUES

RAISED BY THE CONTROVERSIAL MOVIE

MIRAMAX BOOKS

ISBN 1-4013-5959-0

COPYRIGHT © MIRAMAX FILM CORP.

PRINTED IN THE UNITED STATES OF AMERICA

FOR INFORMATION ADDRESS:

HYPERION

77 WEST 66TH STREET

NEW YORK, NEW YORK 10023-6298

FIRST EDITION

10 9 8 7 6 5 4 3 2 1

CONTENTS

❖

JESUS OF HOLLYWOOD

Reinhartz is Dean of Graduate Studies at Wilfrid Laurier University,
Ontario, Canada, where she is also Professor in the Department of
Religion and Culture. A specialist in first-century Judaism and
Christianity, she has written extensively on the Gospel of John, anti-
Judaism in the New Testament, biblical narrative, and the Bible and film.
Her most recent book, *Jesus of Hollywood,* will be published by Oxford
University Press.

COMMITMENT TO COMMUNITY: INTERFAITH RELATIONS AND FAITHFUL WITNESS

Both authors, members of the original ad hoc scholars group that exam-
ined Gibson's script, are clergymen as well as leaders and community
organizers for interfaith relations. Korn, an Orthodox rabbi, is Adjunct
Professor of Jewish Thought in the Department of Christian-Jewish
Studies at Seton Hall University and former director of Interfaith Affairs
at the Anti-Defamation League; Pawlikowski, a priest of the Servite
Order, is Professor of Social Ethics at Catholic Theological Union in
Chicago.

FIRST TAKE THE LOG OUT OF YOUR OWN EYE: DIFFERENT VIEWPOINTS, DIFFERENT MOVIES

Levine is the E. Rhodes and Leona B. Carpenter Professor of New
Testament Studies at Vanderbilt University, and one of the original contributors to the Scholars Report.

JONATHAN BURNHAM

❖

FOREWORD

The Passion of the Christ is a remarkable phenomenon. One of the highest-grossing films of all time, it has acted as a cultural lightning rod, provoking devotion and revulsion, admiration and loathing. It has evoked strongly opposed responses in people within religious communities, and, at the same time, has helped to forge new bonds across denominational lines. Exposing significant differences in the way that diverse readers—historians, theologians, churchgoers of various kinds—understand the New Testament, it has also renewed questions about the literal reading of Scriptures and the spawning and sponsoring of anti-Semitism. Across the board, it has stirred up fresh debate over the significance of the mission and message of Jesus Christ.

THE EIGHTEEN ESSAYS GATHERED HERE represent some of the broad-ranging responses *The Passion* has inspired. We have brought together journalists, historians, and theologians, rabbis, priests, and ministers to comment on this movie and the troubling—and vital—questions it has raised. Protestants from the Evangelical, Episcopalian, United Church of Christ,

Methodist, and Lutheran communities have contributed, as have Catholic laypeople and Catholics in religious orders. So have Reform, Conservative, and Orthodox Jews. No single perspective on the movie dominates this collection. But all the contributors share a commitment to the importance of using this charged cultural moment as an occasion to reflect on ideas and ideals, beliefs and traditions, that matter to all of us.

JON MEACHAM

❖

WHO REALLY KILLED JESUS?

It is night, in a quiet, nearly deserted garden in Jerusalem. A figure is praying; his friends sleep a short distance away. We are in the last hours of the life of Jesus of Nazareth, in the spring of roughly the year 30, at the time of the Jewish feast of Passover. The country—first-century Judea, the early-twenty-first-century's Israel—is part of the Roman Empire. The prefect, Pontius Pilate, is Caesar's ranking representative in the province, a place riven with fierce internal disputes. Jesus comes from Galilee, a kind of backwater; as a Jewish healer and teacher, he has attracted great notice in the years, months, and days leading up to this hour.

His popularity seemed to be surging among at least some of the thousands of pilgrims gathered in the city for Passover. Crowds cheered him, proclaiming him the Messiah, which to first-century Jewish ears meant he was the "king of the Jews" who heralded the coming of the Kingdom of God, a time in which the yoke of Roman rule would be thrown off, ushering in an age of light for Israel. Hungry for liberation and deliverance, some of those in the teeming city were apparently flocking to Jesus, threatening to upset the delicate balance of power in Jerusalem.

The priests responsible for the Temple had an understanding with the Romans: the Jewish establishment would do what it could to keep the peace, or else Pilate would strike. And so the high priest, Caiaphas, dispatches a party to arrest Jesus. Guided by Judas, they find him in Gethsemane. In the language of the Revised Standard Version of the Bible, there is this exchange: "Whom do you seek?" Jesus asks. "Jesus of Nazareth." The answer comes quickly. "I am he."

Thus begins the final chapter of the most influential story in Western history. For Christians, the Passion—from the Latin *passus,* the word means "having suffered" or "having undergone"—is the very heart of their faith. Down the ages, however, when read without critical perspective and a proper sense of history, these Christian narratives have sometimes been contorted to lay the responsibility for Jesus' execution at the feet of the Jewish people, a contortion that has long fueled the fires of anti-Semitism.

Into this perennially explosive terrain comes a controversial new movie directed by Mel Gibson, *The Passion of the Christ,* a powerful and troubling work about Jesus' last hours. "The Holy Ghost was working through me on this film," Gibson has said. The movie, which was released on February 25, 2004, Ash Wednesday, has provoked a pitched battle between those who think the film unfairly blames the Jewish people for Jesus' death and those who are instead focused on the emotional power and piety of Gibson's depiction of Jesus' torment. "It is as it was," the aged Pope John Paul II is said to have remarked after seeing the film, and Billy Graham was so moved by a screening that he wept. One can see why these supremely gifted pastors were impressed, for Gibson obviously reveres the Christ of faith, and much of his movie is a literal-minded rendering of the most dramatic passages scattered through the four Gospels.

But the Bible can be a problematic source. Though countless believers take it as the immutable word of God, Scripture is not always a faithful record of historical events; the Bible is the product of human authors who were writing in particular times and places with particular points to make and visions to advance. And the roots of Christian anti-Semitism lie in overly literal readings—which are, in fact, misreadings—of many New Testament texts. When the Gospel authors implicated "the Jews" in Jesus' Passion, they did not mean all Jewish people then alive, much less those then unborn. The writers had a very specific group in mind: the Temple elite who believed that Jesus might provoke Pilate.

Gibson is an ultraconservative Roman Catholic, a traditionalist who does not acknowledge many of the reforms of the Second Vatican Council (1962–1965). He favors a much older version of the Latin mass, does not eat meat on Fridays and adheres to an unusually fundamentalist interpretation of Scripture and doctrine—a hard-line creed that he grew up with and that he rediscovered about a dozen years ago. "He began meditating on the Passion and the death of Jesus," said James Caviezel, the actor who played Jesus in *The Passion*. "In doing so, he said the wounds of Christ healed his wounds. And I think the film expresses that." Gibson set out to stick to his view of the Gospels and he has made virtually no nod to critical analysis or context. As an artist, of course, he has the right to make any movie he wants, and many audiences will find the story vivid and familiar.

The film Gibson has made, however, has revived an ancient and divisive argument: Who really killed Jesus? As a matter of history, the Roman Empire did; as a matter of theology, the sins of the world drove Jesus to the cross, and the Catholic Church holds that Christians themselves bear "the gravest responsibility for the torments inflicted upon Jesus." Yet for nearly two thousand years, some Christians have persecuted the Jewish people on the grounds that Jews were responsible for the death of the first-century prophet who has come to be seen as the Christ. Now, four decades after the Second Vatican Council repudiated the idea that the Jewish people were guilty of "deicide," many Christian theologians and Jewish leaders fear the movie, with its theatrically contrasting portraits of the Jewish high priest Caiaphas leading an angry mob and of Pilate as a reluctant, sympathetic executioner, may slow or even reverse forty years of work explaining the common bonds between Judaism and Christianity. Gibson has vehemently defended the film against charges of anti-Semitism, saying he does not believe in blood guilt and citing the Church teaching that the transgressions and failings of all mankind led to the Passion—not just the sins of the Jewish people. "So it's not singling them out and saying, 'They did it.' That's not so," Gibson told the Global Catholic Network in January. "We're all culpable. I don't want to lynch any Jews... I love them. I pray for them."

The fight about God, meanwhile, has been good for Mammon: Gibson has made what is likely to be the most watched Passion play in history. Sales are roaring along and breaking all records for R-rated and subtitled movies. Evangelical congregations have bought out screenings, and religious leaders of all denominations have urged believers to see the film. This surprising alliance between Gibson, as a traditionalist Catholic, and evangelical Protestants seems born out of a common belief that the larger secular world—including the mainstream media—is essentially hostile to Christianity. Finding a global celebrity like the Oscar-winning Gibson in their camp was an unexpected gift. *The Passion of the Christ*, Billy Graham has said, is "a lifetime of sermons in one movie."

Shot in Italy, financed by Gibson, the $25 million film is tightly focused on Jesus' final twelve hours. Some flashbacks give a hint—but only a hint—of context, with episodes touching on Jesus' childhood, the triumphant entry into Jerusalem, the Sermon on the Mount, the Last Supper. The characters speak Aramaic and Latin, and the movie is subtitled in English, which turns it into a kind of artifact, as though the action is unfolding at a slight remove. To tell his story, Gibson has amalgamated the four Gospel accounts and was reportedly inspired by the visions of two nuns: Mary of Agreda (1602–1665) and Anne Catherine Emmerich (1774–1824). The two nuns were creatures of their time, offering mystical testimony that included allusions to the alleged blood guilt of the Jewish people.

Jesus' arrest, scourging, and crucifixion are depicted in harsh, explicit detail in the movie. One of Jesus' eyes is swollen shut from his first beating as he is dragged from Gethsemane; the Roman torture, the long path to Golgotha bearing the wooden cross, and the nailing of Jesus' hands and feet to the beams are filmed unsparingly. The effect of the violence is at first shocking, then numbing, and finally reaches a point where many viewers may spend as much time clinically wondering how any man could have survived such beatings as they do sympathizing with his plight. There are tender scenes with Mary, Jesus' mother, and Mary Magdalene. "It is accomplished," Jesus says from the cross. His mother, watching her brutally tortured son die, murmurs, "Amen."

As moving as many moments in the film are, though, several scenes raise important historical issues about how Gibson chose to portray the Jewish people and the Romans. To take the film's dramatized account of the Passion as history will give most audiences a misleading picture of what probably happened in those epochal hours so long ago. In Gibson's version, the Jewish priests and their followers are the villains, demanding the death of Jesus again and again; Pilate is a malleable governor forced into handing down the death sentence.

In fact, in the age of Roman domination, only Rome crucified. The crime was sedition, not blasphemy—a civil crime, not a religious one. The two men who were killed along with Jesus are identified in some translations as "thieves," but the Greek that stands behind the English actually means "insurgents" or "brigands," attesting to politically-motivated forms of "theft," like raiding Roman supply lines. This New Testament word supports the idea that crucifixion was a political weapon used to send a message to those still living: beware of revolution or riot, or Rome will do this to you, too. The two earliest and most reliable extra-biblical references to Jesus—those of the historians Josephus and Tacitus—say Jesus was executed by Pilate. The Roman prefect was Caiaphas' political superior and even controlled when the Jewish priests could wear their vestments and thus conduct Jewish rites in the Temple. Pilate was not the humane figure Gibson depicts. According to Philo of Alexandria, a contemporary of Jesus, the prefect was of "inflexible, stubborn, and cruel disposition," and known to execute troublemakers without trial.

So why was the Gospel story—the story Gibson has drawn on—told in a way that makes "the Jews" look worse than the Romans? The Bible did not descend from heaven fully formed and edged in gilt. The writers of Matthew, Mark, Luke, and John shaped their narratives several decades after Jesus' death to attract converts and make their young religion—understood by many Christians to be a faction of Judaism—attractive to as broad an audience as possible.

The historical problem of dealing with the various players in the Passion narratives is complicated by the exact meaning of the Greek words usually translated as "the Jews." The phrase does not include the entire Jewish population of Jesus' day—to the writers, Jesus and his followers were certainly not included—and seems to refer mostly to the Temple elite. The Jewish people were divided into numerous sects and parties, each believing itself to be the true or authentic representative of the ancestral faith and each generally hostile to the others.

Given these rivalries, we can begin to understand the origins of the unflattering Gospel image of the Temple establishment: the elite looked down on Jesus' followers, so the New Testament authors portrayed the priests in a negative light. We can also see why the writers downplayed the role of the ruling Romans in Jesus' death. The advocates of Christianity—then a new, struggling faith—understandably chose to placate, not antagonize, the powers that were. Why remind the world that the earthly empire which still ran the Mediterranean had executed your hero as a revolutionary?

The film opens with a haunting image of Jesus praying in Gethsemane. A satanic figure—Gibson's dramatic adaptation from Emmerich—tempts him:

no one man, the devil says, can carry the whole burden of sin. As in the New Testament, the implication is that the world is in the grip of evil, and Jesus has come to deliver us from the powers of darkness through his death and resurrection—an upheaval of the very order of things. Though in such anguish that his sweat turns to blood, Jesus accepts his fate.

In an ensuing scene, Mary Magdalene calls for help from Roman soldiers as Jesus is taken indoors to be interrogated by the priests. "They've arrested him," she cries. A Temple policeman intervenes, tells the Romans "she's crazy" and assures them that Jesus "broke the Temple laws, that's all." When word of the trouble reaches Pilate, he is told, "There is trouble within the walls. Caiaphas had some prophet arrested." It is true that the Temple leaders had no use for Jesus, but these lines of dialogue—which, taken together, suggest Jewish control over the situation—are not found in the Gospels.

The idea of a nighttime trial as depicted in Gibson's movie is also problematic. The Gospels do not agree on what happened between Jesus' arrest and his appearance before Pilate save for one detail: Jesus was brought before the high priest in some setting. In the movie, Jesus is interrogated before a great gathering of Jewish officials, possibly the Sanhedrin, and witnesses come forth to accuse him of working magic with the devil, of claiming to be able to destroy the Temple and raise it up again in three days, and of calling himself "the Son of God." Another cries: "He's said if we don't eat his flesh and drink his blood, we won't inherit eternal life." Gibson does indicate that Jesus has supporters; one man calls the proceeding "a travesty," and another asks, "Where are the other members of the council?"—a suggestion that Caiaphas and his own circle are taking action that not everyone would agree with. The climax comes when Caiaphas asks Jesus: "Are you the Messiah?" and Jesus says, "I am..." and alludes to himself as "the Son of Man." There is a gasp; the high priest rends his garments and declares Jesus a blasphemer.

There is much here to give the thinking believer pause. "Son of God" and "Son of Man" were fairly common appellations for religious figures in the first century. The accusation about eating Jesus' flesh and blood—obviously a Christian image of the Eucharist—does not appear in any Gospel trial scene. And it was not "blasphemy" to think of yourself as the "Messiah," which more than a few Jewish figures had claimed to be without meeting Jesus' fate, except possibly at the hands of the Romans. The definition of blasphemy was a source of fierce Jewish argument, but it turned on taking God's name in vain—and nothing in the Gospel trial scenes supports the idea that Jesus crossed that line.

The best historical reconstruction of what really happened is that Jesus had a fairly large or at least vocal following at a time of anxiety in the capital, and the Jewish authorities wanted to get rid of him before overexcited pilgrims rallied around him, drawing down Pilate's wrath. "It is expedient for you," Caiaphas says to his fellow priests in John, "that one man should die for the people" so that "the whole nation should not perish."

As the day dawns, Jesus is taken to Pilate, and it is here that Gibson slips farthest from history. Pilate is presented as a sensible and sensitive if not particularly strong ruler. "Isn't [Jesus] the prophet you welcomed into the city?" Pilate asks. "Can any of you explain this madness to me?" There is, however, no placating Caiaphas.

The scene of a crowd of Jews crying out "Crucify him! Crucify him!" before Pilate has been a staple of Passion plays for centuries, but it is very difficult to imagine Caesar's man being bullied by the people he usually handled roughly. When Pilate had first come to Judea, he had ordered imperial troops to carry images of Caesar into the city; he appropriated sacred Temple funds to build an aqueduct, prompting a protest he put down with violence; about five years after Jesus' execution, Pilate broke up a gathering around a prophet in Samaria with cavalry, killing so many people that he was recalled to Rome to explain himself.

Jesus seems very much alone before Pilate, and this raises a historical riddle. If Jesus is a severe enough threat to merit such attention and drastic action, where are his supporters? In Gibson's telling, they are silent or scared. Some probably were, and some may not have known of the arrest, which happened in secret, but it seems unlikely that a movement that threatened the whole capital would so quickly and so completely dwindle to a few disciples, sympathetic onlookers, Mary, and Mary Magdalene.

In his memorable if manufactured crowd scene, Gibson originally included a line that has had dire consequences for the Jewish people through the ages. The prefect, the picture of the just ruler, is again improbably resisting the crowd. Frustrated, desperate, bloodthirsty, the mob says: "His blood be on us and on our children!" Gibson ultimately cut the cry from his subtitles, and he was right to do so. Again, consider the source of the dialogue: a partisan Gospel writer. The Gospels were composed to present Jesus in the best possible light to potential converts in the Roman Empire—and to put the Temple leadership in the worst possible light. And many scholars believe that the author of Matthew, which is the only Gospel to include the "His blood be on us" line, was writing after the destruction of the Temple in 70 and that he inserted the words to help explain why such misery had come upon the people of Jerusalem. According to this argument, blood had already fallen on them and on their children.

A moment later in Gibson's movie, Pilate is questioning Jesus and, facing a silent prisoner, says, "You will not speak to me? Do you not know that I have power to release you, and power to crucify you?" Jesus then replies: "...he who delivered me to you has the greater sin." The "he" in this case is Caiaphas. John's point in putting this line in Jesus' mouth is almost certainly to take a gibe at the Temple elite. But in the dramatic milieu of the movie, it can be taken to mean that the Jews, through Caiaphas, are more responsible for Jesus' death than the Romans are—an implication unsupported by history.

The Temple elite undoubtedly played a key role in the death of Jesus; Josephus noted that the Nazarene had been "accused by those of the highest standing amongst us," meaning among the Jerusalem Jews. But Pilate's own culpability and ultimate authority are indisputable as well. If Jesus had not been a political threat, why bother with the trouble of crucifixion? There is also evidence that Jesus' arrest was part of a broader pattern of violence or feared violence this Passover. Barabbas, the man who was released instead of Jesus, was, according to Mark, "among the rebels in prison, who had committed murder in the insurrection"—suggesting that Pilate was concerned with "rebels" and had already confronted an "insurrection" some time before he interrogated Jesus.

Except for the release of Barabbas, there is no hint of this context in Gibson's movie. *The Passion of the Christ* includes an invented scene in which Pilate laments his supposed dilemma. "If I don't condemn him," he tells his wife, "Caiaphas will start a rebellion; if I do, his followers will." Caiaphas was in no position to start a rebellion over Jesus; he and Pilate were in a way allies, and when serious revolt did come, in 66, it would be over grievances about heavy-handed Roman rule, not over a particular religious figure, and even then the priests would plead with the people not to rebel. In the movie, far from urging calm, the priests lead the crowd, and Pilate, far from using his power to control the mob, gives in. And so Jesus is sentenced to death.

Clear evidence of the political nature of the execution—that Pilate and the high priest were ridding themselves of a "messiah" who might disrupt society, not offer salvation—is the sign Pilate ordered affixed to Jesus' cross. The message is not from the knowing Romans to the evil Jews. It is, rather, a scornful signal to the crowds that this death awaits any man whom the pilgrims proclaim "the king of the Jews."

The Roman soldiers who torture Jesus and bully him toward Golgotha are portrayed as evil, taunting, and vicious, and they almost certainly were. Without authority from the New Testament, Caiaphas, meanwhile, is depicted as a grim witness to the scourging and crucifixion. After Jesus, carrying his cross, sees the faces of the priests, he is shown saying: "No one takes my life from me, but I lay it down of my own accord." Is this intended to absolve the priests? Perhaps. From the cross, Jesus says: "Forgive them, for they know not what they do."

As clouds gather and Jesus dies, a single raindrop—a tear from God the Father?—falls from the sky. A storm has come; the gates of hell are broken; back in the Temple, Caiaphas, buffeted by the earthquake, cries out in anguish amid the gloom. Then there is light, and a discarded shroud, and a risen Christ bearing the stigmata leaves the tomb. It is Easter.

Are the gospels themselves anti-Semitic? Not in the sense the term has come to mean in the early twenty-first century. But they are polemics, written by followers of a certain sect who disdained other factions in the way the Old Testament was dismissive of, say, Israelite religious practices not sanctioned by Jerusalem. Without understanding the milieu in which the texts were composed, we can easily misinterpret them. The tragic history of the persecution of the Jewish people since the Passion clearly shows what can go wrong when the Gospels are not read with care.

Most of the early Christians *were* Jews and saw themselves as such. Only later, beginning roughly at the end of the first century, did some Christians start to view and present themselves as a people entirely separate from other Jewish groups. And for centuries still—even after Constantine's conversion in the fourth century—some Jewish people considered themselves Christians. It was as the church's theology took shape, culminating in the Council of Nicaea in 325, that Jesus became the doctrinal Christ, the Son of God "who for us men and our salvation," the council's original creed declared, "descended, was incarnate, and was made man, suffered and rose again the third day, ascended into heaven and cometh to judge the living and the dead."

As the keeper of the apostolic faith, the Roman Catholic Church has long struggled with the issue of Jewish complicity in Jesus' death. Always in the atmosphere, anti-Semitism took center stage with the coming of the First Crusade in the eleventh century, when Christian soldiers on their way to expel Muslims from the Holy Land massacred European Jews. By the early Middle

Ages, Christian anti-Semitism lent a religious veneer to political decisions by the secular authorities of the day, decisions that often penalized or curtailed the rights of the Jewish people. The justification for anti-Semitism was articulated by Pope Innocent III, who reigned in the early years of the thirteenth century: "The blasphemers of the Christian name," he said, should be "forced into the servitude of which they made themselves deserving when they raised their sacrilegious hands against Him who had come to confer true liberty upon them, thus calling down His blood upon themselves and their children."

After the horror of Hitler's Final Solution, the Roman Church began to reassess its relationship with the Jewish people. The result from Vatican II was a thoughtful and compelling statement on deicide. "True, the Jewish authorities and those who followed their lead pressed for the death of Christ; still, what happened in His passion cannot be charged against all the Jews, without distinction, then alive, nor against the Jews of today…in her rejection of every persecution against any man, the Church, mindful of the patrimony she shares with the Jews and moved…by the Gospel's spiritual love, decries hatred, persecutions, displays of anti-Semitism, directed against Jews at any time and by anyone."

The council went on to make another crucial point undercutting the use of the Passion to fuel anti-Semitism, either in fact or in drama. "Besides, as the Church has always held and holds now," *Nostra Aetate* (*In Our Time*) says, "Christ underwent his passion and death freely, because of the sins of men and out of infinite love, in order that all may reach salvation." And his mercy is not limited to those who confess the Christian faith. "The Church reproves, as foreign to the mind of Christ, any discrimination against men or harassment of them because of their race, color, condition of life, or religion."

If pointing to a forty-year-old church teaching is not enough, we can also look back more than four hundred years to find the seeds of reconciliation and grace. At the Council of Trent in the sixteenth century, the Roman Church stated as a theological principle that all men share the responsibility for the Passion—and that Christians bear a particular burden. "In this guilt [for the death of Jesus] are involved all those who fall frequently into sin..." read the catechism of the council. "This guilt seems more enormous in us than in the Jews since, if they had known it, they would never have crucified the Lord of glory; while we, on the contrary, professing to know him, yet denying him by our actions, seem in some sort to lay violent hands on him."

In the battle over his project, Gibson has veered between defiance and conciliation. "This film collectively blames humanity [for] the death of Jesus," he said in his Global Catholic Network interview. "Now there are no exemptions there. All right? I'm the first on the line for culpability. I did it. Christ died for all men for all times." Of critics who think his film could perpetuate dangerous stereotypes, he said: "They've kind of, you know, come out with this mantra again and again and again. You know, 'He's an anti-Semite.' 'He's an anti-Semite.' 'He's an anti-Semite.' 'He's an anti-Semite.' I'm not." In a letter to Anti-Defamation League national director Abraham Foxman last week, Gibson wrote: "It is my deepest belief, as I am sure it is yours, that all who ever breathe life on this Earth are children of God and my most binding obligation to them, as a brother in this waking world, is to love them." The news of the letter broke on Tuesday; late last week David Elcott, the U.S. director of interreligious affairs for the American Jewish Committee, reported that he had been present at a screening when someone asked Gibson, "Who opposes Jesus?" Gibson's Manichaean reply: "They are either satanic or the dupes of Satan."

Was there any way for him to have made a movie about the Passion and avoided this firestorm? There was. There are a number of existing Catholic pastoral instructions detailing the ways in which the faithful should dramatize or discuss the Passion. "To attempt to utilize the four passion narratives literally by picking one passage from one gospel and the next from another gospel, and so forth," reads one such instruction, "is to risk violating the integrity of the texts themselves...it is not sufficient for the producers of passion dramatizations to respond to responsible criticism simply by appealing to the notion that 'it's in the Bible.'" The Church also urges "the greatest caution" when "it is a question of passages that seem to show the Jewish people as such in an unfavorable light." The teachings suggest dropping scenes of large, chanting Jewish crowds and avoiding the device of a Sanhedrin trial. They also note that there is evidence that Pilate was not a "vacillating administrator" who "himself found 'no fault' with Jesus and sought, though in a weak way, to free him." A reference in Luke, instructions point out, and historical sources indicate that he was, rather, a "ruthless tyrant," and "there is, then, room for more than one dramatic style of portraying the character of Pilate and still being faithful to the biblical record." The United States Conference of Catholic Bishops has reissued these teachings in book form to coincide with the release of Gibson's movie.

In the best of all possible worlds, *The Passion of the Christ* will prompt constructive conversations about the origins of the religion that claims 2 billion followers around the globe, conversations that ought to lead believers to see that Christian anti-Semitism should be seen as an impossibility—a contradiction in terms. To hate Jews because they are Jews—to hate anyone, in fact—is a sin in the Christian cosmos, for Jesus commands his followers to love their neighbor as themselves. On another level, anti-Semitism is a form of illogical and self-defeating self-loathing. Bluntly put, Jesus had to die for the Christian story to unfold, and the proper Christian posture toward the Jewish people should be one of respect, for the man Christians choose to see as their savior came from the ancient tribe of Judah, the very name from which "Jew" is derived. As children of Abraham, St. Paul said, Christians and Jews are branches of the same tree, linked together in the mystery of God.

Let us end where we, and Gibson's movie, began—in the garden, in darkness. The guards have come to arrest Jesus. He watches as his disciples come to blows with the troops. Punches are thrown, and one of Jesus' men lashes out with a weapon, slashing off the ear of a servant of the high priest. Watching, removed from the fray, Jesus intervenes, commanding: "Put up thy sword," making real the New Testament commandment to love one another as he loved us, even unto death—a commandment whose roots stretch back to the nineteenth chapter of Leviticus: "You shall love your neighbor as yourself; I am the Lord."

Amid the clash over Gibson's film and the debates about the nature of God, whether you believe Jesus to be the savior of mankind or to have been an interesting first-century figure who left behind an inspiring moral philosophy, perhaps we can at least agree on this image of Jesus of Nazareth: Confronted by violence, he chose peace; by hate, love; by sin, forgiveness—a powerful example for us all, whoever our gods may be.

JAY TOLSON AND LINDA KULMAN

❖

THE OTHER JESUS

HOW A JEWISH REFORMER LOST HIS JEWISH IDENTITY

The audience gathering for a prerelease screening of Mel Gibson's *The Passion of the Christ* at an Arlington, Virginia, cineplex had few apprehensions about the film they were getting ready to see. Most belonged to one of the area's largest evangelical churches. And even before the lights were dimmed, many said they were eagerly anticipating an "accurate" and "truthful" version of the Passion story. A number also admitted to being puzzled and even skeptical about the allegations of anti-Semitism that had been swirling around the film for months. "Some of my friends who are Jewish are planning to see the movie," one young woman said.

The lobby chatter after the viewing suggested that the film more than lived up to the high expectations. "I could see it ten more times," raved Sara Correa, a mortgage banker, as she left the theater. She found no anti-Semitism in the film, she said, and even the violence seemed justified to her. "It's hardly more graphic than the junk many adults allow their kids to see on TV. And this violence," she added, "has a purpose."

As months of carefully stoked controversy have made clear, not everyone who has seen the movie—either before or after the official opening—has given it such a thumbs-up. Prominent Jewish leaders including Abraham Foxman, head of the Anti-Defamation League, while not accusing Gibson or his film of being anti-Semitic, feel that it will fuel or reinforce anti-Jewish sentiments—no small matter when such sentiments appear to be on the rise around the world.

And Jews are not the only ones who think Gibson's portrayal of the events leading up to and including Christ's crucifixion is an exploitative and sensationalistic distortion of the story. To some viewers of the film, the alleged accuracy is itself highly questionable. "What on earth do people mean by accurate?" asks W. Barnes Tatum, a professor of religion at Greensboro College. "A lot of people mean that it's faithful to the Bible, but accuracy from my point of view means being able to present a historical argument. Gibson's film is very sensitive to how somebody who's been arrested might be treated and what it's like to be crucified. But that very accuracy is counter to the New Testament." James Carroll, a former Catholic priest and author of *Constantine's Sword: The Church and the Jews*, describes the film as "a pornographic celebration of suffering."

At the very least, the film raises big questions—even for faithful Christians—about how people are to read, interpret, and understand the Scriptures on which Gibson has selectively and uncritically based his film. Gibson himself came close to saying as much in his remarks to Diane Sawyer during an ABC interview shortly before the film opened. "You know, critics who have a problem with me don't really have a problem with me and this film. They have a problem with the four Gospels. That's what their problem is."

Gibson might more accurately have said that people—including most Jews, quite a few Christians, and many who claim no religious affiliation at all—have long had a problem with the way Jesus' life and teachings have been represented and interpreted. And not just in the four Gospels but in the rest of the New Testament, as well as in the subsequent teachings of the many branches and sects of Christianity. For many devout Christians, in fact, struggling with those matters is a major part of their religious lives.

And little wonder, given that there are few other religions in which the claims of historical and theological truth are more confusingly mixed. Paramount among those confusions is the connection between Christianity and the religion of Judaism from which it emerged and with which it still claims a special if problematic tie. Specifically, Christians have always had to deal with the fact that the founder of their religion, the Jesus of Nazareth whom they declare to be both the Messiah ("Christ," in Greek) and the second part of the triune God was himself not a Christian but, indisputably, a Jew. From the earliest years of the Christian movement, followers of Jesus have tended to handle this fact in various ways: Some, particularly in the first centuries after the crucifixion, simply saw themselves as part of Judaism, or at least as one of the many contending versions of Judaism that then existed. Increasingly, though, Christians simply ignored or minimized Jesus' Jewishness, or else qualified it in such a way as to make Jesus seem at odds with mainstream Judaism. Yet others, more radically, came to deny that he was Jewish at all. To be sure, for the last five hundred years a growing number of clerics, theologians, and scholars have made the recovery of the historical Jesus a central concern. To the leaders of the Protestant Reformation, this effort was part of the struggle to throw off the "corrupted" misreadings and interpretations of the Catholic Church and to return to the real Jesus and his teachings. Yet even amid such attempts, a blend of church politics, long-held prejudice, and limited evidence impeded a full or fair examination of the specifically Jewish context of Jesus' prophetic ministry, well into the twentieth century.

That has begun to change during the last fifty years or so. Aided by the rise of the academic study of religion and by major textual and archaeological finds (including the mid-century discoveries of the Dead Sea Scrolls), scholars have made great strides in reconstructing the world of late Second Temple Judaism, particularly during those years around the life of Jesus. These efforts have helped to restore the fully Jewish context of Jesus' mission, even while revealing how the later church distanced their founder and his movement from their Jewish roots.

Geza Vermes, emeritus professor of Jewish studies at Oxford University, is arguably the dean of this recent scholarly enterprise. Three decades ago, in *Jesus the Jew*, he led the way by reading the Gospels of Mark, Matthew, and Luke (the so-called Synoptic Gospels, as distinct from the highly theological Gospel of John) as part of what he calls a "continuously evolving Jewish religious and literary creativity." Among other things, Vermes showed how the Synoptic Gospels drew on many of the same oral and written sources that later rabbinic writings would draw on. In one such source, the first-century BC Psalms of Solomon, for example, the psalmist evokes the coming Kingdom of God and anticipates a "Jewish savior-king establishing divine rule over Gentiles."

Vermes's reading of the Synoptic Gospels yields a figure who fits perfectly into first-century Galilee, an outstanding exemplar, he writes, of "the charismatic Judaism of wonder-working holy men such as the first-century BC Honi and Jesus' younger contemporary, Hanina ben Dosa, modelled on the biblical prophets such as Elijah and Elisha."

The Gospels can be read in many ways, Vermes acknowledges, and he does not disparage orthodox Christian interpretations. "But if you read them literally," he cautions, "without knowledge of what they describe in terms of institutions and politics, then suddenly the Jews can become different, the enemies, the opposition. What is really going on in them is a family quarrel within Judaism."

This is not strictly an academic matter for Vermes. In his view, a willful disregard of the Jewishness of Jesus and his teaching has been partly responsible for "all the nasty things" that are associated with Christian anti-Semitism. And it is not only Jews who share that concern. New Testament specialist Margaret Mitchell, a professor of religion at the University of Chicago and a

Roman Catholic, worries that Gibson's movie, like uncritical, ahistorical readings of the Gospels, will potentially "flatten what ought to be a curriculum for each generation of Christians to struggle with, including this strange fact of a religion starting in Judaism and then moving away from it." E. P. Sanders, a professor of religion at Duke University and a Methodist, puts it even more bluntly: "Most things Christians say about Jews are scandalous."

What, then, are some of the highlights of the corrective "curriculum" that recent scholarship has provided?

The first, certainly, is a fuller understanding of the political context of ancient Israel. The conquest of that land by Pompey in 63 BC, only the last in a succession of imperial conquests since Nebuchadnezzar's destruction of the Temple in Jerusalem in 597 BC, inaugurated an era of shared Roman-Jewish governance. During that time, as Sanders recounts in *The Historical Figure of Jesus*, able and compliant local leaders such as Herod the Great (37–4 BC) enjoyed considerable autonomy; less adept leaders such as his son Archelaus, who inherited a third of Herod's lands—namely, Judea and the city of Jerusalem—fared less well. After tolerating ten years of his incompetence, Roman prefects took over Archelaus' territory, though they continued to share the running of Jerusalem with the high priests of the Temple. The two other portions of Herod's former lands, including Jesus' Galilee, remained under Jewish rulers (known also, confusingly, as Herods as well as by their proper names). This arrangment lasted until a major Jewish revolt brought on a harsh Roman reaction and the destruction of the Second Temple in AD 70 .

The delicate governing arrangements and the political volatility of Judea are crucial to understanding Jesus' fate. History, for example, reveals a Pontius Pilate very different from Gibson's (or the Gospels') somewhat benign figure puzzled by the high priests' insistence on punishing Jesus. Indeed, according to the accounts of the first-century historian Josephus, Pilate was a notoriously harsh prefect, quick to crucify even potential political rebels. It is not clear whether Jesus' followers thought he was the Messiah—and there

were many competing Jewish ideas of the Messiah at that time, as Bard College's Jacob Neusner has shown—or an apocalyptic prophet declaring the
imminent coming of God's Kingdom. The fact that his arrival in the city
stirred up popular interest among the holiday crowds in Jerusalem would
have set off Pilate's fears of a seditious leader. Caiaphas and the high priests
of the Temple were also certainly concerned about anyone disturbing the
peace, although declaring oneself the Messiah, Vermes has pointed out, was
not blasphemy by any Jewish law. Indeed, if Jesus's sin had truly been blasphemy, as certain Gospels assert, then the priests would have rightfully condemned Jesus to death by stoning—and not handed him over to Pilate for
crucifixion, a punishment reserved for political crimes. As Boston University
scholar Paula Fredriksen puts it, "I see Roman concerns exceeding priestly
ones. If Pilate didn't have an itchy trigger finger, the crucifixion, which was a
specifically political punishment, probably would not have happened."

Another point the new scholarship emphasizes is the variety within
Judaism at Jesus' time. To be sure, there were certain constants: all Jews worshiped only one God and all believed in the divine election of Israel, the
divine origin of the Torah, and repentance and forgiveness. Apart from that,
there were many different emphases associated with, variously, the priestly
class and lower-order clergy (Levites), the various religious parties (Pharisees, Sadducees, and Essenes), and, not least, the great majority of obser-
vant, unaffiliated Jews.

The Pharisees, for instance, a party of some six thousand strong, shared
with most other first-century Jews (except the Sadducees) the belief in life
after death—"an idea," writes Sanders, "that is hard to find in the Hebrew
Bible (the only clear reference is Daniel 12: 2)." The Pharisees also developed a collection of non-biblical traditions governing the proper observance
of the law. The Gospels, particularly Matthew's, would later caricature the
Pharisees as inflexible legalists in order to suggest a spurious divide between
their emphasis on the law and Jesus' emphasis on spirit and grace. Yet as the

discovery of post-biblical Jewish texts has helped to establish, the concern with mercy, love, and forgiveness was widely shared throughout Judaism, and certainly was not unique to Jesus' teaching. In fact, Pharisaic interpretations often made biblical laws less restrictive. And in any case, even the Gospel of Mark shows Jesus sharing the Pharisees' belief that the love of God and of one's fellow man constitute God's greatest commandments. They would have drawn this conclusion because both Jesus and his Pharisaic contemporaries would have found these commands in the same source: Deuteronomy ("Love the Lord your God with all your heart") and Leviticus ("and your neighbor as yourself: I am the Lord.")

Why the caricature, then? Because, Sanders explains, the Gospel of Matthew was probably written at a time (ten years or so after AD 70, when the Gospel of Mark, probably the earliest of the Synoptic Gospels, was written) and in a place (Syria) where early Christian gatherings, still predominantly Jewish, were in direct competition with other Jewish communities associated with Pharisees. Matthew projected his own situation of competition and controversy back onto the period some sixty years earlier, to the lifetime of Jesus. But in AD 30, in Galilee and Judea, relations had probably been different. "I don't think Jesus can accurately be cast in enmity with the Pharisees," Sanders says.

The distancing of Jesus from his Jewish context and the denial of the similarities between his teachings and those of other Jewish holy men and even whole schools of Jewish thought is a complex story— and anything but smoothly linear. In broad strokes, though, that story follows the gradual separation of the Christian movement from Judaism both in Palestine and the rest of the eastern Mediterranean world, beginning shortly after the crucifixion of Jesus.

Yet as the new scholarship emphasizes, even the belief in Jesus' resurrection should not be considered a Christian novelty. "The resurrection of the dead was one of the redemptive acts anticipated in Jewish traditions about the End of Days," Paula Fredriksen explains in *Jesus of Nazareth, King of the Jews*. Jesus' individual resurrection was thought by his early followers to herald a more general resurrection of the dead and transformation of the living that would come with the establishment of the Kingdom of God. Another tenet of apocalyptic Judaism—one still echoed in Orthodox Jewish prayer services to this day—was the belief that Gentiles would abandon their idols and turn to the true God once he established his Kingdom.

And indeed, as the movement spread through synagogue communities on the coast and throughout the Jewish Diaspora, it drew more and more Gentiles. In response, leaders of the Christian movement in Jerusalem decided that these Gentiles-in-Christ did not have to convert to Judaism as long as they abandoned all forms of idolatry.

Soon, though, there arose a clear and powerful reason for Gentile Christians to distance themselves from Jews and Judaism: the Jewish revolt of 66–74 and the Roman levelling of the Second Temple in 70. All four Gospels—or at least the three after Mark's—were most likely written in the afterglow of the Temple's destruction, when anti-Jewish sentiment was running high throughout the eastern Roman Empire. Since a large part of the intended audience was Gentile, Vermes argues, it would have been unwise and counterproductive to claim that Rome was responsible for killing the Messiah. Jerusalem, and its Temple, had stood at the epicenter of the revolt against Rome. No surprise, then, that the Gospel writers place more of the blame on Jerusalem's Jews and on the Temple leadership than on the Roman governor.

Sanders, for his part, does not completely exonerate the Jewish high priests, noting that they were also responsible for maintaining public order in Jerusalem. Yet when the Gospels were written, he says, the Chistian authors "had to make the church appear innocuous to Rome. They didn't want their leader to be thought of as a criminal."

It would be wrong to think that the close ties between Christians and Jews were instantly or fully severed. For centuries, many Christians from Asia

Minor to North Africa continued to attend synagogue services or observe Jewish high holidays. "Fourth-century Gentile Christians," writes Fredriksen, "despite the anti-Jewish ideology of their own bishops, kept Saturdays as their day of rest, accepted gifts of matzo from Jewish friends, indeed still celebrated Easter according to when Jews kept Passover." As late as 387, the exasperated bishop of Antioch, John Chrysostom, excoriated his synagogue-attending congregation: "Don't you understand that if the Jews' way of life is true, then ours must be false?"

However intertwined Christianity and Judaism remained in the world of late antiquity, politics increasingly divided them. In 312, Constantine, one of the four Caesars at the time, reputedly had a vision that led to his conversion. "Up to that point, the Christians were much more persecuted than the Jews," says Donald Akenson, a professor of history at Queen's University in Canada. For Christians, Akenson adds, Constantine's decision "was like winning the lottery." Fighting under the insignia of the cross, Constantine defeated his last rival to become the emperor of Rome in 324, and, having unified the empire politically, he moved swiftly to do the same ecclesiastically. In 325, he convened the Council of Nicaea, where at least 250 bishops met to formulate the official articles of faith, including Jesus' place in the Holy Trinity, in the first Nicene Creed. (Those bishops who disagreed with the creed were promptly exiled.) Under his regime, Sunday became the Christian Sabbath, and Christians were prohibited from consulting with the rabbis on the date of Easter. Any Jew who obstructed the conversion of another Jew to Christianity was to be put to death; any Gentile Christian who converted to Judaism was to have his property seized by the state. "As the Roman Empire goes Christian, Jesus is increasingly seen as the divine incarnation of the second person of the Trinity and less as a Jew from Nazareth," says Amy-Jill Levine, a professor at Vanderbilt Divinity School. "When his Judaism is noted, it is only to say that he was 'rejected by his own' or that he came 'to demolish the old system from within.'"

While imperially sponsored Christianity coalesced into a community quite distinct from Judaism, many Christians still felt uncertain about their beliefs. The "Jewish rejection of Christian claims [that Jesus was the Messiah] was a mortal threat to the spreading of Christianity among pagans and also to what Christians believed," says Carroll in his book *Constantine's Sword*. "They would ask themselves, 'Is what I believe true?'" And over the next several centuries, he says, this uncertainty translated into blaming the Jews for killing Christ.

Some 750 years after the Council of Nicaea, in 1098, St. Anselm, a bishop and theologian, penned the treatise *Why God Became Man,* which put the crucifixion at the center of Christian faith. Why, St. Anselm asked, did God become a man? To be crucified to atone for the sins of humankind, the author responded. "It's not a coincidence it was written when it was," Carroll states. St. Anselm was a friend of Pope Urban II, who had called for the First Crusade. "It was a time of plagues, of savage war, of millennial fever," he says. The notion of Christ's sacrifice was "a way of coping with a very violent and brutal world, and it's a way of making sense of it. Crusaders are promised a life in heaven if they die on the crusades." En route to liberate the Holy Land, however, the soldiers stopped in the Rhineland, where they left a third of northern Europe's Jews dead in their wake.

Although the Church condemned the attack—and the official line was tolerance of Jews—nothing staunched the powerful tides of anti-Jewish violence. Jews were first accused of "ritual murder," the killing of Christian boys as a reenactment of the crucifixion, in 1144—a charge leveled repeatedly over the next several centuries, each time provoking brutal popular reactions. The incident occurred during Holy Week, in England, when a tanner's apprentice was found dead in the woods. Blame was fixed on local Jews, and in "retaliation" Christians murdered a Jew on Good Friday. The "blood libel," a related accusation that Jews kill Christian children to drink the blood at Passover or to make matzo, originated in the thirteenth century. Ever since, this libel has been a constant fixture in anti-Jewish rhetoric. Anne Catherine Emmerich, a source for much of Gibson's non-scriptural material in his movie, repeated it in the early nineteenth century; just this past year, 2003, the state-sanctioned media of modern Arab countries repeated it yet again.

Even official tolerance of Jews and Judaism was suspended in 1215, when a council convened by Pope Innocent III called for the existence of one universal church. No one outside the Catholic Church, the council pronounced, would be saved. New laws required Jews to dress a certain way—a precursor to the yellow armbands of Nazi Germany—and banned them from public office. Among the council's critical theological innovations was its teaching that the consecrated Communion wafer was, in some real sense, the body of Christ. As much to convince Catholics of the literal correctness of this view as to vilify Jews, scholars say, Jews were charged with desecrating the host— that is, stealing and stabbing the Communion wafer with a knife in a bizarre reenactment of the crucifixion. The blood that miraculously trickled from the wafer, these stories held, would convince the Jews of the truth of Christianity and lead to their conversion. "It shows the connection between a high-level theological doctrine and a low-level belief," says Marc Saperstein, a professor of Jewish history at The George Washington University. Even the Black Plague of the mid-1300s, which killed one in three Europeans, was blamed on a Jewish plot.

Throughout much of the Middle Ages, and especially during the troubled and traumatized fourteenth century, Passion plays dramatically enacted the medieval Christian demonization of the Jews. Focused precisely on the suffering, death, and resurrection of Jesus, these performances often triggered mob violence, sending Jews into hiding as Christian neighbors ransacked their homes and murdered their occupants. The plays were largely suppressed after the Reformation—mainly because of their lewdness, not their anti-Jewish content—but a production in Oberammergau, Germany, is still performed every ten years. Only recently, though, did the

Oberammergau producers revise the script and delete the line from Matthew 25:27—"His blood be upon us and upon our children!"—that Christian tradition had long interpreted as an eternal blood curse on Jews who refuse Christian conversion. Responding to prerelease criticism, Gibson took this line out of his subtitles, but kept it in the sound track of the final cut of *his* Passion.

Christian ambivalence about Jesus' Jewishness, and Christian discomfort over the Jews' continued Jewishness, became most evident with Martin Luther and the Reformation. Six years after he posted his 95 Theses, Luther wrote a defense of the Jews called "That Jesus Christ Was Born a Jew." He believed that his purified form of Christianity would finally bring the Jews around. "He, too, needed the Jews to convert," says Carroll. When they failed to respond to what Luther saw as a magnanimous gesture, he retaliated in 1543 with another tract, called "On the Jews and Their Lies." "He thought Catholics were like Jews only worse," says Mary Boys, a professor of practical theology at Union Theological Seminary. For its part, the Catholic Church declared in 1545 that all sinners, not just Jews, bore the burden of Christ's death. Yet at the same time, the Church imposed newer and harsher restrictions on Jewish "unbelievers." Ten years later, Pope Paul IV established the first Jewish ghetto in Rome.

The relationship between Christians and Jews in Europe improved only slightly during the Enlightenment. Jews got out of the ghettoes, for instance. "But the desire to keep Jesus away from any Jewish contamination at this point becomes actually greater," says Levine. This desire was in part stimulated precisely by steady advancements in the quest for the historical Jesus, the effort on the part of New Testament scholars to see Jesus not as a figure in church doctrine, but as a human being who lived within his own time and culture. By the second half of the nineteenth century, that quest was in full swing. While of great interest to scholars, the resulting picture of Jesus as a Jewish teacher of his day was troublesome to many Christian theologians, especially in Germany. "Scholars said there's nothing new in Jesus," says Susannah Heschel, a professor of Jewish studies at Dartmouth. "So then what's new about Christianity? Where does it differ from Judaism? It touched a sensitive nerve."

The questions began to take on racial overtones in the early twentieth century, fanned by the writings of British-born Houston Stewart Chamberlain, a notorious anti-Semite who claimed that Jesus was not Jewish but Aryan. Theologians took up the cause in the 1920s, arguing on the basis not of Jesus' physiognomy but on his intimacy with God. Jews were not close to God, they said, hence the Jews depended on the law; but Jesus was close, uniquely close, to God, and therefore he overthrew the Jewish law. By 1939, Protestant Germans were at work on a de-Judaized hymnal, deleting Jewish words like "Zion," "hosana," and "hallelujah" from their songs. As Heschel recounts in her forthcoming book, *When Jesus Was an Aryan: Protestant Theologians in Nazi Germany*, "Eliminating the Old Testament was relatively easy, compared to the next major undertaking: purifying the New Testament of positive Jewish references."

Heschel adds in an interview that these theologians "identified the German people with Christ. Jesus had a message, which was to destroy Judaism. He struggled to accomplish that, but the Jews got the better of him and killed him. [Now] Germans, too, are engaged in a life or death struggle, but they are going to be victorious, destroying Judaism and the Jews." Hitler, in fact, became the Christ figure, says Heschel, "the one sent by God."

In response to the Holocaust, in large part, Vatican II issued its famous *Nostra Aetate* in 1965, which fully repudiated the older teachings about Jewish guilt for the death of Jesus, and launched a serious Catholic scholarly reconsideration of Jesus' Jewish context. These theological and scholarly initiatives led, in turn, to more practical questions about Catholic dramatizations of the Passion story. In 1988, the U. S. Conference of Catholic Bishops issued specific guidelines reminding Catholics "that the correct presentation of the Gospel accounts of the Passion and death of Jesus Christ do not sup-port anti-Semitism."

It is a well-publicized fact that Gibson, like his father, is happy neither with the reforms nor the spirit of Vatican II. But it would be too easy—or cyni-cal—to say that Gibson's movie simply reflects a yearning for pre–Vatican II approaches to the relationship between Jews and Christians. It does, how-ever, quite pointedly ignore any of the new understandings of that relation-ship brought forth by dedicated Catholic, Protestant, and Jewish scholars of the last fifty years.

Gibson, of course, can hardly provide centuries of background in a two-hour movie—or all of the scholarship that deals with it. And yet, says Bard College's Jacob Neusner, "The entire corpus of the work has been com-pletely dismissed by Gibson." Focusing strictly on the Passion, Gibson did not provide much-needed context. Nor did he apologize for that. "I know how it went down," he told Sawyer in the ABC interview. "Not everybody does, maybe they'll find out. It's not my job, you know. My job is to make a film as well as I can make it." Maybe so. But, at the very least, Gibson has helped to perpetuate some of the same misunderstandings that have plagued Christian-Jewish relations for close to two thousand years.

PAULA FREDRIKSEN

❖

GOSPEL TRUTHS

HOLLYWOOD, HISTORY, AND CHRISTIANITY

Christians whom I know and respect, both Protestants and Catholics, have loved *The Passion of the Christ* and have spoken to me of how moved they've been by it. The wide gap between the movie's story elements and the New Testament Gospels, if they noticed it, has not troubled them. Nor did its hostile characterizations of Jerusalem's Jews and of the high priest really seem, to them, to be anti-Semitic. Some Jewish viewers, too, have commented positively on *The Passion*'s visual and dramatic power, opining also that they detected nothing particularly anti-Semitic in Gibson's rendition. And the violence that stands at the heart of the film, since put to good purpose—a proclamation of Christian faith—has caused no offense to the countless numbers of people who otherwise would never think of seeing an R-rated movie, or of taking small children to see one.

As for Gibson himself, for the past year now he has dodged all criticism of his movie like the action-flick hero he is. When promoting *The Passion*, he proclaimed its historical veracity: the script, he said, was based on the "rock-solid" eyewitness reporting of the evangelists themselves. Presented with the long list of the film's goofs, at odds with both Scripture and history—the spoken Latin; the outsized, impossible cross that James Caviezel's Jesus lugs along the way to Gibson's Golgotha; the improbably softened character of Pontius Pilate; the destruction by earthquake of the Temple—he's shrugged, "It's a movie, not a documentary." His only obligation, he claims, was to make the best movie he could, exercising his right to artistic freedom of expression. Asked if so much gore were really necessary, he responds, "That's just what's in the Gospel. I know how it went down." When pressed on his potentially harmful depiction of Jews, he blocks with a counter-punch: "People like this don't have a problem with me, they really have a problem with the Gospels."

But *The Passion* is *not* a movie based on the Gospels. And it is certainly not a movie about the historical Jesus. Gibson has said that he drew on the Gospels and then filled in "details" by using the visions of the early-nineteenth-century stigmatic nun Anne Catherine Emmerich. The reverse is closer to the truth. The scaffolding of his story, the reorganization of events presented in different sequences in the evangelists, the characterizations of Caiaphas, Pilate, Mrs. Pilate, and Mary the mother of Jesus—the meat of the movie, in brief—are pure Emmerich. So too are the numerous visual touches—Jewish children morphing into demons, Satan stalking among the Jews, the crow plucking out the bad thief's eye—that have alarmed even sympathetic viewers. Where the movie seems to be biblical, it's the Bible as filtered through *The Dolorous Passion of Our Lord Jesus Christ*.

Gibson's reliance on Emmerich accounts for two of the film's main features: all that blood, and all those very wicked Jews (those Jews who are not followers of Jesus). As her own stigmata attest, Emmerich herself meditated long and hard on the wounds of the crucified Christ. She was guided in her meditations by the traditional Catholic practice of the Stations of the Cross. The Stations are a narrative meditation on Jesus' pain, in the context of a theology of pain whose roots extend back to the Middle Ages. They retrace, in a sequence of fourteen episodes, Christ's progress from Pilate to the tomb. The walls of older Catholic churches are lined with depictions of these episodes. Converging on the altar, the Stations literally lead to the Mystery of the Sacrament—Christ's Eucharistic Body—which rests upon the altar, beneath a representation of its visual and historical counterpart: Christ in Agony, dying on the Cross.

This Church architecture, this Catholic meditative practice of the Stations, and these baroque visions of Emmerich's all express a theological proposition: that Christ saved humanity not so much through his death and resurrection (which would be closer to the New Testament's understanding) as through his endless, unspeakable, unbearable suffering. Christ suffered more than anybody else ever did, and ever could, because he suffered not for his own sins (he had none), but for the sins of the whole world. By his stripes (so Isaiah 53, in this understanding) we are healed. The visual violence of the movie is thus more than yet another instance of Gibson's standard cinematic fare. Because he gets his story through Emmerich, the violence is essential, because the story itself is all about pain.

The bad Jews, presented so theatrically in Gibson's movie, are also native to Emmerich's imagination. In her visions, Satan and Caiaphas are constantly linked. Hell yawns at the high priest's feet; he witnesses Jesus' torture by Romans with implacable satisfaction; he and his minions bay for Jesus' death. Why? Emmerich did not need to answer: she simply imagined Judaism as the eternal opposite of Christianity, and Jews as the eternal enemies of Christ. In other memoirs, she unself-consciously repeated another classic canard—namely, that Jews killed Christian babies in order to use their blood for Jewish rituals.[1] Emmerich's visions, in brief, enunciate an anti-Semitism typical of her time and place.

Gibson's dependence on Emmerich does not in itself confer her anti-Semitism on him. But his own expertise as a master of the action movie com-

1. Carl E. Schmöger, *The Life and Revelations of Anne Catherine Emmerich* (Rockford, IL: Tan Books, 1976) 1: 547–48.

bined with these two strong characteristics of Emmerich's work: the extreme suffering of the good, the extreme villainy of the bad. The combination accounts for his heavy-handed scripting of the bad Jews in his movie. Action films in general, Gibson's in particular, are encumbered neither by realism nor by moral subtlety. Actors routinely "bleed" in medically remarkable ways, thanks to the makeup artist's skill. Bad guys are *very* bad, good guys *very* good: anything more complex interferes with the story line. Sensational violence carries the story, substituting for character development and plot. Gibson took the skills honed in *Lethal Weapon, Conspiracy,* and *Braveheart* (a medieval action flick) and used them to construct *The Passion.* This time, Jesus was William Wallace, and Caiaphas was Longshanks.

Gibson's reliance on Emmerich, combined with the Good Guys/ Bad Guys strictures of his own favorite genre of storytelling, determined the exaggerated features of his movie. Had he actually stuck closer to the Gospels, his film would have suffered much less from the visual violence that it inflicts on its audience: the three Gospels that mention Jesus' flogging do so in one brief sentence. It would have been much less anachronistic, since the evangelists, as first-century writers, reflect much more faithfully the life and times of Jesus than nineteenth-century meditations, refracted through the prism of twenty-first-century Hollywood heroic stereotypes, ever could. And had Gibson actually put his research department to work, he could have produced a story of much greater moral subtlety and power.

IF YOU READ THE GOSPELS one after the other, straight through, what will probably strike you is their similarity. But if you then read them as students and scholars typically do—printed in parallel columns, with the bits that correspond ranged next to each other—what emerges with startling clarity is their many differences.

Some examples: Mary and Joseph's hometown, according to Matthew, is

Bethlehem; in Luke, it's Nazareth. Mark's Jesus proclaims that the Kingdom of God is at hand; Luke's Jesus tells a parable so that his followers will not think that it is at hand. Luke's temple veil tears before Jesus dies; Matthew's and Mark's, after Jesus dies. John's Jesus "cleanses" the Temple at the very beginning of his mission; Mark's (and, following him, Matthew's and Luke's) at the very end. Mark and Matthew feature two trials before a full Jewish court, a charged dialogue between Jesus and the high priest, and an accusation of blasphemy. Luke has a single trial, no role for the high priest, no blasphemy charge. And John has no Jewish trial scene at all. Jesus dies after the Passover seder in the first three Gospels; before the seder in John.

I could go on. The above paragraph stands not as an argument but as a simple observation: the Gospels differ as to issues of "fact." If we insist on measuring the Gospels with the standards of empirical science, we will get a mental cramp. Mary and Joseph cannot have been living all along in Nazareth and also moved there for the first time after their flight to Egypt. Jesus cannot have died both before the seder and after.

Ancient theologians did not need parallel columns to be aware of all the differences in the Gospel texts. They knew them by heart. They believed that the Holy Spirit had planted each and every word in the body, or "flesh," of the text. Where stories conflicted, where numbers did not add up, it was the Spirit's signal to the believer that he had to think harder, to see past the text's flesh—its plain sense—into its "soul," its symbolic, eternal import. Free of modern people's preoccupation with empirical knowledge, the heroes of the ancient church—Origen, Chrysostom, Augustine—found deep spiritual significance in all the twists and eddies of the great river of biblical prose. They did not deny the challenges of Scripture's stories. Where they found variety, they made meaning.

In contrast to ancient theologians, modern-day fundamentalists have reduced meaning to facticity. Despite their dislike of modern science ("godless evolutionism" and so on), fundamentalists, curiously, seem wedded to the proposition that all Scripture, since "true," must be true as empirical sciences define truth. (This is what Gibson means, I imagine, when he proclaims that all four Gospels are "rock solid.") When reading Genesis, fundamentalists come up with Creationism: the ancient poetry about God's work that ends with His resting on the first Shabbat must yield a factual description of the way that the physical universe actually came into being. In defense of Scripture's facticity—the measure of meaning adapted from science, where empirical description and "hard facts" are the gold standard of knowledge—fundamentalists throw complexity aside.

With the Gospels, where the conflict stands not between science and story but between the different versions of the biblical stories themselves, the tension is potentially even greater. Fundamentalists, facing the Gospels' many variations on the themes of who did what to whom, when, where, insist that no such differences exist. Or they say that these differences are not significant. Or they acknowledge these differences only in order to explain them away. Non-fundamentalist Christians—the vast majority—find other ways to see meaning in their sacred texts that require neither the suspension of critical thinking nor a cooling of religious attachment. Such Christians, to fundamentalists, seem "soft": impious, weakly committed, "liberal." What seems like a simple difference in styles of interpretation actually codes a test of faith.

Historians, meanwhile, of whatever denominational stripe or of none, study the Gospels' differences closely and rejoice in their strong contrasts. These bumps and ridges in ancient Christian tradition are what give us our toehold up Scripture's slopes. We use them to ascend the surface of the evangelists' stories, to sense the tectonic forces—historical, social, theological, political—that shaped their different presentations. When did they write? Why? In what circumstances? What did they inherit, what did they alter, what do they seem to create? And finally, once we have mastered these questions as best we can, we stand atop the evangelists' writings to peer out across the haze and distance—four to seven decades of it—that lies between them and the events that called them into being: the mission and message of Jesus of Nazareth.

THE GOSPEL OF MARK AND THE GOSPEL OF JOHN provide us with two very different, and equally canonical, traditions about Jesus' final days in Jerusalem. Both begin the same way: Passover pilgrims joyfully greet Jesus and dance him into the city, singing about the coming Kingdom of David (Mark) and of the coming King of Israel (John). Thereafter, their stories diverge significantly. Mark's Jesus, who never goes to Jerusalem in the course of his mission, proceeds to the Temple mount. There he dramatically overturns the tables of the money changers and incurs the enmity of the priests (though he nonetheless continues to teach at the Temple every day). John's Jesus, by contrast, has taught frequently in Jerusalem during his mission. This final time, he also teaches in the Temple, but he causes no scene there: John places the Temple disturbance toward the beginning of his Gospel, at the outset of Jesus' mission.

In Jerusalem, Mark's priests, angry, plot to arrest Jesus and to kill him, but secretly, so that "the people" will not riot (Mark 14:2): Jesus is so popular that they dare not move against him openly. John's priests, by contrast, are anxious about Jesus even before he arrives. Prior to Jesus' triumphal entry, they had already decided that Jesus had to die. They reached this decision not because they are offended and resentful, as in Mark, but because they fear that Jesus' great popularity will call down the wrath of Rome upon the Temple and the people. Thus at an earlier council, well before Jesus' arrival for this Passover, John's Caiaphas decides that it is better that Jesus die than that the whole nation suffer (John 11:47). In short, if Mark's Jesus dies for "religious" reasons (the offense of the Temple scene, the confusing charge of blasphemy), John's Jesus dies for a political reason: Rome's notorious impatience with popular leaders of subject peoples.

In Mark, Passover begins on Thursday night. After a seder with his disciples, Jesus walks out on the Mount of Olives to Gethsemane, where he is ambushed by a civilian "crowd" armed with knives and clubs, sent by the chief priests. In John, Passover does not begin until Friday night, so on Thursday night, Jesus has a last meal (though not a seder) with his disciples. Walking with them in a garden after dinner, Jesus is arrested by a contingent of *Roman* soldiers, guided there by a few of the priests' Temple guard. In Mark, Jesus is led to the first of two full meetings of the Sanhedrin. He faces off with the high priest, who condemns him for blasphemy. In John, the Roman soldiers lead Jesus to Annas, Caiaphas' father-in-law, for a brief interview; thence, again briefly, to Caiaphas. No council, no confrontation, no charge of blasphemy.

Before Pilate, Jesus is ultimately condemned to the cross. Both Mark and John, each in his own way, emphasize Jewish initiative behind Pilate's decision. And both report, finally, that Jesus' cross declared his crime: He was sentenced to die as the "King of the Jews."

How do we sort through these two quite different traditions? If we want to make sense of them historically, we must see which pieces of the Gospels' accounts cohere with others, and we must grab on to what we can learn from other sources. We also have to be aware of places where the individual stories are internally inconsistent. This can be difficult. These stories can be hard to read precisely because they are so familiar that we easily miss where their own logic breaks down. For example, in Mark, Jesus is so popular that, Thursday night, he has to be arrested by stealth so that Jerusalemites will not riot in his defense; yet by Friday dawn, Jesus is so unpopular that "the crowd" demands his death, specifically by crucifixion. Mark provides no explanation at all.

If we suppose that Jesus was extremely popular with Jerusalem's pilgrims, a lot fits together: the triumphal entry, Mark's priests' decision to ambush, and Pilate's decision to crucify. A public execution—especially this particular Roman one—is addressed less to the victim than to a sympathetic watching audience. A crucifixion effectively tells a crowd to calm down: The man on the cross is *not* your king. No regime change is in the offing (as the pilgrims had sung during the triumphal entry). Anyone who thinks otherwise will end up dead the same way. Gibson's movie, of course, would have us believe that Jews sympathetic to Jesus were in short supply, while vast numbers demanded his death. Historically, the opposite is more likely. Had Jerusalem's population actually been so hostile to Jesus, he would not have died by crucifixion. There would have been no need. Rome did not bother to crucify leaders without followers.

If we suppose that Jesus was too popular for Pilate's comfort, then we also have a nice fit with John's priests' motivations for wanting him dead: popular prophets could prompt swift Roman action against pilgrims. For this possibility we have evidence in abundance outside of the Gospels, from the histories of Josephus, a contemporary of the evangelists. We know from Josephus that Pilate was eventually recalled to Rome in AD 36 precisely for losing control of such a situation. Pilate had called out his troops against a Samaritan prophet and inflamed the region with his use of excessive force: both the prophet and his followers, though unarmed, had been slaughtered.

Christian tradition, as it develops, steadily rehabilitates this feckless Roman prefect. In Mark, Pilate hesitates, unhappy at the priests' importuning. In Matthew, Pilate acquires a wife, who warns him not to harm Jesus; and he washes his hands of the affair while the crowd in Jerusalem calls Jesus' blood down on themselves and their children. In Luke, Pilate pronounces Jesus "innocent" of a charge of sedition (brought by the perfidious priests) no fewer than three times. Pilate's representative at the foot of the cross, a centurion, passes the same judgment ("Surely this man was innocent"). In John, Pilate tries hard to secure Jesus' release, to no avail. (John's picture clashes, needless to say, with the other elements of his own story.) Eventually, in the Coptic Church, both Pilate and his wife become saints. By the time Emmerich-Gibson are through with them, Pilate has become Hamlet, and Mrs. Pilate is a proto-Christian even before the crucifixion.

How then do we answer the question, Who killed Jesus? Were it not for (much) later traditions of Christian anti-Judaism, the answer, even from the Gospels, would be clear: Pilate ordered Jesus executed. We also know from the *mode* of Jesus' execution who killed him: only Rome had the authority to crucify. "Crucified under Pontius Pilate" even stands in the Creed. So whence this question, and why does it cause so much turmoil?

The answer is that more troubling questions—ones that touch upon issues of religious identity—lurk beneath this simple one. At whose *initiative* was Jesus killed? And why? The Synoptic ("seen-together") Gospels, Matthew, Mark, and Luke, all insist that the initiative came from the priests, for religious reasons. Jesus, through the scene at the Temple, had challenged their authority, and they resolved to have him killed. Unable (for whatever reason) to execute a sentence of capital punishment themselves, they persuade Pilate to do the job for them. Absent the priests' ill will (so goes this reconstruction), Jesus would have survived the holiday. So while Pilate is culpable legally, the priests are culpable morally.

But what about the tradition in the no-less-canonical Gospel of John? Why disregard that altogether? John, too, posits a type of priestly initiative, but he configures the priests' motivations completely differently. In John, Caiaphas makes a practical and principled decision to minimize bloodshed. He fears that Jesus' enthusiastic and growing following is going to provoke Rome. He reasons that, if he turns Jesus over to Pilate, Jerusalem might be spared a more general slaughter.

John's unique tradition that Roman soldiers, rather than a Jewish crowd, captured Jesus coheres with this line of thought too. Of course, in real life, only Pilate, not Caiaphas, could command Roman troops. So if Roman soldiers actually had been the ones to arrest Jesus, Pilate would have been in on the plan to crucify him all along. Caiaphas would still have stood behind

Pilate's action: the high priest facilitated Jesus' arrest. (His Temple guards, who know the city, guide Pilate's soldiers to the garden.) But Caiaphas and his priestly colleagues, in this reconstruction, are motivated not by any religious objection to Jesus, but by their responsibility to avert mayhem during a major pilgrimage feast (cf. John 11:50). Absent the priests (so goes this reconstruction), Pilate would have killed Jesus anyway. But if Caiaphas had not acted, a lot of other Jews might have died that Passover, too.

Why, given this countertradition that is right in the Bible, has Christian tradition kept so focused on the Synoptic story line? Why is it so important for Christianity to insist that "the Jews" killed Jesus? And how did this belief transmute to a standing indictment, so that Christians throughout their generations have insisted that Jews throughout their generations were and are guilty of Jesus' death?

"IF YOU THINK THAT *The Passion of the Christ* is anti-Semitic, then you are saying that the Gospels are anti-Semitic." I have heard this thought endlessly repeated in the course of the controversy over Gibson's movie. The proposition implies a defense: "But since the Gospels are not anti-Semitic, then neither can this movie be anti-Semitic."

The Gospels are *not* anti-Semitic, though that fact says nothing about Gibson's movie. The Gospels, in their original context, are Jewish writings. Their authors most probably were Jews themselves. The Christian movement, when they were written, was a species of Judaism. And streams of Christianity would remain Jewish for long centuries after their composition.

The Gospels base their interpretations of the life and teachings, death and resurrection of Jesus by explicit appeal to Jewish Scriptures, which in their period would have been available only in Jewish communities. They evince typically Jewish concerns: What is the right way to be Jewish? How is one to worship (the Jewish) God? How is one to understand his laws, and to walk in

his ways? What constitutes keeping the Sabbath? What is a person's obligation to others: one's parents, one's own family, and especially to the poor?
These stories depict Jesus in ferocious argument with other Jews about precisely these questions. He debates with Pharisees, with Sadducees, with
scribes, with Jews of no party affiliation. They argue about the Sabbath,
about sacrifices, about behavior. They quote Scripture to each other. When
Jesus, on the Temple Mount, tells the scribe that the greatest commandment
is to love the One God of Israel with "all your heart and with all your mind
and with all your strength, and your neighbor as yourself" (Mark 12:29–31),
he's not having a deep and original religious insight; he's quoting Deuteronomy and Leviticus.

Jesus shows up frequently in synagogues on the Sabbath. He's in Jerusalem
in order to keep the feast of Passover—which means that he'll eat from a blood
offering made at the Temple. He's a practicing Jew, and so too are the evangelists who later write about him. Is their practice different from the practice of
some other Jews? Yes. Do they—the Jesus of history, his apostles who carry
the movement forward after him, the evangelists who eventually write up these
traditions from and about him—argue about practice, claiming that *their* way
is the only right way, and that other ways are wrong? Unquestionably. All the
noise, all the argument, all the fraternal name-calling, is one of the most
unmistakably Jewish things about the Jesus movement, and about the Gospels.
Compared to some of the things that the Dead Sea Scrolls say about Jerusalem's priests, Matthew is actually kind of mild. Do these texts say bad things
about other Jews? So do all Jewish texts, beginning with Genesis. The Gospels
are no more *intrinsically* anti-Semitic than is Isaiah, or Deuteronomy.

But the Gospels have long been used against Jews as an indictment of
Judaism. Indeed, so has the entire Jewish Bible. And Jews in every generation—including, alas, in this generation of American children—have been
accused of "killing Christ." The evangelists, by naming the priests and the
crowds in Jerusalem as responsible morally for Jesus' death, seem to frame

this accusation in the Gospel texts themselves. But this is where we have to remember when the Gospels were written, and by whom.

Composed after the war with Rome in 66-73 AD, the Gospels were written by authors who placed themselves in the sweep of biblical redemption promised in their own holy scriptures, namely, the Jewish Bible. In quarrying Jewish scriptures for ways to understand Jesus, the evangelists also looked to Scripture to understand how God could have permitted the terrible destruction of Jerusalem to have occurred. As Jews (though "Christian" ones), they name these other Jews, who lived some forty to seventy years earlier, as the real reason behind Jesus' execution: the priests and these others had understood Scripture so poorly that they did not believe, as the evangelists did, that Jesus was the messiah (Greek: *Christos*, hence our word "Christ"). The evangelists thus linked two traumatic events—Jesus' death in 30 AD; the failure of the Christian message to convince the majority of Jews in the period since then—with this third one, the destruction of the Temple. Their scripting of Jerusalem's population as Jesus' opponents is a narrative form of the intra-Jewish argument that defined the Gospels' immediate social context.

Thus, for example, the curse that Matthew's crowd invokes—"His blood be upon us and upon our children!"—had *already*, in Matthew's view, come true. Jesus' generation of Jerusalem's Jews, and the one following ("our children"), had been consumed by Rome's victory in 70. This cry was not Matthew's eternal indictment of all Jews everywhere, but his way of placing Jesus' death in relation to the destruction of the Temple. The linkage palliated the trauma of both events.

Once these documents were read by Christians who were not Jews, their meaning shifted. They were used as condemnations of Judaism itself. This anti-Jewish use of sacred Scripture, and this anti-Jewish accusation, developed slowly over the course of the second through the fourth centuries. Not coincidentally, this is the same period during which various forms of Christianity developed among exclusively Gentile communities, and during which these Gentile Christians, like their Jewish counterparts, fell to furious argument among each other. What was salvation? Was it of the soul, or of soul and body together? Did Christ really have a fleshly body? Was the god described in Genesis, the god of the Jews, actually Christ's opponent? Or was he Christ's divine father? Or was he Christ himself, before his incarnation? And why hold on to Jewish Scriptures if Gentile Christians were not going to assume the practices (Sabbath observance, kosher food laws, circumcision) that these Scriptures commanded?

The Gentile church that "won" these fights in the fourth century, when Constantine became its patron, was continuous, more or less, with the Gentile church that in the course of the second century had argued that Jewish Scriptures, properly understood, were actually about Christ. The Jews' Bible, in its Greek translation, became this group's "Old Testament," completed and properly understood only through and by specifically Christian writings, the "New Testament." Any Gentile Christian groups saying otherwise, this church maintained, were actually heretics, "false" Christians. And, further, the establishment of their own church—the one true or "orthodox" or universal ("catholic") Gentile Church—had been the entire reason for Jesus' coming.

This Gentile Christian community, reading itself back into the Gospel texts, accordingly read "the Jews" out. Judaism shifted from being the medium of Jesus' message to being its bleak contrast. In fact, said these theologians as they pored over their "Old Testament," the Jews had never understood any of their own prophets, and had never done what God had wanted them to do anyway. And what had God wanted them to do? To these Christians, the answer seemed obvious. Christ's resurrection (in 30 AD); the Temple's destruction forty years later (70 AD); Rome's erasure of Jewish Jerusalem seventy years after that (following the Bar Kochba revolt, 132-135 AD)—all these events, they said, clearly indicated that God wanted Jews to become Gentile Christians, dropping Jewish practice and worshiping the Son as well as the Father.

Contemporary Jews were understandably skeptical that these former pagans grasped the meaning of Jewish Scriptures better than they did. Frustrated, their Christian critics argued that as long as Jews did not convert to Christianity, they were themselves guilty of the death of Christ. Meanwhile, many other Gentile Christians went to synagogues, kept the fast of Yom Kippur, and celebrated the Sabbath as well as Passover with their Jewish neighbors. They did so (as they explained to their own furious bishops) in the imitation of Christ: that's what Jesus had done too, they said, according to the Gospels.

Orthodox ideologues of separation argued long and hard against these intimate Jewish/Christian relations. The longer these relations continued, the uglier their rhetoric became. Judaism, they loudly insisted (against the obvious counterevidence of all this comfortable social activity), was intrinsically anti-Christian. All Jews everywhere, urged the bishops, unless they "repented" by joining the church, were Christ-killers. They fumed; they gave bitter sermons; they wrote acid commentaries, especially on the Gospels' Passion narratives. Together with emperors and minor kings, they promulgated laws, century after century, penalizing Christians, whether clerics or laypeople, for worshiping together and interacting religiously with Jews. We can infer from the bulkiness of these legal corpora that their congregations mostly continued to ignore them.

BUT BY THE SEVENTH CENTURY, Roman civil society had largely collapsed. The literary legacy of the ideologues, however, was preserved for the medieval church. Society became meaner and more violent; Jews increasingly became the victims of that violence. (In fairness, I must note that Christian minorities, a.k.a. "heretics," received no less vicious treatment.) By the High Middle Ages, Jews in Christian imagination were "the enemy" par excellence. And so they were scripted, once Passion plays developed. In these dramatic reenactments of the Gospels' Passion narratives, the Jews represented the evil Christ-killers, Pilate their unhappy pawn.

All of which brings us, once more, to Mel Gibson's movie. Is *The Passion of the Christ* anti-Semitic? The question is misconceived. The only thing that matters is that the film is inflammatory, and that its depiction of Jewish villainy—exaggerated well beyond what is in the Gospels and violating what historical knowledge we have of early-first-century Judea—will give aid and comfort to anti-Semites everywhere. For this reason, the bishops of France have officially denounced the film. Decrying it as a mirror of the "obsessions of our times—the dread of evil, the fascination with violence, and the search for the guilty," the bishops condemned *The Passion* both for its distortion of Christian teaching and for its potential support of anti-Semitism.[2]

Almost comically, the Arab world has tripped over itself to endorse *The Passion*. Islam teaches that Jesus was not crucified, and that he did not die in Jerusalem. Arab anti-Zionism teaches that the Jews never had anything much to do with Jerusalem at all. Nonetheless, Yasir Arafat has weighed in with his own version of "it is as it was" ("moving and historically accurate"). Arab countries forbid depictions of prophets in movies, and Islam considers Jesus a prophet. Arab countries frequently persecute their own Christian minorities. Yet Arab censors have given Gibson's movie a pass because "they think that the film is anti-Semitic," Mustafa Darwish, a film critic and former president of the Egypt Censorship Authority, explained to the Western press. His colleague Mohiy el-Din Abdel Aleem, Egyptian professor of media and journalism, was yet more explicit: "I encouraged [allowing] the movie because it withholds from the Jews their claims that they are innocent of Christ's blood."[3]

Thus, while many Christians, and some non-Christians, see no problems with Gibson's movie with regard to anti-Semitism, some Christians (fewer,

2. "French Catholic Bishops blast Gibson's 'The Passion,'" Reuters, April 5, 2004.

3. "Arab censors giving 'Passion' wide latitude," *San Francisco Chronicle*, April 1, 2004.

though, I hope) and many non-Christians (alas, millions in the Arab world) embrace it as they embrace anti-Semitism. And they are joined in this sentiment by anti-Semites of no religious persuasion whatever. What binds this second group together, other than a common hatred of Jews? I do not know. I can observe that, historically, Passion plays (or now, movies) have rarely brought out the best in people; and that anti-Semitism makes strange bedfellows.

Christian anti-Judaism is one of history's most terrible and most bloody ironies. This is so because, of all the world's religions, the one that Christianity is most like is Judaism. One can appreciate this fact intellectually by comparing their Scriptures, their liturgical practices, their calendars, their ethical patrimony. As a professional historian, I do this routinely. And I note that in the earliest, formative period of Christianity, few meaningful distinctions exist between the two.

Why, then, does so much of Christian tradition focus so resentfully, even homicidally, on differences? And why do so many Christians not understand that, by demeaning Jews and Judaism, they demean their own tradition? I can trace the historical reasons for this, but I confess that I have no real answer. Perhaps it is nothing more complicated than a longing for simplicity and an impatience with complexity. By ignoring history, and by thinking simplistically about their own traditions, Christians can hold to a black-and-white contrast between "us" and "them." Who is "us"? Whatever idealized identity you want to define for yourself. Who is "them"? The contrasting group you imagine. For the purposes of affirming Christian identity ("us"), the contrasting group has been "the Jews" of Christian imagination. Real Jews have suffered for it.

The Passion stands as a monument to this sort of simplicity. Stripped of its theological pretensions, there's little more to Gibson's film than the glorification of blood and pain, and a quick and easy moral contrast of "us" and "them." But there is so much more than this to Christianity. When the market-driven furor has died down, I hope that thoughtful people will do what they have usually done: read the Book, and forget the movie.

PHILIP A. CUNNINGHAM

❖

MUCH WILL BE REQUIRED
OF THE PERSON ENTRUSTED WITH MUCH

ASSEMBLING A PASSION DRAMA FROM THE FOUR GOSPELS

FOUR GOSPEL PORTRAITS OF JESUS

Dramatizing the death of Jesus, whether on stage or screen, is a daunting task. The primary sources of information, the four Gospels in the New Testament, are not simply reporters' notes from eyewitnesses. They are narratives composed so that readers "may come to believe that Jesus is the Christ, the Son of God" (John 20:31). To achieve this goal, the Gospel writers—the evangelists—filled their accounts with a wealth of symbols, sophisticated literary devices, quotations or allusions to the Scriptures of ancient Israel, and, Christians believe, divinely inspired insights. In narrating the life and death of Jesus, the evangelists were wonderfully creative in conveying their conviction that the Crucified One had been raised to Lordship.

How, then, are modern authors of Passion plays to convey the full richness of each author's inspired vision if they combine diverse elements from the four Gospels? How are they going to present the Gospels' multiple religious perspectives about Jesus in a single story? How are they going to present spiritual insights that arose only *after* Jesus' death, in the light of the resurrection, without giving the anachronistic impression that characters in Jesus' lifetime were arguing about post-resurrection issues? Will the play be more of a historical docudrama or a theological reflection? Will it seek to address the concerns and attitudes of contemporary audiences through the dramatization?

In fact, there are many ways to devise a Passion play script while being "faithful to the New Testament" in the process. Each way requires making conscious, careful choices, though, because the four different Gospels present four related but different stories.

Two component parts of a script are characters and plot. While the four Gospels tell similar stories, their characterizations of Jesus, and their devices for moving the plot along, are distinctive. We see this most clearly when we attend not to the evangelists' similarities, but to their differences.

In Matthew, Mark, and Luke, the Synoptic or "seen-together" Gospels, these differences are less evident because their overall stories are so similar. However, Mark's Jesus is misunderstood even by his own family (his mother included: see Mark 3:21, 31–35) and by his closest disciples (e.g., Mark 8:14–21). Not coincidentally, Mark's overarching theme is that no one can "get" who Jesus really is until they have seen Jesus suffer and die. By definition, this can happen only at the end of Mark's story and so it is noteworthy that the centurion at the foot of the cross is the first human character in the Gospel to perceive Jesus' identity (Mark 15:39). For this reason, Mark's Passion narrative dominates his work, and gives shape to the way that everything else is presented. Disciples must be ready to take up their own crosses and follow Jesus (Mark 8:34). And, most dramatically, the evangelist presents his and his community's *post*-resurrection beliefs about Jesus as the reason why the high priest, by definition in the period *before* the resurrection, condemns Jesus: for claiming to be the Son of God.

Matthew is a much longer Gospel, and offers many more of Jesus' sayings and teachings than does Mark. In Matthew, Jesus' family and his disciples (unlike their counterparts in Mark) do "know" who Jesus is before his death. And Matthew's Jesus faces off much more with other Jewish authorities, most notably the Pharisees during his mission, and especially the priests during his Passion. This is partially because, for Matthew, Jesus is preeminently the supreme teacher who definitively instructs how God wants people to live. The priests, in Matthew's view, were instrumental in Jesus' death, and had led the people of Jerusalem astray by encouraging them to reject Jesus. Hence Matthew, uniquely, puts into the mouths of Jerusalem's Jews the cry, "His blood be upon us and upon our children!" (Matthew 27:25). Looking back, Matthew could argue that the "curse" had been realized, with devastating result: the Romans destroyed the Temple in Jerusalem in AD 70, exactly one generation after Jesus' crucifixion.

Luke, by contrast, is the first volume of a two-volume work: Part II is the Acts of the Apostles. Written later, and with a significant number of Gentile Christians in view, this two-volume work makes the case that Christianity is a religion for Jews and Gentiles both, worthy of recognition by the governing authorities of the empire. Luke offsets the embarrassing fact that the Church's founder had been executed for sedition by a Roman prefect by showing that Pilate declares Jesus "innocent" not once, but three times (Luke 23:4, 14, 22). So too does the centurion at the foot of the cross who, unlike the same character in Mark and Matthew, declares, "Surely this man was innocent" (23:47). In addition, Luke portrays Jesus as bringing healing and reconciliation wherever he goes. Thus, only in Luke does Jesus heal the injured ear of someone in the arresting party (Luke 22:51); cause Pilate and Herod to become friends (Luke 23:12); pray for his crucifiers (Luke 23:34); and inspire the repentance of a man crucified with him (23:39–43).

John's Gospel, finally, is quite unlike the first three. His Jesus is clearly an exalted divine character, who speaks openly of his special status throughout his mission. He is literally not "of this world" (e.g., John 1:9; 8:23; 16:28; 18:36). In

John's Passion, therefore, Jesus is clearly the one in control. He confronts those coming to arrest him, causing them to swoon. He dominates his conversations with Pilate, and carries his own cross (unassisted, as in the Synoptics, by Simon of Cyrene). And he brings his own crucifixion to a close by declaring, authoritatively, "It is finished." By being "lifted up"—crucified and raised—(John 3:14; 8:28; 12:32), John's Jesus makes the life that unites the Father and the Son in the world above available to believers on earth (John 17:26).

MEL GIBSON'S PORTRAIT OF JESUS' DEATH

It must be stressed that the hasty sketches given above only scratch the surface of the spiritual richness of each Gospel's presentation. They minimally consider, for instance, how each Gospel writer distinctively understands what it means to be a disciple of Jesus. However, even such a necessarily partial overview should indicate the difficulties confronting authors of modern Passion play scripts. How does one choose among this wealth of material and negotiate the varying theological interests, contexts, and time frames?

Mel Gibson's screenplay for *The Passion of the Christ* was the result of his choices. By comparing his movie to the Gospels, we can see what he dropped, what he retained, and how he interpreted what he chose to keep. In the following quick look at some scenes in the movie, we will note especially those elements that are not found in the Gospels at all. In principle, there is nothing wrong with supplementing the fairly sparse New Testament accounts; in fact, to create a coherent narrative, this is almost unavoidable. However, the choice of extra-biblical materials can also disclose the viewpoints that shaped Gibson's selections from among the four Gospels.

The Arrest in the Garden

In the garden, Jesus prays for the cup of suffering to pass him by as in the Synoptic Gospels. He returns to three disciples twice to find them sleeping (in Mark and Matthew he returns twice, in Luke once, absent in John). At one point his prayer is so intense that his sweat becomes bloody (some versions of Luke).

The men who come to arrest him are all Jews (Synoptics, not John), and they are all soldiers (neither the Synoptics nor John). Jesus confronts them with the question, "Whom do you seek?" (John). However, they do not then swoon when Jesus declares "I am he." Instead, Judas redundantly identifies Jesus by kissing him (Synoptics).

After violence erupts (all Gospels), Jesus heals the ear of one of the arresting party (Luke). Everyone flees (Mark and Matthew), including one disciple who leaves behind some clothes (an adaptation of Mark).

The film's arrest scene includes other elements found in no Gospel. Satan questions Jesus in the garden, asking, "Who is your father? Who are you?" Satan also makes a revealing theological statement: "No one man can carry this burden of sin, I tell you." As Jesus is dragged away in chains, he is thrown off a bridge under which a demon lurks. Among other injuries one of his eyes is swollen shut. He is regularly struck with chains, violence unattested in any of the Gospels. While this is happening, agents of the high priests bribe other Jews to assemble to demand Jesus' death.

Jesus before the High Priests

Matthew and Mark are the only Gospels that depict a nighttime "trial" of Jesus before a Jewish council. Luke describes a gathering of elders only the next morning, while John recounts simply an interrogation by the two high priests Annas and Caiaphas without any council present. Gibson selects the Marcan/Matthean approach, but embellishes the physical abuse of Jesus beyond any of the Gospels. Some of the charges that Gibson's tribunal levels against Jesus come not from the evangelists' trial scenes but from elsewhere in the Gospels (curing the sick with the help of devils) or from no Gospel at all (calling himself king of the Jews). Gibson never explains why the priests are so hostile to Jesus. The implication that their hostility stems from some sort of claim for his divine Sonship misrepresents Mark's post-resurrection theology as pre-resurrection history.

An additional non-biblical feature is an attempt by Mary Magdalene to get Roman soldiers to intervene. "They are trying to hide their crime from you," she pleads. A Temple guard tells the Romans that it is merely an internal affair over someone who broke unspecified Temple laws.

Jesus before the Roman Prefect

When they bring him before Pilate, Caiaphas and Annas accuse Jesus of various crimes: being a malefactor (John), curing the sick on the Sabbath (not in any Passion narrative), forbidding the tribute to Caesar (Luke), being the leader of a large and dangerous sect that hails him as Son of David (non-biblical), and claiming to be the Messiah (Luke). Pilate's wife had earlier told him of a dream about the righteous Jesus (Matthew), and Pilate had spoken of his fear that Caiaphas would instigate a revolt if Pilate did not assent to Jesus' crucifixion (non-biblical, as well as non-historical).

In a private exchange, Jesus tells Pilate that his kingdom is not of this world and that he has come to testify to the truth (John). Then Pilate sends Jesus to Herod for judgment, but the ruler of Galilee refuses to get involved (Luke).

Gibson next chooses to follow the Gospel of John by having Jesus scourged as part of Pilate's effort to placate the Jewish crowd. In Matthew and Mark, Jesus is scourged only *after* Pilate pronounces his sentence, in other words as part of the normal Roman crucifixion process. Luke has no scene of scourging.

In the film, Pilate presents the flayed Jesus to a huge Jewish crowd, saying, "Behold the man" (John). Caiaphas leads the crowd in chanting "Crucify him!" (all four Gospels, but at this point only in John). Pilate, gesturing to the bloody Jesus, asks, "Isn't this enough?" (non-biblical). The crowd is unappeased. "Shall I crucify your king?" asks Pilate. Caiaphas declares ironically, "We have no king but Caesar" (John). Pilate turns to Jesus, seeking some escape. "Speak to me. I have the power to crucify you or to set you free." Jesus reassures him, "He who delivered me to you has the greater sin" (John). If there is any doubt about to whom this refers, Caiaphas immediately exclaims, "If you free him, governor, you are no friend of Caesar's" (John, adapted). Violence breaks out between the crowd and the soldiers. A riot appears imminent (Matthew). Pilate summons a servant to bring him a bowl of water. Dramatically lifting his hands, Pilate announces, "It is you who want him crucified, not I" (non-biblical). He washes his hands. Caiaphas, angrily pointing to Pilate, exclaims in Aramaic (not in subtitles), "Let his blood be on us and our children!" (Matthew, adapted). Pilate commands his aide, "Do as they wish" (non-biblical). This combination of the Johannine scourging at Pilate's effort to free Jesus with Matthew's scene of Pilate washing his hands of responsibility results in a depiction of Jewish hostility that is more relentless, implacable, and evil than either Gospel on its own conveys.

The Execution of Jesus

In the movie, as Jesus is being crucified, he prays for the forgiveness of his executioners (Luke). One hand does not line up with predrilled holes in the cross, so Jesus' arm is dislocated to force it into place (non-biblical). The entire cross is then flipped facedown in order to bend back the protruding nails, yet somehow Jesus is not crushed under its weight (non-biblical). Jesus prays a second time for his crucifiers (Luke, repeated), and one of those crucified with him yells at the high priest, Caiaphas, "Listen, he prays for you!" (non-biblical). The Lucan conversation among the three crucified men ensues, followed by the non-biblical scene of a raven pecking out the eye of the one who mocked Jesus. Gibson's Jesus then works through his last words in Mark, John, and Luke in succession.

Upon Jesus' death, a teardrop from heaven strikes the ground (non-biblical), triggering an earthquake (Matthew). The earthquake causes destruction in the heart of the Jewish Temple (non-biblical and non-historical). The camera cuts immediately to Satan screaming in defeat as hell is apparently emptied of its righteous dead (non-biblical).

CONSEQUENCES OF THESE CHOICES

By filming his movie with the soundtrack in Aramaic and Latin, Gibson creates the impression of offering a sort of historical docudrama. The effect is aesthetic: Greek, not Latin, was the chief non-Jewish language of Roman Judea. Also, far from being "true" to the Gospels in some literal sense, the screenplay selects and combines various features from the four Gospel accounts. It omits other verses and elements of Scripture, and blends them with material from outside the New Testament.

Most, but not all, of Gibson's non-biblical material draws on visions attributed to Anne Catherine Emmerich (1774–1824). An Augustinian nun in Westphalia, Germany, who was renowned as a mystic and stigmatic, her dreams or visions of the life of Christ were published after her death. Living when most European Christians simply took it for granted that Jews were collectively cursed for the crucifixion of Jesus, her visions emphasize Jewish evildoing and associate Jews with demonic powers. Gibson drew not only particular elements, but also his arrangement of scenes, from this nineteenth-century source. *The Passion of the Christ* is less a movie based on the Gospels than it is a filmed version of Emmerich's imaginative interpretation of them. The movie's credits should have stated "Based on a story by Anne Catherine Emmerich."

Despite all the dramatic techniques that make the movie seem historical, Gibson's film, by relying so much on Emmerich, ignores undisputed and well-established historical facts about the time period it purports to depict. Most egregiously, the film totally reverses the relationship of Pilate to Caiaphas. Caiaphas was dependent on the Roman prefect, Pontius Pilate, to retain his position as high priest. Since Caiaphas held the high priesthood throughout Pilate's eleven-year tenure as prefect, it seems clear that the two collaborated closely. Caiaphas, as all the other chief priests from this period, routinely urged patience and cool tempers to their fellow Jews, since they feared that the Romans could be provoked into destroying the Temple (see John 11:48–50). Gibson's portrayal of Pilate impossibly fearing a Caiaphas-led revolt contributes to the film's placing the onus on Jews for Jesus' execution. Gibson draws this idea from Emmerich.

Also significant is the historical fact that the Passover festival was an especially volatile time since it celebrated freedom from foreign domination. Jerusalem overflowed with Jewish pilgrims from around the empire. The city's population swelled so significantly during these festivals that the Roman governors, who usually lived on the coastline, would also come to Jerusalem and station soldiers around the Temple precincts to discourage any restiveness. When rebellion threatened or actually erupted, the Romans knew what to do: they regularly used crucifixion to instill fear and impose order. Jesus was only one of thousands of Jews whom the Romans crucified.

Yet the film attempts to make Jesus' sufferings unique, not only with the addition of materials not found in the New Testament, but in the way it chooses to portray other aspects of his execution. Jesus is the only one of the three crucifixion victims who is scourged, even though scourging was part of the standard Roman crucifixion process for everyone. Jesus is made to carry an enormously heavy complete cross, while the other two victims only carry a crossbeam, as is more historically accurate. The Roman executioners inexplicably single Jesus out for endless torments on the way to Golgotha, but such violence against the other two victims is minimal or absent.

The cumulative effect of all of these choices—choices that were *not* inevitable; choices that were *not* dictated by fidelity to the New Testament texts—is that the diversity and wealth of the evangelists' inspired perspectives is flattened to a glorification of pain that seems the only thing that will placate God. Other parts of the Gospels are summarily ignored, as are any historical considerations; and the evildoing of Jewish characters is exaggerated while the complicity of Roman leaders is minimized. Nothing forced these choices on Gibson: as he has insisted repeatedly, he exercised his artistic freedom to make his movie the way he wanted to.

TWO OTHER OPTIONS

How else could the final hours of Jesus be depicted in a biblically grounded manner? There are many possible script arrangements, but any dramatist would have to first decide whether to try to present primarily a historical account or a theological one informed by the post-resurrection insights of the evangelists. In either case, scriptwriters must determine what principles of selection will guide the assembling of different Gospel elements and what materials from outside the Bible will be used to fill out their sparse accounts.

A Historical Approach

We begin with a script for a Passion play that aims to give a sound historical presentation of Jesus' final hours. This will only be a sketch indicating major decisions and overall tone. Again, it should be stressed that such a historical reading of the Gospels is *not* what makes them most important for Christian faith. But such readings are important if we also want to know the historical circumstances of Jesus' life.

My historical dramatization of Jesus' death would take as its starting point the statement in Mark 14:2: "The chief priests and the scribes were looking for a way to arrest Jesus by stealth and kill him, for they said, 'Not during the [Passover] festival, or there may be a riot among the people.'" This verse testifies to Jesus' popularity with a great number of pilgrims. That popularity also coheres with what we know from other historical sources: namely, that during the festivals, and especially at Passover, rioting could break out.

What Mark's verse does not explain is the reason why the priests are worried about Jesus. On that question, John 11:45–53 is important. Set before the

Passover celebration, this passage describes a council of chief priests and Pharisees who are alarmed by Jesus' popularity. "If we let him go on like this, everyone will believe in him, and the Romans will come and destroy both our holy place [the Temple] and our nation" (11:48). The high priest Caiaphas then declares that it is better for one man to die rather than the whole nation be destroyed (11:50). This motive of preserving the Temple from Roman destruction connects with the fact that Caiaphas' service as high priest depended on Pilate's approval. Caiaphas was responsible to Pilate for maintaining order during the festival. Also according to John 18:3, the arresting party was comprised of Roman soldiers, led by several of the high priest's guards. This joint contingent conveys the degree of cooperation between Caiaphas and Pilate. Both sought to maintain order during Passover.

The decision to present the arrest in the garden more historically would tend to favor the Marcan tone rather than the Johannine one. Anxiety, rather than superhuman total control, seems a more plausible emotion in these circumstances. In this script, then, Jesus would indeed pray that the cup of suffering might pass him by, and the words of the Lord's Prayer might be added; namely, that Jesus might persevere in the time of trial ahead (Luke 11:4).

None of the Gospels describes violence inflicted on Jesus by whichever group arrests him, whether Jewish civilians (the Synoptics) or Roman soldiers (John). We have no warrant, scripturally or historically, to depict violent abuse at this point in Jesus' story.

Next, we must decides about the calendar. In the Synoptics, Jesus is arrested after the Passover feast has already begun; in John, he is dead the afternoon before Passover begins. So: is the Thursday night of his arrest the first night of Passover (as in the Synoptic Gospels) or the eve of the Day of Preparation, with Passover beginning sundown on Friday (as in John 19:14, 31)? Our script will follow the Gospel of John: once arrested, Jesus is questioned simply by the high priest about his disciples and his teaching (John 18:19). This choice also sidesteps the difficult challenge of how to deal with the post-resurrection awareness of Jesus' divine Sonship that underlies the high priest's question in the synoptic accounts: "Are you the Son of God?" (Matthew 26:63).

Since we want our dramatization to be as historically plausible as we can make it, we presume the close working relationship of Pilate and Caiaphas. Our scene before Pilate, then, will derive chiefly from the Gospel of Mark, which does not really posit much of a conflict of wills between the two.

What about the next scene, the strange episode of Barabbas? In the Synoptic Gospels, the release of a prisoner at Passover is Pilate's custom; in John, it is a Jewish custom that Pilate observes. In either case, there is no extra-biblical evidence to support the existence of such a practice in areas under Roman rule. Furthermore, how likely is it that Pilate would release a convicted murderer or, worse, an insurrectionist (Mark and Luke) under any circumstance, much less simply to please his Jewish subjects? Moreover, in certain versions of Matthew's Gospel, Barabbas' personal name is Jesus, so that Pilate asks whether he should release Jesus son of the Father (= "Barabbas") or Jesus the messiah (Matthew 27:17). This strongly indicates that a theological argument is being mounted by the evangelists at this point. Therefore, this historical drama will omit the Barabbas episode.

It should be observed that once in Roman captivity, Jesus simply could have been made to "disappear." The fact that Jesus was crucified indicates that Pilate decided to make an example of him to deter Passover unrest. The fact that Jesus was crucified also coheres with the idea that he was popular with Jerusalem's pilgrims. The Romans would have had no reason to crucify an unpopular figure. But Jesus' crucifixion would deter pilgrims, seeing him agonizing on a cross on public display, from thoughts of violence: crucifixion warns those viewing it that they would share Jesus' fate if they caused trouble. This is plainly a Roman calculation.

Next question: How large a Jewish "crowd" before Pilate should we portray? Since Mark's account closely links this crowd to the high priests, a group of Temple employees seems more plausible than the vast multitude suggested by the collective Johannine "the Jews" (e.g., John 18:18). A small crowd is also consistent with Jesus' popularity and avoids the vexing question of why the people at large—so "pro-Jesus" that the priests felt that they could only arrest him by stealth—would suddenly turn against him. Answer: they didn't.

In all the Gospels, Pilate questions Jesus about whether he thinks he is a king. This makes good historical sense. It is a question, first of all, that would concern a Roman governor. (Quarrels between Jews over Jewish religious issues would not.) Since Jesus, during his mission, had constantly announced the arrival of God's kingdom, and since the title over the cross read "King of the Jews" (all four Gospels), Pilate's question is historically plausible. Flashbacks to Jesus' preaching about the kingdom could be effective here, and would also introduce some content from his teaching that would provide some balance to a Passion play's concentration on his death. And flashbacks to the Triumphal Entry, when the pilgrims herald Jesus in messianic terms, would also give content and depth to this part of our story: Jesus' death makes sense only in light of his life.

Pilate would be concerned about a prophet of a new kingdom arriving in Jerusalem at Passover, not because he represented a real threat of a revolt, but because of the potential for rioting and bloodshed that would make Pilate's rule appear weak. Crucifying a popular figure in such a mocking fashion ("King of the Jews"), Pilate would calculate, might help forestall unrest at this particular Passover, and might deter genuine revolts by more threatening Jewish figures in the future. And as we know from Luke 13:1 and from extra-biblical sources, Pilate was known to use violence to impose order.

If all these historical considerations seem too "political" and thus insufficiently "religious," we should pause to reflect that, in the ancient world, religion, politics, military matters were all intertwined. The Temple was both a religious center and a military fortress, and the economic lifeblood of Jerusalem. Jesus' preaching of the coming of God's Kingdom was not simply a spiritual proclamation, but had political implications for human empires.

Finally, once Pilate issues the order to execute, and since the Gospels give us such little detail on the crucifixion, this Passion play would unfold according to what we know about Roman practices. Jesus would be scourged after the sentencing, as would any others executed with him. All would carry only crossbeams to the crucifixion site, where the upright beams would be permanently mounted. Since Jesus' crime is specified in all the Gospels as "King of the Jews," some Roman mocking of him along these lines is plausible, but his torments would not be utterly unique. Everything would be done in haste (Mark 15:25), especially if the Johannine chronology is followed and the Passover begins at sunset that day (John 19:31). At Jesus' death, the crowds of Jerusalem's pilgrims—Pilate's intended audience for this public execution—would grieve and lament Jesus' death (Luke 23:48).

Our screenplay would be faithful to the Gospel material. It would also responsibly take account of current historical research. And its drama would not be limited to a near-endless spectacle of blood because it would engage the crescendo of hopes unleashed by Jesus' teachings, the serial reversals between his joyous entry and brutal execution, and the calculations of Pilate contrasted to the hopes, inspired by the Passover celebration itself, that energized Jerusalem's crowds.

And, of course, if we continue our screenplay through to Easter morning, we have the most dramatic reversal of all: oppression, but then freedom; darkness, but then light; death, but life again—indeed, the life of resurrection and the triumph of hope.

Theological Approaches

However, if we want to produce a Passion drama in order to express or provide a Christian faith experience, then we must pay greater attention to the distinctive theological perspectives of each evangelist. A choice must be made whether to feature one Gospel's inspired ideas or to try to present the faith perspectives of all four. The latter would not be easy. The four Gospel portraits could be simplistically summarized as Jesus as the suffering servant whose solidarity with human mortality reveals God's love (Mark), Jesus as the definitive teacher and rejected Wisdom of God that abides in the church (Matthew), Jesus as the healing reconciler whose death transcends human divisions (Luke), and Jesus as the one from above whose "lifting up" unites God and believers (John). These theological portraits are not contradictory; but they are nonetheless distinctive.

In this respect, live staged Passion dramas perhaps have an advantage over their cinematic counterparts. Staged productions could make use of a chorus to express an evangelist's theological interests or to relate the performance to the faith of the Christian believer. If the Marcan Peter curses Jesus, the chorus could ask, "Do we curse you, today, Lord? Do we abandon our convictions when convenient?" When the Lucan Jesus prays for his crucifiers, the chorus might chant, "The healing savior offers life even to those who take his life."

Filmed Passion plays can use narrations to similar effect, though this would immediately remove any façade of being a historical docudrama. But perhaps that would be more faithful to the Gospels that, after all, never set out to be mere historical records but rather are inspired and inspirational faith testimonies about living in relationship with Christ crucified and raised.

CONCLUSION

Different readers—and different artists—will all find different ways to be faithful to the New Testament when they seek to re-present the story of Jesus. But as the history of Passion plays in Europe makes very clear, it is possible to violate the teachings of Jesus by understanding "fidelity" in such a naive manner that dramatic interpretations of Jesus' death, by generating hostility and hatred, end up betraying the message of his life. For this reason, a script faithful to the "Gospel," to the "Good News" of Christ, makes moral as well as dramatic demands of its author. The Gospels' spiritual richness defies any single dramatic rendering. Nonetheless, their status as sacred Scripture means that they must be respected in all their complexity and diversity. Interpreting the Gospels "faithfully" means embracing that responsibility. After all, "Much will be required of the person entrusted with much" (Luke 12:48).

LAWRENCE E. FRIZZELL

❖

THE DEATH OF JESUS
AND THE DEATH OF THE TEMPLE

In *The Passion of the Christ*, between his scene of Jesus' death and his brief glance at Jesus' resurrection, director-writer Mel Gibson placed two more scenes. This time the violence was directed not toward humans but toward their buildings. A tear, dropped from heaven, causes an earthquake. Suddenly, we are whisked from Calvary back to Jerusalem. We see a worried Pilate glance around: his quarters rattle. We then see the Jewish priests gathered together: their space, by contrast, is devastated. Braziers tip, torches flame crazily, and flagstones rip in two: the priests' space is no more. The earthquake, Gibson invites us to think, is a sign of divine judgment. In consequence of Jesus' death, Rome is shaken; but the Temple is destroyed.

This scene of the destruction of the Temple seems to refer, in Hollywood manner, to an episode mentioned in three of the New Testament's four Gospels: that, whether before Jesus died (Luke), or after (Mark, Matthew), the "curtain of the temple was torn in two." (John has no such scene.) Gibson's movie enlarges the image from a torn curtain to a torn Temple. And this amplified image might seem to carry with it a theological message:

As the priests brought about the death of Jesus, so Jesus' death brought about the death of Judaism, or at least of Temple Judaism.

Whether he knew it or not, Gibson touched on themes long traditional in Christian theology and meditations on these Gospel scenes. Most of these theological traditions, however, were formed long *after* the lifetime of Jesus. To have them shape a movie that purports to tell a story set *during* the lifetime of Jesus—even if only in his last twelve hours—adds a confusing kind of anachronism to Gibson's effort to "tell it like it was." It (the movie) is as it (the history) wasn't.

To understand the place of the Temple in the lifetime and the piety of Jesus of Nazareth, we have to look beyond later Christian traditions, to the religious and cultural context in which Jesus himself lived. In other words, to understand where Gibson's closing images of the Temple's destruction come from, we have to begin where the Jerusalem Temple enters Christian tradition itself: with the religious devotion of Jesus.

THE TEMPLE IN JEWISH LIFE

Photographs of Muslim pilgrims in Mecca can give the modern person a sense of the crowds and congestion that were part of ancient Jewish pilgrimage festivals in Jerusalem. In absolute numbers, of course, first-century crowds in Jerusalem would have been smaller than their modern counterparts in Mecca, though the excitement would have been much the same. We can imagine Jewish men, many with their families, ascending to Jerusalem and gathering at the Temple for their feasts. Once Rome administered Judea as a province of the empire (beginning in AD 6), the governors would weigh in with their troops to help with crowd control. Rome's representative would march up from the seacoast, where he lived, and stay in the city while these holidays ran their course. In holidays such as Passover, which celebrated God's redemption of the people of Israel from oppressive foreign powers, the Roman presence may have agitated pilgrims as much as it served to keep things calm.

For Jews, Jerusalem was the center of the earth. According to Jewish traditions, the Creator had sealed His own name on the rock that would stand beneath the Temple, in order to keep the waters of the abyss from inundating the world. The prayers and offerings of each generation were linked with the binding of Isaac by Abraham upon this very spot (Genesis 22:1–18; see 2 Chronicles 3:1). The various offerings of animals and other gifts from the land were the means prescribed in Jewish scripture for enacting the people's devotion to God. Temple offerings were accompanied by psalms and other prayers. Pilgrims found that community worship in the Temple elevated their faith and gave them a means of atonement, enabling them to return home with a renewed experience of God's love and mercy. Those many Jews who, by Jesus' day, lived much too far from Jerusalem to make such a pilgrimage nonetheless contributed to the Temple's sacred function. They annually sent contributions from all over the empire and beyond to help with the Temple building and to defray the costs of the sacrifices. In all these ways, even for Jews who were never able to go there, the city and the Temple remained the center of their nation.

Judaism in Jesus' lifetime was far from uniform. Different Jews had different opinions on what constituted the right way to be Jewish, and sometimes these clashed. The Sadducees, for example, were priests and aristocrats whose attention focused on keeping international relations positive, so that they could ensure the smooth operation of the Temple. It was from these aristocratic families that the high priest was appointed. When Rome administered Judea, this meant that the high priest had to cooperate with Rome. Another Jewish group, the Pharisees, were educated laymen who honored the priestly functions in the Temple but declared that they too could interpret and apply the commandments to daily life. (We also know of some priests who were Pharisees.) A third group, associated with the people of Qumran (whose library, the Dead Sea Scrolls, was recovered in 1947), declared that the wrong priesthood was in office, and that the current priests used the wrong calendar. These Jews held the Temple in such high esteem that they would not worship there while the Sadducee priests ruled. These groups that we know about comprised a tiny fraction of all the Jews living at the time of Jesus. The vast majority of Jews belonged to no one "party," but all (except the Jews of Qumran) nonetheless came together at the Temple. According to the Gospels, among these Jews were Joseph, Mary, and Jesus; according to the Acts of the Apostles, many of Jesus' later followers worshiped there too.

JESUS AND THE TEMPLE

Jesus of Nazareth participated in these traditional pilgrimages, and the Gospel accounts present many of his teachings within that context. According to the first three Gospels, Jesus went to Jerusalem only once, and the culmination of his public mission was his journey for the festival of Passover. The evangelists saw this last pilgrimage as Jesus' conforming to the will of God the Father. According to the Gospel of John, by contrast, Jesus made several trips to Jerusalem, and taught frequently at the Temple. Given that these equally canonical traditions tell stories that differ, we need to study each separately in order to understand their differences before we can take them together to try to understand what Jesus himself did and taught.

Despite their disagreement about how many times Jesus taught in Jerusalem, all four Gospels relate a scene known in tradition as "the cleansing of the Temple." The first three Gospels use this scene to begin the events that will lead to Jesus' Passion. The evangelists present Jesus as overturning the tables in the Temple courtyard where pigeons were sold and money changed. Jesus, they say, did so quoting the prophets: "My house shall be a house of prayer…" (Isaiah 56:7) "but you are making it a den of thieves" (Jeremiah 7:11). The fourth Gospel placed this encounter between Jesus and the Temple authorities in the first of Jesus' visits to Jerusalem (John 2:13–21). Politely, the authorities asked for a sign to explain this bizarre action. His reply was enigmatic: "Destroy this temple and in three days I will raise it up" (John 2:19). The evangelist notes: "He was speaking about the temple of his body." This identification is consistent with the biblical message. Besides the Tabernacle (and Temple), the only other earthly reality made according to the heavenly model is the human being (see Genesis 1:26–28; Exodus 25:40). Of course, John and his community understood the exchange presented here in the light of the resurrection (2:22).

The Gospel writers thus have two different perspectives on Jesus, and also on the Temple. They know something about Jesus that the people in the story they tell about Jesus do not know: Jesus will be raised. And they know something about the Temple that people in the year AD 30 did not know: that the Romans would destroy the Temple in AD 70. They indicate that Jesus, like the prophet Jeremiah, manifested a deep affection for Jerusalem and lamented its impending destruction. "Behold your house will be abandoned, desolate" (Matthew 23:37–38; see Luke 13:34–35 and 19:41–44). When the disciples marveled at the beauty of the Temple, Jesus remarked: "Amen, I say to you there will not be left here a stone upon another that will not be thrown down" (Matthew 24:2 and parallels). The evangelists also presented such prophecies as figuring in the trial of Jesus, where they are interpreted as threats: "This man said, 'I can destroy the Temple of God and within three days rebuild it'" (Matthew 26:61; see Mark 14:58).

The Temple is associated with the death of Jesus again in the first three Gospels. Whether just before (as in Luke) or just after Jesus' death (Matthew, Mark), "the veil of the Sanctuary was torn in two from top to bottom." Matthew alone went on to tell, immediately after his statement about the Temple's curtain: "The earth quaked, rocks were split, tombs were opened and the bodies of many saints who had fallen asleep were raised" (27:51–52). These additional elements in Matthew's story seem drawn from his understanding of traditions concerning the resurrection of the saints, an event that Jews associated with the establishment of God's Kingdom. So too, for example, in the visions of Daniel, a book written some two centuries before Matthew's gospel, the prophet foresees that "many of those who sleep in the dust of the earth shall awake" (12:2).

None of the other Gospels mentions such an earthquake, nor do the letters of Paul. Nor does any of the other ancient sources we have that describe Jerusalem in this time—Josephus, the Jewish historian; Tacitus, the Roman historian—mention any earthquake in Judea in this period (again, Matthew's unique tradition), or anything occurring to the Temple or its curtain. These stories evidently were also unknown to the fourth evangelist, John. We may appreciate all these different Gospel stories as each writer's way of dramatically expressing his faith that God, in the life, death, and resurrection of Jesus, had in some special way ushered in his Kingdom.

JEWS AND CHRISTIANS IN EARLY CENTURIES

A generation after Jesus' death in Jerusalem, Jews in Galilee and Judea rebelled against the empire. In 70, their defeat was sealed with the burning of the city and the destruction of the Temple. It was in the period following this destruction that the evangelists wrote the Gospels. As we have just seen, they wove statements about the Temple's destruction into their stories about Jesus' life. In a sense, they used the death of Jesus as a way to understand the "death" of the Temple. And, consequently, their retelling of traditions about Jesus' Passion increasingly emphasized a role for the Temple elite, the chief priests.

Jews in Judea rebelled against Rome again in 132, when Hadrian was emperor. The great Rabbi Akiba declared the leader of this revolt, Simon bar Kochba, to be a messiah. This rebellion also met with defeat, and Hadrian built a new pagan city, Aelia, over the ruins of Jerusalem. From this period in the second century onward, we begin to find many different Christian traditions about the significance of the destruction of the Temple seventy years earlier, during the first revolt. And we also see theologians claiming that (pagan) Rome's defeat of the Jews, twice, said something theologically about Christianity and about Judaism. Some of these Christian authors were also Jews, others were Gentiles.

An apocryphal text, *The Ascent of James*, partially preserved in the Pseudo-Clementine *Recognitiones* of the late second century, reported that all nature suffered with Jesus. The Temple veil was torn as if in lamentation for the future destruction of Jerusalem. This idea resonates with the Jewish practice of rending garments in mourning: perhaps through the medium of his temple, the Father was lamenting the death of the Son.

Jerome, a fourth-century Latin Christian and translator of the Bible, knew of a "Gospel of the Hebrews" that recorded that the great stone lintel (rather than a curtain) was split in two. This is the only example in ancient Christian literature of a Temple stone being damaged by Matthew's earthquake. Over the centuries, the vast majority of interpreters have understood the torn curtain to symbolize God's abolition of his covenant with the Jewish people. Jerome remarked: "The veil of the Temple is torn and all the mysteries of the Law which were hidden previously are revealed and passed to the people of the nations." In other words, for Jerome, the torn veil becomes a condensed symbol for the shifting of divine favor from Jews to Gentiles in the Church. Through Jesus' death, Jerome said, knowledge of the true God, previously the unique privilege of the Jews, was revealed as well to the Gentiles.

Other interpretations were less benign. In the late second or early third century, a treatise attributed falsely to Cyprian, Bishop of Carthage, "Concerning the two mountains Sinai and Zion," linked the tensions between (Gentile) Christians and Jews to the crucifixion.

From the high tree he [that is, Jesus on the cross] watched them both as images of two evil-doing peoples: the Gentiles who do evil deeds in the world and the Jews who kill the prophets. These are the two evil-doing peoples whose images are the two criminals between whom an innocent man hung: one of them blasphemed, but the other truly confessed that an innocent was suffering injustice.... He saved the one who confessed and abandoned the one who blasphemed just as he did in the case of two peoples.

Then the exacerbated Father opened the heavens and there was unbearable thunder, the earth moved, graves opened and released their corpses, the veil of the temple was torn. Such a great roaring in the heaven and the movement of the earth made all who stood before the tree—some of them suffering, but some blaspheming and mocking—lay down prostrate trembling like the dying.

(A. M. Laato, *Jews and Christians in De duobus montibus Sina et Sion* [Abo, 1998], p. 176.)

After the victory of Constantine in 312, attributed to his response to a vision of the cross, some Christians found themselves in a favored position: eventually, their church became the official religion of the empire. Constantine himself began a major building program in the Holy Land, and especially in Jerusalem. There he built the splendid Church of the Holy Sepulchre, which subsequent Christian writers referred to as the "New Temple." A major setback for the newly state-sponsored church occurred when Constantine's nephew, Julian, became emperor. Raised Christian, Julian converted to the religion of ancient Greece and Rome. He revoked Christian privileges, sponsored state paganism, and even tried to initiate a program to rebuild the Jewish temple in Jerusalem. (How the rabbis felt about a pagan emperor trying to rebuild their temple, we may only speculate!) Would this contravene the predication of Jesus that no stone would rest upon another? Some Christian writers told gleefully that the assembled building materials were destroyed in an earthquake. The death of Julian in battle, soon after, enforced the Christians' view that they had been vindicated by heaven.

As the Christian Roman Empire faded, and as Western Christendom itself fragmented, Gentile Christians had their own reasons to lament over

Jerusalem and the "temple." In the seventh century, a new, Eastern monotheism, Islam, conquered the formerly Christian city. Jerusalem was now Muslim. Respecting the Christian sacred space of the grand Constantinian basilicas, the Muslims eventually built a mosque over the older Jewish sacred space, the still-leveled surface on the Temple mount. But Christians in both halves of the old Roman world mourned the loss of Jerusalem. To express their grief, they turned to the Jewish lamentations in the Old Testament that had voiced similar pain over the loss of the city with the ancient Babylonian destruction of Solomon's temple by Nebuchadnezzar (BC 586).

Almost four centuries later, Christians had an even more precise experience of "Jewish" loss. In the year 1009, the Caliph of Jerusalem, Al-Hakim, destroyed the Church of the Holy Sepulchre, Christendom's Constantinian "temple." European Christians responded by denouncing Al-Hakim as a new Nebuchadnezzar. Some Christians found a way to vent their rage closer to home. Blaming Europe's Jews for the Muslim destruction of Christian holy sites, some communities confronted their Jewish neighbors with a choice of conversion or exile; in some cases, violence led to murder.

The fever peaked, then subsided. Europe stabilized; Al-Hakim repented his action and rebuilt the basilica, and things returned to normal. By the end of the century, however, the Pope called for a Crusade to liberate Jerusalem from the Muslims. Marching along the Rhine, the Crusading army fell upon resident non-Christian communities, this time slaughtering European Jews.

Popular Christian devotion and theology, meanwhile, began to shift in emphasis from Jesus' resurrection as the key moment in salvation history, to the pains that Jesus suffered in the course of his brutal death. This theological shift placed attention less on the narratives of Christ's resurrection and more on the events of his Passion. And in their retelling of the Passion story, medieval theologians came to emphasize the actors in the Gospels' drama: Pilate the (neutral) governor, and the "wicked Jews." But more than the Jews in Jerusalem in Jesus' day were thereby condemned as evil. The community of contemporary Jews, their neighbors, seemed to medieval Christians to be continuous with the Gospels' actors. As long as any Jew of any generation refused to convert to Christianity, he or she was thought to be as guilty of slaying the Christ as were the Jews of centuries earlier depicted in the Passion narrative.

THIS RAPID REVIEW OF A THOUSAND YEARS of Western theological development might seem to have taken us far from Gibson's 2004 movie. In fact, without these developments, *The Passion of the Christ* would have told a very different story. Only three of our four first-century Gospels even mention the incident with the Temple's curtain. And early Christians, as we have seen, interpreted that Gospel scene in various ways: as the Temple mourning its own future destruction, or of God perhaps tearing his own "clothes" to mourn the death of his Son. Only after the second unsuccessful Jewish rebellion against Rome, in AD 132–135, do we find Gentile Christians specifically arguing that God, through the Romans, destroyed the Jewish Temple to punish the Jews for the death of his Son. Once Constantine favored the Church, and sponsored the building program in Jerusalem, Christians celebrated the new "Christian" temple as further proof that the Jews, in rejecting both Christ and his Church, had doomed themselves to live forever without a Temple. And with the intensification of politics and theology in the Middle Ages, contemporary Jewish communities were telescoped with the ancient one that Christians heard or read about when they heard or read their own Gospels: modern Jews, in declining Christian conversion, were seen as Christ-killers too. Passion plays dramatized this message, and provoked popular violence. The emphasis on Christ's suffering—an emphasis that visually dominates Gibson's movie—intensified Jewish "guilt."

By casting his characters as he has, by having Pilate so blameless and Caiaphas so wicked, by presenting a citywide hostility to Jesus, by depicting both priests and populace as utterly unmoved—indeed, as further incited—by Jesus' extreme suffering, Gibson has indeed given us an extremely accurate historical presentation of Jesus' passion, *as viewed from the high Middle Ages.* Hence his coda at the end of his film: Rome is shaken, but the Temple is destroyed. No Gospel ever stated that. Much later theology read that meaning into the Gospels. And that is the meaning that Gibson gives us. The movie's destruction of the Temple, caused by Gibson's special-effects divine tear, is God's pronouncement against the priests, and in a larger sense against the Jews.

But Gibson drew the elements of his story from a more modern source as well. His medieval heritage filters through the very detailed visions of an early-nineteenth-century nun. I am speaking, of course, of Anne Catherine Emmerich.

VISIONS OF VENERABLE ANNE CATHERINE EMMERICH (1774–1824)
Emmerich was a stigmatic visionary. That is, her piety was aligned with her identification of Jesus' suffering on the cross: she spontaneously exhibited in her own flesh the sorts of wounds that the crucifix depicted on the suffering Christ. Her visions about Christ's suffering were collected and, eight years after her death, written up in a voluminous work by a German poet, Clement Brentano. He entitled Emmerich's visions *The Lowly Life and Bitter Passion of Our Lord Jesus Christ and His Blessed Mother.* The quotations below draw on the 1915 English translation of the fourth edition of the German original. By looking at Brentano's work, we can see more clearly that the earthquake Gibson brings us at the close of his movie originates not in the Gospel of Matthew but in the visions of Emmerich.

> Terror fell upon all at the sound of Jesus' deathcry, when the earth quaked and the rock neath the cross was split asunder. A feeling of dread pervaded the whole universe. The veil of the Temple was on instant rent in twain, the dead arose from

their graves, the walls in the Temple fell, while mountains and buildings were overturned in many parts of the world (pp. 298–299).

By the earthquake at Jesus' death, when the rock of Calvary was split, many portions of the earth were upheaved while others sank, and this was especially the case in Palestine and Jerusalem. In the Temple and throughout the city, the inhabitants were just recovering somewhat from the fright caused by the darkness, when the heaving of the earth, the crash of falling buildings in many quarters, gave rise to still more general consternation; and, to crown their terror, the trembling and wailing crowd, hurrying hither and thither in dire confusion, encountered here and there the corpses raised from the dead, as they walked about uttering their warnings in hollow voices (pp. 301–302).

The two great columns at the entrances of the Holy of Holies in the Temple, between which hung a magnificent curtain, fell in opposite directions, the left-hand one to the south, the right-hand to the north. The beam which they supported gave way and the great curtain was, with a hissing noise, rent from top to bottom, so that opening on either side it fell. This curtain was red, blue, white and yellow. Many celestial spheres were described upon it, also figured like the brazen serpent. The people could now see into the Holy of Holies (pp. 303–304).

Jeremias appeared at the altar and uttered words of denunciation. The sacrifice of the Old Law was ended, he said, and a new one had begun (p. 304).

The description of widespread damage from the earthquake fills several more pages. The importance for our study is that the work of Emmerich-Brentano emphasizes the devastating impact that the earthquake had on the Temple. The mother of Jesus together with some companions visited the area in the wee hours of the next morning. She wept, "for its ruin and its desolate aspect on that day...bore witness to the sins of her people" (p. 350). Thus the judgment is explicit: the concept of Jewish corporate guilt for the death of Jesus is linked to the cessation of sacrifice in the Temple.

This accusation against all Jews everywhere for the crime of those who collaborated with Pilate is an integral part of the piety of that period in which Sister Anne Catherine lived. We have seen how the idea developed in Western theology. And if we have seen *The Passion*, we know as well how Gibson uses this idea to conclude his movie.

The teaching of the Catholic Church holds that, in the instance of private revelations, such visions may be accepted by Catholics provided they do not contradict the message of the Bible and teaching of the Church. In the case of Emmerich, the question of the authenticity of her visions is compounded by the fact that Brentano, not Emmerich herself, seems to have supplied the detail about Jerusalem that figures so strongly in *The Dolorous Passion*. Much seems to come from Brentano (who availed himself of maps and guidebooks of the Holy Land), and not from Emmerich herself.

Gibson noted in his interview with Diane Sawyer that Emmerich gave him many ideas for his movie that he would not have thought of himself. It is Gibson's prerogative as an artist to draw his inspiration where he will. But we might wish, if Gibson, as he says, knowingly shaped his story by so closely following a nineteenth-century book, that he would refrain from making claims that his movie is true to events in the first part of the first century. He cannot—or should not—be able to have it both ways. And given the sort of anti-Judaism native to Emmerich and Brentano's time and place, we might question Gibson's sense of responsibility. Artists are free, but they are also responsible for the works that they create. In regard to a sacred theme, we would hope that a reflective person would ask, "What are the implications of my choices?"

JUDAISM AS A LIVING RELIGION

The vitality of Jewish faith and practice, despite tragic persecutions in many parts of Europe, has continued across the centuries. Even the horrendous attacks of the Nazi period did not prevent the restoration of Jewish communities to vibrant life. Judaism thrives. Christians who might wish that this were otherwise, or who wish that all Jews would convert to Christianity, should consider the instructions of our own New Testament. In the Acts of the Apostles, the Jewish sage Gamaliel argues that the Sanhedrin should leave the early Church in peace. "For if this endeavor or activity is of human origin, it will destroy itself. But if it comes from God, you will not be able to destroy it; you may even find yourselves fighting against God" (Acts 5:38–39). Any Christian theological judgment that Jews have ceased to have their own role to play in the divine plan should likewise be put under the scrutiny of Gamaliel's dictum in this New Testament book.

In 1965, the Second Vatican Council formally rejected the traditions that held that all Jews of all generations were guilty of the death of Jesus. The following brief statement was not "absolution" (as the secular press has stated ad nauseam), because Jews were not being "absolved" of any sin or crime: the point was that Jews as a people had committed no sin or crime. Rather, the Council Declaration *Nostra Aetate* stated that the general indictment of Jews and of Judaism, a long-standing staple of popular preaching and teaching of Christian tradition, was wrong.

> Even though Jewish authorities and those who followed their lead pressed for the death of Christ (see Jn 19:6), neither all Jews indiscriminately at that time, nor Jews today, can be charged with the crimes committed during his passion. It is true that the Church is the new people of God, yet the Jews should not be spoken of as rejected or accursed as if this followed from holy Scripture. Consequently, all must take care, lest in catechizing or in preaching the word of God, they teach anything which is not in accord with the truth of the Gospel message or the spirit of Christ.
>
> (Vatican Council II, *Nostra Aetate:* Declaration on the Relationship of the Church to Non-Christian Religions, October 28, 1965)

This teaching must be reiterated in the religious education of both adults and children. At the same time, the diversity and richness of Jewish spirituality during the Second Temple period should be known. The danger of Christians reverting to old stereotypes of Judaism as a ritualistic, legalistic religion of hypocrites will be offset by the emphasis on the rich context within which Jesus and his followers built their teachings.

The council dealt with the past. Slowly, over the decades, the Holy See's Commission for Religious Relations with the Jews also grappled with questions regarding Judaism contemporary with the Church and the State of Israel. After Rabin and Arafat met in 1993, fears concerning the lot of small Christian communities in Arab lands subsided and the stage was set for the *Fundamental Agreement* between the Holy See ("The Vatican") and Israel (December 30, 1993). This laid the foundation for the exchange of ambassadors, a sign of the highest level of diplomatic recognition of Israel by the Holy See. But this agreement was more than a link between two small states. It was a sign of "the unique nature of the relationship between the Catholic Church and the Jewish people, and of the historic process of reconciliation and growth in mutual understanding and friendship between Catholics and Jews" (Preamble).

No one, whether in symbolic gestures or in words, has done more than has Pope John Paul II to show respect for the Jewish people and their faith. His address to the Jewish community of Mainz, Germany (November 17, 1980), described the encounter between the Church and "the people of God of the old Covenant, *never revoked by God* (see Romans 11:29), and those of the New Covenant" as involving a dialogue with the Church between the first and second parts of her Bible. "A second dimension of our dialogue...is the meeting between present day Christian Churches and the present day people of the Covenant concluded with Moses." From this foundation, the Church in recent decades has developed a series of statements to assist preachers and religion teachers to present a positive vision of Judaism and of the Jewish people. This vision must reach all parts of the Catholic world, including places without a significant Jewish population. These teachings should inform all artistic work as well, including efforts to dramatize the Passion of the Christ. American bishops have reiterated their commitment to this teaching, specifically on the issue of presentations of the Passion with the promulgation of *Criteria for Evaluation of Dramatizations of the Passion* (1998).

The words of Pope John Paul present a challenge for both faith communities:

As Christians and Jews, following the example of the faith of Abraham, we are called to be a blessing for the world (cf. Gen 12:2ff). This is the common task awaiting us. It is therefore necessary for us, Christians and Jews, to be first a blessing to one another.

("Reflections on the Fiftieth Anniversary
of the Uprising of the Warsaw Ghetto," April 6, 1993)

BEN WITHERINGTON III

❖

NUMBSTRUCK

AN EVANGELICAL REFLECTS ON MEL GIBSON'S *PASSION*

Numb. That is about the only word I can use to describe how I felt after seeing Mel Gibson's *The Passion of the Christ*. And I gather from the exit poll interviews that many Evangelicals would agree that "numb" aptly describes their response. The other word that keeps being mentioned is "overwhelmed." You have to be a "braveheart" indeed to watch this movie, especially if you love Jesus as much as most Evangelicals do. Who wants to see their best friend beat up for two straight hours?

But, as Mel Gibson explained in his televised interview with Diane Sawyer, his movie was not intended to produce a warm fuzzy feeling in the viewer. It is an example of using the "direct method" of confronting the audience with the price Christ paid for the redemption of the world. Some of the people watching may be as affronted with and scandalized by this portrayal as were the original viewers of Jesus' crucifixion. Yet even those who are sympathetic to the portrayal leave numb and overwhelmed. Is this a good thing?

Does Gibson's movie have any redeeming value, or is it just another display of the video violence for which our culture has such an appetite? In other words, is the source both of the film's violent idiom and of the audience's positive response to it not so much the story in the Scriptures as the fashions of pop culture? Why are Evangelicals so sympathetic to a portrayal that in some respects is closer to Catholic traditions about the Passion than to the Gospels themselves? These are issues worth probing.

HISTORICAL OR HYSTERICAL: THE LIBERTIES OF POETIC LICENSE

For those who know the Gospels well, and in their original languages, this movie is one of those cases where you say "Oh yes!" at some junctures in the film, and "Oh no!" at others. For example, it was actually very refreshing to hear the characters speak in Aramaic, and the subtitles really were not a distraction. This attempt at creating distance between the culture of the characters and that of the audience is both effective and a good thing. It has been rightly said that the past is like a foreign country—they do things differently there. Doubtless, however, it went right over the heads of most Evangelicals that in the flashback scene depicting Jesus at home in the carpentry shop, he spoke with his mother in Hebrew, not Aramaic; and that, in the middle of his discussion with Pilate, Jesus broke into medieval Latin! The former scene is plausible, but the latter simply vitiates Gibson's attempt at historical authenticity. Most assuredly, if Pilate and Jesus had conversed without the help of a translator, it would not have been in medieval Latin. More probably their shared language would have been Greek. But of course, 99 percent of all the Evangelical audience would not recognize this blunder.

Does this historical gaffe matter? If, as Mel Gibson says, he wanted to portray Christ's Passion "as it actually was," and indeed if, as he has frequently claimed, he felt led by the Holy Spirit to film his movie as he did—that is, by striving for a high level of historical authenticity—then his mistakes of language, especially regarding Latin, are problematic. What they suggest is that Gibson's attraction to medieval Catholic ideas, rather than his concern for historical authenticity, was the real driving force behind the way that he wrote, filmed, and edited this movie.

Another good example of this problem is Gibson's presentation of Mary Magdalene. Though her portrayal is dramatically effective, it is also historically and scripturally unfortunate. Gibson blunders by identifying her, through a flashback, with the woman caught in adultery in the Gospel of John. Is this just poetic license? No, it is a Catholic tradition that, in Evangelical perspective, is again at variance with the biblical text. We have no reason whatsoever to think that the woman portrayed in John 7:53–8:11 is Mary Magdalene. That story speaks of an anonymous woman. Since John 20 portrays Mary Magdalene at length and identifies her quite explicitly by name, how likely is it that the fourth evangelist would present the same woman as an anonymous figure in the former story (which in any case is textually problematic), and as the named woman at the cross and at the empty tomb?

A more extreme example of Gibson's fondness for medieval Catholic traditions is evident in his introduction of Veronica, a young woman wiping Jesus' face when he falls on the route to Golgotha. Miraculously, a true image of his face appears imprinted on her veil. We see here, again, that what controls Gibson's presentation is not commitment to historical authenticity or his fidelity to the Gospel narrative accounts (which contain no stories about Veronica), but his desire to offer up a visual version of the medieval Catholic traditions about what happened on the Via Dolorosa. Evangelicals are largely ignorant of these traditions. They might be mildly puzzled by these non-Gospel elements in this filmed Gospel story, but they are willing to permit them as small aberrations that do not detract from the overall authenticity of the film.

But it is not just the poetic license of inserting later Catholic traditions into the story—some of which distort the story—that is at issue here. There is also the issue of inserting motifs that have no basis either in the Gospels or apparently in ancient Catholic tradition. For example, in one scene Jesus, having been taken captive in the Garden of Gethsemane, is marched off to

Caiaphas' house and then pushed off a bridge and left dangling there as Judas, quivering, lurks below. This scene comes straight out of the nineteenth-century visions of Anne Catherine Emmerich. They are not even part of ancient Catholic tradition. The problems then extend beyond the historical difficulties raised by the use of certain long-revered Catholic traditions.

But there is more. Gibson not only presents a story of the struggle between good and evil: he also introduces the figure of Evil as a character in this movie. It is of course true that it is difficult to portray Satan in a movie about a historical chain of events, and I think that Gibson's gamble paid off from a dramatic point of view. I found the androgynous Satan figure spooky enough and believable enough to be effective in this movie. Gibson's devil was disturbing in the right sense, even though the Gospel accounts say little about the role of Satan in the story except in relationship to Judas Iscariot.

That said, I feel strongly that there can be no excuse for portraying children as demons who taunt Judas into hanging himself, and in particular it is especially inexcusable to portray Jewish children with head coverings taking on this demonic task. Though I do not think that Mel Gibson intends for his movie to be an inducement or endorsement of any kind of anti-Semitism, this particular scene should certainly have been altered or deleted, because it definitely can be construed in that way. His source for this unhappy scene is again the visions of Anne Catherine Emmerich. This is a case where poetic license becomes reckless and lacking in sensitivity and understanding of how such a scene will be viewed by non-Christians, especially by Jews. Here Gibson cannot invoke his defense of Biblical literalism, since demons are nowhere in evidence in any of the canonical Gospel accounts of these events, not even in the story of Judas' hanging. Had Mel Gibson taken more counsel or wiser counsel from some scholars, including Evangelical scholars, this blunder, and the hurt it causes, could have been avoided. Among other things it might have prevented some of the complaints that Mel Gibson reflects the same insensitivity to Jews as some of his father Hutton's remarks, trivializing the Holocaust, do.

This brings us to the two scenes in the movie most puzzling for Evangelicals: (1) the devil's carrying around a very spooky looking child, and (2) Mrs. Pilate's handing linens to Mary Magdalene and the mother of Jesus so they may sop up his blood after the flagellation. Neither of these scenes come either from the Bible or from ancient Catholic tradition but, again, from the visions of Anne Catherine Emmerich. Not surprisingly, these scenes made no sense to Evangelicals, not least because they were not grounded in the biblical text at all. The former scene seems to be an anti-Madonna and anti–Christ child scene, and the latter has to do with the concept of Christ's blood being sacramental or precious, and so Jesus' blood is sopped up. The former scene is especially disturbing because of the wicked grin that appears on the child's face. Apparently we are meant to see how Satan twists and distorts the truth about the mother of Jesus and her child. These scenes are talismans of the engine that is driving this depiction: not the Gospels themselves, but Emmerich's mystical imagination. The former scene has the same liabilities as the Judas scene in that it appears to depict demons as children. The latter scene seems to treat Jesus' blood as a holy relic.

If we turn now more fully to the depiction of Jews in this movie, two things can be said immediately: (1) it is the Romans who flagellate Jesus; (2) it is the Romans who execute Jesus. So far so good, in terms of historical accuracy and biblical fidelity. Nor should there be objections to the notion that some Jews, including some in the Sanhedrin, opposed Jesus and wanted him off the scene. This also is supported in the biblical texts. To his credit, Gibson portrays a mixed response in the Sanhedrin to Jesus, with some Jews not wanting any part of the travesty that is happening.

Now of course many non-Evangelical scholars will argue that this whole scene is fiction because the Sanhedrin would not meet under such circumstances and at night. I am unconvinced by such arguments, since they are based largely on much later Jewish sources about the Sanhedrin's procedures. There is no good historical reason that I can see why there could not have been at least a sort of preliminary hearing, if not an emergency meeting, of the Sanhedrin because of the seriousness of the situation. (John 11 presents such a meeting.) So it is not this material that should cause offense, beyond whatever one may think of what the Gospels themselves suggest. The Gospels are certainly not anti-Semitic, and thinking that Jesus was condemned by the Sanhedrin does not make a person an anti-Semite.

But what of some of the other contrived scenes in the movie? Is it really necessary to have Jesus abused by Jewish Temple police when they take him captive in Gethsemane? There is absolutely nothing in our earliest account in Mark to suggest such abuse (Mark 14:43–52), nor in the Matthean account (Matthew 26:47–56) nor in the Lukan account (Luke 22:54), nor in the Johannine account (John 18:1–11). John's Gospel actually tells us that the soldiers sent to arrest Jesus were Romans (18:12). In other words, here as elsewhere, Gibson has taken the liberty to add violence to the depiction that is not found in the Bible itself. In this case it is at the expense of Jews.

But perhaps by more than anything else in the movie, the alarm bell warning of anti-Semitism has been set off by Gibson's depiction of Pontius Pilate and Caiaphas. Pilate seems to be a vacillating and weak governor, while Caiaphas and his entourage are determined pursuers of the death of Jesus. Let us take the harder path here and allow for a moment that perhaps Caiaphas was determined to do away with Jesus. Even if this were so, it does not allow one to tar all Jewish officials, much less all Jews in Jerusalem, much less all Jews in general as being opposed to Jesus. In other words, we would be dealing with the actions of a few, which cannot be globalized into collective guilt of some kind.

But the portrait of Pilate is another matter. Pilate, we know both from the New Testament (Luke 13:1) and from the Jewish historian Josephus, was a vicious governor. Has Gibson gone beyond the portrayal of Pilate in the three principal accounts he is drawing on (Matthew, Luke, and John)? The answer here is yes. Gibson does so by amplifying the role of Pilate's wife well beyond the brief mention of her in Matthew 27:19. Gibson portrays her as a compassionate and fair-minded person who even gives the Marys the linens so that they may soak up Jesus' blood. This goes well beyond the one Gospel verse that indicates Pilate's wife had a dream that informed her Jesus was innocent. Gibson also distorts the record by not depicting the fact that Pilate was indeed vicious, regardless of the character of his wife. Once again, his reliance on the visions of Anne Catherine Emmerich has led Gibson astray.

There is a plausible historical scenario, however, as to why Pilate might hesitate to execute Jesus, and it is not because he cared about truth and fairness. He could have done so simply to tweak the nose of Caiaphas. Precisely because he despised Jews, he may have played with not giving Caiaphas what he wanted. This seems to me to be historically plausible; but Gibson, alas, suggests no such scenario. Rather, his Pilate seems weak, indecisive, even tormented, if not just and committed to due process. This recasting of Pilate's character is particularly telling when we actually get to the biblical motif of Pilate's washing his hands. In Gibson's portrayal, this symbolic act seals the deal in terms of signaling Pilate's fair-mindedness, as opposed to his simply giving up in disgust. Throughout Gibson's movie, the people most ardently pursuing the death of Jesus do not include Pilate. If one asks why the high priest might want Jesus crucified instead of just executed by some other means, it surely has to do with the fact that crucifixion was the most shameful way to die; and if the high priest wanted to scotch the rumor that Jesus was Messiah, this was by far the most effective method to demonstrate the contrary.

Perhaps as compensation for portraying Pilate as meek and mild we have the literal overkill when it comes to the flagellation of Jesus by some really sadistic Roman soldiers. Here, for a change, Gibson's exaggerations come at the expense of the Romans. In Matthew and Mark, Jesus' flagellation comprises all of one verse, while in Luke it is omitted altogether, although Luke adds that Jesus was abused and mocked by those guarding him (presumably Jewish guards) at the house of the high priest (Luke 22:63–65). In John as well (John 19:1), only one verse speaks of Jesus' flogging. In short, nothing whatsoever in the Gospel accounts suggests the long and gory spectacle that we have to endure in Gibson's movie where Jesus is brutalized beyond all recognition. Realistically, Jesus should never have even survived that onslaught, much less been able to carry or help carry an extra-large, entire cross (not just the crossbeam) all the way to Golgotha.

What makes Gibson's depiction of this torture all the worse is that there is very little relief from the violence in the entire movie. The flashbacks are too few and too short. This causes a further problem for those who see this movie and do not really know the Gospel story: such people have no context by which to understand why in the world all this abuse is being heaped on this man. We do not even have the story of the cleansing of the Temple to give us a clue.

It is the flagellation scene especially and its excesses that has led to the charge that Gibson's movie glorifies violence. Whether one wants to go this far or not, when Gibson diminishes Pilate's responsibility and at the same time amplifies the flagellation to the breaking point, he is certainly guilty of historical distortion, going well beyond what poetic license should allow for. I should add that, from a Christian theological point of view, there is no good reason to exaggerate the flagellation, since it is *not* flagellation, or a superhuman ability to endure extreme pain, that accomplishes atonement for our sins. The death of Jesus on the cross is what atones for our sins.

Why then, in light of all we have just considered, are Evangelical Christians so fervently embracing this movie, especially in view of their professed commitment to sticking to the historical substance of the Bible? The answer is complex, and we must turn to it now.

PASSION MYSTICISM AND PASSIONATE FAITH

It is of course easy to point out that many Evangelicals do not know their Bibles all that well, so that they are likely to miss the small historical incongruities. They may even be willing to overlook the larger ones as long as they feel the essence of the story is told accurately. Since the essential message of the great price Christ paid for the redemption of the world is indeed portrayed clearly here, as is Christ's forgiving love, and since there is actually a brief resurrection scene, most Evangelicals may be tempted to think that complaining about other aspects of the movie is an exercise in majoring in minors. This, in my judgment, is a mistake, but it is an understandable reaction given the Evangelical mind-set.

A second important factor is that Evangelicals are zealous to evangelize, to tell the world about the Gospel. Any bold attempt to portray the essence of the story of Jesus in the public forum is likely to be applauded even if it involves some historical distortions. Evangelicals often have a great suspicion of the media, and believe that the media do not treat Christianity fairly. Thus, the opposition to Gibson and his film, many Evangelicals think, is just another example of the media's anti-Christian bias.

But the most powerful reason, in my judgment, why Evangelicals are embracing this very Catholic portrayal of Christ, his suffering, and his death is something that many non-Christians may not understand. Some non-Christians will even find this reason repugnant if they do understand it, and make accusations of sadism or masochism. All these reactions, positive and negative, have to do with the deeply offensive notion of suffering love. Some explanation is required.

We live in a therapeutic culture. Our culture sees suffering as always a bad thing, and lacking in redeeming value. Indeed, suffering is something that health professionals rightly try to eliminate from human life. Perhaps this modern attitude is an extreme over-reaction to the medieval notion that suffering is, in many ways, an inherently good thing. Such valorizing of suffering in itself in turn led to the distortions of corporal mortification, physically abusing oneself, instead of mere mortification of sinful desires. But to leave the matter at that does not really explain why Evangelicals are so passionate about this movie. Let me illustrate with a poem I once wrote.

Wounds That Heal
Updike says it's fertile
To open an old wound
Like plowing up the scab of earth
Upon a harvest moon.

The wound itself
A tender spot
Becomes the source of salve
A balm itself from deep within
A pleasant pain to have.

A wound may fester,
Or may heal,
A bitter, better pill
It more reveals a depth of soul
Than a pure pleasure will.

Healing's not always the goal
Within this vale of tears,
What draws you closer to the Lord,
Is nothing we should fear.

St. Paul was told
When he besought
The thorn to be plucked out
That he'd do better keeping it,
Than healing from without.

His power is made perfect
Within this mortal shell,
When we most own our weakness
Is when we are most well.

So unbind your wounds
Examine
And see what truths they tell.
Short of resurrection
Your wounds will serve you well.

There are many dimensions of the concept of suffering love, and how suffering can actually be of benefit to a person. For Christians, these concepts ultimately go back to the story of Christ's redemptive suffering on the cross, which in turn led people like Paul to speak of being crucified with Christ or to speak of God's power being perfected in weakness. The theological underpinnings of this reasoning are multifaceted.

First of all, Evangelicals have a vibrant and strong belief in the afterlife, which includes not just a belief in dying and going to be with the Lord in heaven, but also a belief in receiving a resurrection body like Christ's when he returns. Such beliefs render it quite unnecessary to try and prop up this body forever, or to see this life as the be-all and end-all of existence. To the contrary, Evangelicals see this life as a temporal and temporary situation on the way to eternity. This conviction relativizes many things. It even leads to the conclusion that to die as a Christian can be a good thing, since one then gets to move beyond this vale of tears. It is not necessary to cling to this life at all costs: this life only points forward to a later, better life.

Secondly, Evangelicals strongly believe that God works all things together for good for those who love Him (see Romans 8). This means that suffering in this life can be used for good, even when it may not, in itself, be a good thing. More than that, they see suffering as a means of sanctification and purification for fallen human beings. This is one of the truths that I tried to convey in my poem. This Evangelical belief is unlike medieval Catholic meditation on Christ's wounds, or longing to bear the actual stigmata in one's own flesh. Rather, it involves an acceptance that God can make one a better person through one's suffering if one will submit the suffering into God's hands.

There is, furthermore, the important point that since the Gospels themselves urge disciples to take up their own crosses (not Jesus') and follow him, disciples are warned that they too may be called to suffering love. The imitation of Christ, even in his sufferings, though not to be sought after in some masochistic way, is part of the call to discipleship.

But the mystery of suffering love goes even further when one considers the pattern of Christ's life, which exhibits the principle of enduring wrong rather than perpetrating violence on others. Here we have come to the nub of the matter.

The Gospel of suffering love involves not only a call to be prepared to suffer, but also a call to be prepared to renounce violence altogether. This is exhibited in the Passion story itself, when Jesus rebukes the use of a weapon that severed the high priest's servant's ear. In other words, the Gospel involves a call to nonviolence. Many of the earliest followers of Jesus, like Jesus himself, felt the implication of the Gospel was a call to nonviolence. Now this should have made Gibson's strong emphasis on violence in this movie objectionable; but since it is not Jesus or, in the main, his followers who perpetrate the violence, this has not been the response. Yet there should have been some qualms expressed about the degree to which the movie displayed such mind-numbing violence. Perhaps the American gospel of "peace through war," the *Gladiator* sort of approach to life, has trumped the real Gospel in the hearts of some. Or is it just that the real Gospel of peace, and a depiction of the Passion of Christ more accurate than the one that Gibson made, would not have impressed Americans in the way that this film has?

CONCLUSIONS

Whatever one makes of these reflections, it should at least be clear that there are powerful and deep-seated reasons why Evangelicals would embrace Mel Gibson's movie even with its Catholic excesses. Evangelicals believe that the death and resurrection of Jesus are the most important events in human history, indeed are the fulcrum of human history. They believe strongly that Christ's death provided redemption from sin for all human beings. This being so, this movie, especially with many non-Christians watching, is likely to be strongly supported by the Evangelical community for a long time to come.

Still, upping the quotient of physical abuse that Jesus had to take seems an odd way to exalt the Prince of Peace, and the Gospel of Peace. Furthermore, Evangelicals really love the Gospel as presented, not at the multiplex, but in the New Testament. This movie, which is a mishmash of traditions (ancient and modern) and of the Gospel, is no substitute for the real Gospel.

JAMES MARTIN, S.J.

❖

THE LAST STATION

A CATHOLIC REFLECTION ON *THE PASSION*

The variety of reactions to *The Passion of the Christ* on the part of American Catholics astonished me. After seeing Mel Gibson's film shortly before it opened, I figured that most Catholics would have more or less the same reaction that I did. (More about my own take later.) But the responses ranged widely. One friend, a Jesuit priest and film scholar (yes, there are such persons) expressed a common sentiment: he found the film far too violent and gory. ("Yuck," said another friend with admirable simplicity.) Others objected to an abbreviated resurrection scene that, they said, seemed tacked onto the end of the picture as an afterthought. Some found the Jewish leaders presented almost as caricatures, and deemed the movie anti-Semitic. Another thought that the overly sympathetic portrayal of, as she called her, "Mrs. Pilate," strained believability. After hearing similar reactions, some Catholics decided to forgo seeing it.

On the other hand, an erudite priest who has spent years studying Catholic spirituality found the movie intensely moving, and told me that it was difficult for him to understand the criticisms. A friend teaching in a

Catholic school said that his tenth-grade religion class engaged in a spirited discussion over the movie, with the majority agreeing that it helped them to appreciate the physicality of Jesus' sufferings. In another Catholic school, a Jesuit came across a student in the school's chapel who said, through tears, that he felt drawn to prayer after seeing the movie. "Piercing" was what one elderly man called the film, saying that it led him to reflect on his own sinfulness. Finally, a Latina Catholic friend rushed up to me after seeing the film. "I loved it!" she said. "How could anyone not?"

CATHOLIC AND NOT-SO-CATHOLIC

That *The Passion of the Christ* would serve as a lightning rod for Catholics is not surprising. For, in a way, the film is both strongly Catholic and strongly non-Catholic.

The film's Catholic sensibility is clear. American Catholics would already be familiar with the architecture of the film. For the film's structure locates itself not simply in the Gospel narratives and European Passion plays, but in the Stations of the Cross—the formalized pictorial depiction of the trial, death, and crucifixion of Jesus that appears as murals, mosaics or statues in every Catholic church. The traditional fourteen-part iconography begins with "Jesus is Condemned to Death," and concludes with the Station "Jesus Is Placed in the Tomb." Catholics would also recognize those Stations singled out for attention in the movie, for example, "Jesus Falls for the First Time." During Lent, most Catholic churches sponsor special services centered on the Stations, accompanied by prayers and music. *The Passion*, then, is a filmed representation of what Catholics see every Sunday on the walls of their churches.

The film's Catholic roots are evident as well in its graphic representation of the crucifixion. Centuries old, the tradition of meditating on the physical and spiritual sufferings of Jesus, "the Man of Sorrows," is firmly grounded in the Catholic piety of almost every culture. In his classic work *The Spiritual Exercises*, the sixteenth-century mystic St. Ignatius Loyola counseled reflection on the Passion as a means of understanding not only the willingness of Jesus, out of love, to accept suffering, but also the ways that one's own sins contribute to an already sinful world.

Consequently, in Catholic churches one typically finds a crucifix (that is, Jesus hanging on the cross), in contrast to the empty cross (signifying the resurrection) common in churches of many Protestant denominations. A Jesuit novice recently told me that after working in a hospice run by the Missionaries of Charity (Mother Teresa's religious order), one sister offered him a small crucifix as a gift. Pointing to the body of Jesus, she remarked that one nun regularly applied extra red paint to their crucifixes, because the wounds of Jesus simply weren't realistic enough.

The important role of the mother of Jesus in the film likewise reflects traditional Catholic piety. While Mary is recognized and honored in other Christian denominations, she lies at the heart of much Catholic popular devotion. (The use of the Rosary, for example, which is comprised mainly of Marian prayers, is an almost exclusively Catholic devotion.) Mary is central to the film: the disciples consistently refer to her as "Mother." All these themes—the structure of the Stations of the Cross, the appreciation of the physical sufferings of Christ, and the prominence of Mary—point to a heightened Catholic sensibility.

At the same time, one could argue that *The Passion of the Christ* also demonstrates a non-Catholic sensibility. In some places the script sets aside advances made in Catholic biblical scholarship since even before the Second Vatican Council. It neglects insights by Catholic scholars regarding the role of the Jewish leaders in the trial and crucifixion. And the film's brutally graphic violence flies in the face of repeated pronouncements by the Vatican (and the U.S. bishops) against the excessive use of violence in films.

Throughout the film, Mel Gibson also adds to the Gospel accounts of the Passion by weaving in stories taken from the writings of the nineteenth-century mystic Anne Catherine Emmerich. In what were called her "visions," the German nun reportedly had the gift of being able to offer almost eyewitness accounts of the crucifixion of Jesus, based on her meditations. These visions, transcribed by the German poet Clemens Brentano, were published some eight years after her death. Gibson's scene of Pilate's wife offering Mary a cloth to wipe up her son's blood is taken from Emmerich's *The Dolorous Passion of Our Lord Jesus Christ*. Later scholarship revealed that Brentano himself had probably supplied some of the details of the landscape of the Holy Land that so impressed readers with their veracity. Certainly a filmmaker may take artistic liberties with a story. But beyond the reliability of Emmerich's visions, the Catholic Church has resisted conflating what it calls "private revelation" with Scripture, which Gibson freely does in a film whose accuracy was a main selling point.

In other words, while Gibson offers viewers a decidedly "Catholic" film, he does so at the cost of setting aside some contemporary Catholic teachings and scholarship.

Ironically, this most "Catholic" film has been eagerly embraced by many evangelical Protestant denominations, some of which have historically been critical of the very themes it highlights, such as the centrality of Mary. Evangelicals who often insist on strict adherence to Scripture seemed equally untroubled by the liberties that Gibson took with the Gospel stories—for example, his addition of scenes from Anne Catherine Emmerich's visions. (One wonders what the devout Catholic nun would make of so many Protestants enjoying the fruits of her writings.) If the film's Catholic sensibilities begin to influence members of these denominations, new questions may be raised. How long before an evangelical church decides to include the Stations of the Cross or replace their formerly empty cross with a crucifix? (Or before fundamentalist Christians start praying the Rosary?)

But the movie's jaw-dropping box-office returns indicate a fascination with its subject that crosses denominational and even religious lines. There are a number of possible reasons for the film's appeal among the general public. First, one can't dismiss the American cult of celebrity (this is Mel Gibson, after all, once named *People* magazine's "Sexiest Man Alive") or the surrounding controversy, which drew even agnostics and atheists to their local multiplexes. Further, there have been almost no mainstream Jesus movies since *Jesus of Montreal* in 1989. The movie's popularity may reflect a pent-up desire for cinematic treatments of biblical themes. And despite the perception that we live in a secular age, religion is of continuing interest to most Americans. Other ticket-buyers may just have been curious about a novelty: a new look at an old story.

The movie appeals on another level as well. Since the Gospels describe only a small part of the life of Jesus (the years between the ages of twelve and thirty, often referred to as the "Hidden Life," are entirely absent) and because the Gospels differ on even important aspects of his ministry, the full story of Jesus of Nazareth remains essentially unknowable. And people are naturally drawn to a mystery. As an aside, this partially explains the popularity of Dan Brown's best-selling novel, *The Da Vinci Code*, which posits a Jesus married to Mary Magdalene. (Needless to say, Emmerich and Gibson would both disagree with that imaginative addition.) While representing two different genres of pop culture, the thriller *The Da Vinci Code* and the movie *The Passion of the Christ* both appeal to the human instinct to find answers to mysterious questions.

But let's consider the appeal of the film from a more "spiritual" vantage point. Catholics believe that the very attraction to Scripture, to descriptions of the life of Jesus, as well as to artistic representations of religious themes, are themselves ways that God has of drawing us into a deeper relationship with the divine. In other words, the very desire to know more about God comes from God. So the attraction for Christians to *The Passion of the Christ* may be a response to a deeply felt, even if largely unarticulated, desire to know Jesus more fully.

FAITH SEEKING UNDERSTANDING

Another reflection of the Christian desire to know the story is the scholarly venture called the "quest for the historical Jesus." In brief, scholars of the "historical Jesus" study the historical context and sociopolitical realities that were part of the life of Jesus of Nazareth. And part of this scholarship focuses on how the Gospels were originally composed, what stories were included and why.

Catholic theology has long recognized the importance of serious Scripture scholarship. Underlying this recognition is the belief that Scripture is one of the primary means through which God is revealed. The Second Vatican Council, which convened bishops from around the world in the early 1960s to consider contemporary theological issues, wrote in its document *Dei Verbum* (*The Word of God*): "Sacred tradition and sacred Scripture form one sacred deposit of the word of God…" This reemphasis on serious Scripture scholarship (long the domain of dedicated Protestant theologians, philologists, and historians) has led to a flowering of Catholic biblical scholarship.

When considering *The Passion of the Christ*, therefore, it is important to take seriously historical research and scholarship. Thinking about the Gospels in a critical fashion is part of Catholic belief: fundamentalist and literalist interpretations of Scripture have no place in a modern Catholic understanding of God's revelation.

This approach also makes sense intellectually. Bluntly speaking, since many Gospel accounts differ with one another, a completely literalist interpretation is an impossibility. Some quick examples: Jesus makes one journey to Jerusalem in the Synoptic Gospels (Matthew, Mark and Luke), while he makes at least five in John. The story of Jesus' birth in the Gospel of Matthew describes Mary and Joseph as living in Bethlehem, fleeing to Egypt, and then moving for the first time to Nazareth, whereas Luke has the two living originally in Nazareth, traveling to Bethlehem in time for the birth, and then returning home again. Mark and John have nothing of such traditions.

More dramatically, some of the resurrection stories, perhaps the most important part of the Christian message, are substantially different. In some accounts, the risen Christ appears as a physical being, in others he can walk through walls.

The various ways of telling the story reflect the different views and concerns of the Gospel writers (and, in the case of the resurrection, the difficulty of expressing what the earlier witnesses had experienced). But they also make it clear that the Gospels are not to be treated as strictly historical chronicles.

Catholics believe that this points out the need for a careful approach to even familiar New Testament stories. The first-century writers of the Gospels presented different views of Jesus Christ, and did so with different communities, concerns, and readers in mind. So when arguing about historical accuracy, it is not enough simply to say, "It's in the Bible."

More to the point, when people raise questions about the accuracy of certain historical contexts, unearth inconsistencies in the narratives, or critique a reliance on literalist interpretations of Scripture, they are not "watering down" the Gospels, they are engaging in an important part of the life of faith. For the Catholic, reason and faith are not in opposition, they are both expressions of God's grace leading human beings to the same goal: Truth. Indeed, one of the best (and oldest) definitions of theology comes from St. Anselm of Canterbury, writing in the eleventh century, who defined theology as *fides quaerens intellectum:* Faith seeking understanding.

IN OUR AGE

All these considerations highlight the requirement to portray accurately the role of the Jewish people and leaders in such films as *The Passion of the Christ*. From as early as the second century, a number of Gospel passages have been used to support the charge of "deicide" (literally, God-murdering) against the Jewish people as a whole. Used most often was Matthew 27:25, where "the people" say, in response to Pilate, "His blood be on us and on our children." (The film, oddly, retains this quote in Aramaic but does not provide an English subtitle.)

Until recently, the history of Christian-Jewish relations has been largely a record of hostility, persecution, and cruelty. Throughout European history, Jews were murdered in the name of the Church, and exiled from their homes. Both anti-Semitism and anti-Judaism were given expression and encouraged by medieval Passion plays sponsored by Catholic churches and organizations. The long history of Christian anti-Semitism and the horrific fate of the Jews during the Second World War are in themselves reason enough for Christians to consider exceedingly carefully the ways in which they understand and present the Passion story.

By the Second Vatican Council, however, decades of work on Catholic-Jewish relations led to the publication of the document called *Nostra Aetate* (*In Our Age*). The council's document, echoing the statements of St. Paul (Rom 9:4), reaffirmed the role of the Jews as "the people to whom the covenants and promises were given." It also repudiated the ancient accusations that charged the Jewish people as a whole as guilty for Jesus' death: "True, authorities of the Jews and those who followed their lead pressed for the death of Christ. Still, what happened in His Passion cannot be blamed upon all the Jews then living, without distinction, nor upon the Jews today." The council also stated that the Church "deplores the hatred, persecutions and displays of anti-Semitism...at any time and from any source."

In our own time, Pope John Paul II has worked diligently on Catholic-Jewish relations. Apologizing for the Church's historic role in Jewish persecutions, he stated, "erroneous and unjust interpretations of the New Testament regarding the Jewish people and their alleged culpability [for the crucifixion] have circulated for too long, engendering feelings of hostility toward this people."

How responsible, then, is *The Passion of the Christ* in its dramatic depiction of Jewish involvement in the death of Jesus? How adequately does it reflect recent scholarship? How much does it share the desire of the Church to avoid "erroneous and unjust interpretations"?

The question of the degree of historic responsibility for the death of Jesus is a complicated one that continues to be studied. While it is clear that some of the Jewish leaders were opposed to Jesus, it is also clear that only Rome had the power to condemn and crucify a man. Significantly, strains of anti-Judaism crept into the New Testament as the early Christians began to move away from Jewish traditions and to embrace non-Jews in their movement. Catholic scholarship therefore treats this issue with justifiable care and attention. In an essay entitled "Who Killed Jesus?" the Rev. Daniel J. Harrington, S.J., a renowned New Testament scholar, answers the question: "Pontius Pilate, cooperating with some Jewish leaders, was responsible for the death of Jesus."

The Passion of the Christ, however, adds scenes and dialogue that, in general, make the Jews look worse and Pilate look better. For example, the Gospels are unclear about the number of Jews who demanded the crucifixion; the movie, however, shows a large mob, visually implying that the Jewish community in general wanted him dead. But scholars point out that Jesus most likely had many Jewish supporters in Jerusalem: one reason he was arrested at night was probably to minimize angering his many supporters (Mark 14:2). In addition, the Palm Sunday narratives present Jesus entering Jerusalem the week before his death to the adulation of celebrating crowds.

About many of these artistic choices, one might say "It's in the Gospels" or, likewise, "It's more or less in the Gospels." But as important as what is included is what is excluded. The film, for example, omits the most famous action of Joseph of Arimathea, a sympathetic Jewish leader, who appears prominently in the Gospel of Mark. Joseph, "a respected member of the council," generously provides the tomb for Jesus (Mark 15:43). Thus an opportunity to portray a specific Jewish leader in a positive light—and one that is found in Scripture—is unaccountably left out.

Pontius Pilate, on the other hand, appears as a much more benign figure in the film than he does in the Gospels as a whole. Historical research into other ancient sources also suggests that Pilate was a brutal Roman governor, who had no qualms about crucifixion, and who was recalled to Rome because of cruelty toward his subjects. In the film, however, he is presented as a pensive and conflicted man, certainly more careful about sentencing a man to death than is the Jewish high priest Caiaphas. Pilate, for example, graciously offers Jesus a drink from his cup (which is not found in Scripture and is dubious given the Roman attitude toward their Judean subjects). Later, he carefully deliberates about his role in sentencing Jesus, in stark contrast to the quick and angry decisions of the Jewish high priests. As if to make the contrast more striking, the film has Pilate ask the high priest (after Jesus, in another non-scriptural scene, has been savagely beaten by the Jewish crowd) the question, "Do you always punish your prisoners before they are judged?" These words appear in Emmerich's writings. They are nowhere in the New Testament.

In these ways, *The Passion of the Christ* shifts the burden of responsibility away from Pontius Pilate on to the Jewish leaders. The film thereby overlooks the insights of modern Scripture scholars and, more sadly, frustrates the desire of the Catholic Church to avoid precisely this kind of misrepresentation. Even viewers moved by this representation of Jesus' suffering should understand that they are not watching an authoritative account of the Passion.

ANSELM'S LEGACY

Beyond the treatment of the Jewish leaders and Jews, what is the underlying theological approach of the film?

Many Catholics have said that the movie prompted them to reflect on their own sinfulness and on the willingness of Jesus to "die for our sins." This is not surprising. The movie pointedly opens with a quote from Isaiah 53 (written around 537 BC, not in 700 BC as the movie claims). "He was wounded for our transgressions...and by his wounds we are healed." This image in Isaiah is known as the "Suffering Servant," the one who bears the sins of his people, and finds particular emphasis, in its application to Jesus, in the Gospel of Mark.

The theological question of the meaning of Jesus' death has been the subject of thousands of books, articles, homilies, and treatises, and is difficult to encapsulate in a few paragraphs. In brief, however, Gibson's film emphasizes the theological issue of "redemption," the way in which the death and resurrection of Jesus liberate humankind from the bondage of sin.

The idea of redemption finds its roots in the Old Testament, where God redeems, or saves, the Jewish people, by leading them out of slavery in Egypt. In the New Testament, Jesus is seen, through his life, death, and resurrection, as leading his followers out of the slavery of sin and death. The Gospels express this idea of Jesus as redeemer by recounting his miracles, which constitute a "sign" of God's presence among his people, and which also—in a real way—liberate people from suffering.

But there are many ways of understanding redemption, and each Gospel shades the theme differently. The Gospel of Mark expresses the notion of the death of Jesus as a vicarious sacrifice for others. "For the Son of Man came not to be served, but to serve," Jesus says, "and to give his life as a ransom for many" (10:45). For Matthew, Jesus' Passion and death represent the fulfillment of the Scriptures, and thus the will of God. Luke emphasizes not simply the Passion, but also Jesus as an example of fidelity to the Father and to his mission. All of his actions are "redemptive," particularly the resurrection, which manifests the saving power of God. In John, the incarnation of the Word of God (that is, God becoming human) is a central factor in God's plan for humankind. The death of Jesus emphasizes the Son's obedience to, and union with, the Father. And the resurrection represents the ultimate triumph of light over darkness. For John, redemption comes from one's participation in the Son's union with the Father.

Gibson's film relies heavily on what is known as "satisfaction" theology. Though already present in both the Old and New Testaments, the idea was later developed by St. Anselm in 1098, in his treatise *Cur Deus Homo* (*Why God Became Man*). In Anselm's conception, based on feudal law, human sin is an offense against the honor of God, and can be removed only by reparation. In other words, expiation for sin is roughly paralleled by a vassal's payment of debt to his feudal lord. (A modern analogy, drawn from tort law, might be the idea of paying damages.) But, argued Anselm, the human race can never undertake enough penance for all its sins, because men and women already owe everything to God, who created them. Only Jesus, as God become human and born without sin, can offer his life of infinite worth as a satisfaction to the Father. This brings about our "redemption," with Jesus paying the price for humanity's sins.

There are important spiritual insights in this theological construct, which are well explicated in Gibson's film. This theology emphasizes the sacrifice of the sinless Jesus in and for a sinful world. The message shapes one of the film's most powerful moments, when Mary, cradling her dead son, stares insistently into the eyes of the viewer, inviting moviegoers to reflect on their own complicity in the continuation of sin.

However, "satisfaction" theology, while an integral part of the Christian tradition, cannot by itself explain the full mystery of the death of Jesus. Theologians after Anselm reminded Christians that *all* the activities in the life of Jesus—his incarnation, his ministry and miracles, his teachings, as well as his death and resurrection—were redemptive, because all of these ways enable believers to experience the saving love of God.

Anselm's approach also runs the risk of turning God into a sort of cruel judge, who demands retribution or satisfaction for human sinfulness. But, as one of my theology professors used to say, an encounter with Jesus Christ is an encounter with God. And in that light, the notion of God as a cruel judge contrasts strongly with the Gospel portrait of a loving Jesus, in whom justice reaches its fullness in mercy. So how we understand the death of Jesus has as much to do with our conception of God as it does with our conception of Jesus.

THE LAST STATION

This reflection raises another question for moviegoers, particularly in light of the sparse flashbacks to the ministry of Jesus and the extremely brief resurrection scene. Can one grasp the meaning of Jesus' death without understanding his ministry and the Resurrection? The answer is no. Jesus came not simply to die, but to live and to show his followers how to live. The essential message of Jesus is not his role as a sacrificial victim, but rather the proclamation of what he called "the Kingdom of God," and the revelation of himself as the Son of God. Certainly, his Passion is a central part of his message. But it cannot be separated from the rest of his life. There is, of course, no Easter without Good Friday; but Good Friday is meaningless without Easter.

The resurrection gives ultimate meaning to the entire story of Jesus. "If Christ has not been raised," as St. Paul said to the Christians in Corinth, "then your faith is in vain" (1 Corinthians 15:17). The resurrection, truly the last Station of the Cross, shows that sin and death do not have the last word, and that the loving power of God will always triumph.

This is one reason why the short and surprisingly garbled resurrection scene is problematic for the entire film. Not only does it reduce Jesus' rising from the dead to a kind of cinematic afterthought, it also diminishes the rich Gospel traditions of the various "post-resurrection" appearances, when the risen Christ meets his disciples and offers them forgiveness, peace, and hope. After such a violent two hours, such a message would have been both appropriate and welcome. Its absence is puzzling.

My own reaction to the movie was mixed, but mainly critical. Much of the visual imagery I found captivating. As the character of Jesus slowly made his way to Calvary, I found myself thinking, "This is probably close to what it looked like." As a Jesuit, I have spent many hours contemplating such scenes from the Gospels, and the film made some of these moments more vivid. And it was exciting to hear Jesus and his disciples speaking in Aramaic, and to wonder whether these cadences and inflections were near to what his followers might have heard. (On the other hand, Pilate's soldiers would likely have spoken a common form of Greek, not Latin.)

However, I found the movie excessively violent, going far beyond what was needed to tell the story. Certainly crucifixion was brutal, and the movie serves as a corrective to candy-coated cinematic representations of the death of Jesus. But the film's almost obsessive fixation on blood, guts and gore, especially during the scourging, was, in my opinion, a poor artistic choice. The overuse of slow-motion photography, strangely lingering close-ups and pounding music during these bloody scenes seemed gratuitously grue-some, and prevented me from entering into a story that I love. I was also very disturbed by the portrayal of the Jewish leaders. *The Passion* represents an enormous lost opportunity for a more accurate and nuanced presentation of that topic, especially in light of the call of the Second Vatican Council, Pope John Paul II, and the U.S. bishops to approach this complicated issue with the greatest care.

As a moviegoer, I also found the character of Jesus strangely remote, almost a cipher. Is this because I didn't already know something about the protagonist (his "backstory," as screenwriters say) before the movie began? By no means, as St. Paul would say. Most of my adult life has been spent thinking, studying, and praying about Jesus of Nazareth. In the film, how-ever, Jesus is presented as little more than a body to be tortured. The per-functory flashbacks to his life do little to capture the charismatic appeal of the man for whom his followers gave up everything.

But for me, the most troublesome aspect of the movie was its diminution of Jesus' ministry of teaching and healing, as well as of the resurrection. Now, many Catholics have said, "Well, it was a movie only about the Passion." But this, to me, misses the mark. If one wishes to communicate the message of Jesus, one must proclaim the *full* message—which includes his revolutionary teachings, his astonishing miracles, his intimate relationships with friends and disciples, his bold proclamation of the Kingdom of God and, most importantly, his resurrection. By neglecting or otherwise down-playing these elements, the movie narrows our appreciation of the Gospels and may encourage an overly restrictive focus on suffering. I kept thinking: Fifteen minutes for the scourging, but only one minute for the resurrection?

IN ALL THINGS CHARITY

The Passion of the Christ has already touched many viewers, Catholic and otherwise, and will probably speak to millions more in the coming years. Some Christians may find it a useful tool for meditation and reflection. But it is not the last word on the Gospels, nor, moreover, is it the Gospel. It would be lamentable if this movie came to be seen as an authoritative depiction of the last twelve hours of Jesus' life.

Perhaps the best thing the film may do is to encourage more people to read the Gospels and educate themselves on the complete story of Jesus. To be frank, if one of my parishioners asked me "How can I learn more about Jesus?" I would not send him or her first to this movie, but to the Gospels, to a good Bible commentary, and to books written by people who have spent decades studying and meditating on the life, death, and resurrection of Jesus.

People of goodwill have differed in their reactions to *The Passion*. Many supporters have already declared that those who criticize the movie are "anti-Christian" or are "missing the point." People who find the movie anti-Semitic are deemed "too sensitive." Conversely, some critics have labeled those who like the movie as "anti-Semitic" or "anti-intellectual."

It would be a tragedy if the death of Jesus, or an artistic representation of it, led to hatred and discord. So it is especially important when dealing with such emotional issues to give everyone the benefit of the doubt. Even Catholics committed to Jewish-Christian dialogue may like the movie, and even Catholics devoted to meditating on the Passion may dislike the movie.

Pope John XXIII, who convoked the Second Vatican Council, often quoted a saying attributed to St. Augustine, who himself knew something about controversy. When discussing *The Passion of the Christ* it's an excellent insight to remember: "In the essentials unity; in doubtful things freedom; and in all things charity."

JIM WALLIS

❖

THE PASSION AND THE MESSAGE

I must confess that the cultural and commercial hype surrounding Mel Gibson's movie *The Passion of the Christ* was enough to keep me from wanting even to see it, let alone write about it. The esteemed Lutheran theologian Martin Marty described his own reluctance to see the film in a column he called "Gibson's *Passion* Not My Passion." That's kind of how I felt too as I heard about the film, read of the controversies, and learned about its violence and gore. My brother took his teenagers to see it, then e-mailed the whole family to warn the rest of us about its relentless and mercilessly violent depictions of the sufferings of Christ.

Then I ran into Marty at a pastors' conference. He reiterated what he had said in his column: "In Holy Week I'll be listening to Bach's *Passions*, singing about 'was there ever a grief like Thine?' and meditating on the wounds of Christ, but not in the belief that the more the blood and gore the holier, à la Gibson." He went on to say that "pain is pain, suffering is suffering, torture is torture," but that he didn't think that "there are grades and degrees of these." Marty told me that he supposed there were probably ten thousand people in Chicago (his hometown) who are presently suffering physically as much as the crucified Jesus had. "The point now," said Marty in his column and to me, "is not to accept grace because we saw gore. The issue is not were his the worst wounds and pains ever, but, as the Gospels show, the issue was, and is, who was suffering and to what end. Christians believe that Jesus was and is the Christ, the Anointed, and they are to find meaning in his sacrificial love and death, not to crawl in close to be sure they get the best sight of the worst physical suffering."

Nevertheless, at dinner that evening with several pastors and theologians, I was persuaded to see the film and to write about it. These Evangelical clergy and theologically concerned people were all convinced that the Gibson movie could be a watershed in popular "Christology" (our doctrine of Christ), a milestone in how people view Jesus, and a "cultural marker," as David Neff of *Christianity Today* wrote. All this, I wondered, from a Hollywood movie directed by a B-grade action-flick actor?

One of the pastors at the table was particularly startled and offended by the claim made by *The Passion* movie marketers who described the film as "the greatest outreach opportunity in 2,000 years." But I had heard something similar from my own sister who, together with her husband, is planting a new Evangelical church in the Detroit area. They had attended one of the huge prescreenings for forty-five hundred church leaders at the famed Willow Creek mega-church in suburban Chicago, a congregation of some fifteen thousand. Very moved by the film's power, my younger sister said that the movie opened up a "conversation about faith" among ordinary people in her community unlike anything she has seen "in my lifetime." That seems to be the case, in fact, in many places around the nation. My sister and brother-in-law's new "seeker-friendly church" clearly sees *The Passion* as a unique outreach opportunity.

It is important, then, to ask: What evangelizing message is Hollywood sending? What does this movie say to the world about Jesus, about the Gospel, and about Christian faith? These are important questions, and there was only one way for me to get some answers. I decided to see the film.

At a weekday matinee, the theater in Washington, D.C.'s Union Station was less than half full. I noticed that most people sat toward the back, all of us having been warned by now about how breathtaking the violence and blood would be. (When veteran film critic Roger Ebert says, "This is the most violent film I have ever seen," that is saying something.) And I must admit to feeling vaguely dissociated as I sat with patrons who sipped sodas and munched popcorn while witnessing this modern Passion play. The theater next door was running *50 First Dates*, and I wondered if others were considering switching to Adam Sandler if things with Mel Gibson got too rough. The incongruities mounted as the pre-show ads pushed breath mints, the D.C. lottery, Hershey candy bars, and American Express Cards. I waited for Golgotha with my Diet Coke in my hand. The last movie preview gave us glimpses of carnage amid the war cry "Remember the Alamo!" Perhaps it was preparing us for what we were about to witness in remembrance of the sufferings of Jesus Christ.

I kept my eye on two women sitting in front of me, watching for their reactions. These were middle-aged African-American women and, I learned in talking with them afterward, Pentecostal Christians deeply committed to their faith and their church. They, like my sister, were deeply moved by the film. "I read my Bible every day," one of the women told me, "but just to see it touched my heart." Her reaction is centuries old. The power of the famous medieval Passion plays came from making Christian doctrine and history both *visual* and *visceral*. Yes, Gibson has resurrected an old and very Catholic tradition and brought it to the silver screen. And he is touching many hearts.

In reading the many film reviews, I was struck by one that offered a reflection that I didn't hear anywhere else. It was from my friend Robert Franklin, Presidential Distinguished Professor of Social Ethics at the Candler School of Theology at Emory University. He explained why the film might deeply resonate with many in the black community. Unlike so many of its cinematic predecessors, this film does not present a "sanitized Jesus," which "avoids the brutal manifestations of oppression and violence he experienced." Franklin suggests that the film resists the usual white European "makeover" wherein "the rugged, sun-baked Palestinian Jew of the Bible gets morphed into a manicured, middle-class, model citizen."

He continues, "Since the slave period, blacks have understood and portrayed Jesus as a Suffering Savior and a grassroots leader who was the victim of state-sponsored terror. Black theology has focused on the humanity and socially marginal status of Jesus. More than that, blacks have been attracted to the Jesus who experienced unjust victimization by the authorities and the community." Franklin shows how the rich tradition of the spirituals, gospel music, prayers, and sermons in the black church embrace the realities of political death and liberating resurrection. "When African Americans revisit the Passion scene, we know what the young Jewish mother Mary felt. We know the agony of those disciples who yearned to avenge their leader but were too powerless and afraid to try. We feel the grief and indignation deep in our guts."

At the moment in the film when those few who remain loyal to Jesus until the end—Mary his mother, Magdalene, and John—take Jesus down from the cross and cradle his mutilated body in their arms, my mind did indeed flash to the scene on a Memphis hotel balcony with the young Andrew Young, Ralph Abernathy, and others, in the agony of despair, tearfully holding the bloodied body of Martin Luther King Jr. Franklin's review obviously hit on something. But Franklin had added that "legitimate worries about rousing anti-Semitism have been expressed by Jewish and Christian leaders," and he expressed his hopes that those concerns would be taken most seriously. It would be, he said, "an unfortunate irony to use a film about Jesus to inspire hate and harm toward anyone." I'll get back to his point momentarily.

These comments about black reactions to *The Passion* are significant because they point to what, for me, is the most important issue about this film. That issue is *context*. Black Christians like the two women I spoke with in the theater have a context for viewing the film. Their own experience and their history help them to understand Jesus' own suffering and death. Their own lives provided what the film itself, in my view, failed to provide: any context for understanding what we were watching on the screen. In reading, in seeing, in thinking, context orients us, so that we find meaning. Where was the context for *The Passion?* In fact, the film's lack of context was stunning to me. So my big question, again, is: What will be the content of the "outreach" for this film without the crucial context of the gospel story?

WHERE IS THE KINGDOM OF GOD?

The painfully brief "flashbacks" in Gibson's movie were saving graces for me, and for a few other friends I've talked with who are also Evangelicals with a social conscience. But these flashbacks were way too few, and much too painfully brief. When we saw just a glimpse of Jesus' teaching, "You have heard that it was said, 'You shall love your neighbor and hate your enemy.' But I say to you, Love your enemies and pray for those who perse-cute you," my thirsty heart leaned toward the screen: the Sermon on the Mount was an oasis in the already blood-soaked desert of the film's story. In fifteen seconds it was over. No! No! I silently screamed. Show us more! There is so much more. Blessed are the poor. Blessed are those who hunger and thirst for justice. Blessed are the peacemakers. I thirsted for Jesus' first sermon in his hometown synagogue: his "Nazareth manifesto," echoing dif-ferent verses from Isaiah than the ones from the Suffering Servant passages scrolled in the opening of Gibson's film, was his mission statement. "The Spirit of the Lord is upon me, because he has anointed me to bring good news to the poor. He has sent me to proclaim release to the captives and recovery of sight to the blind, to let the oppressed go free, to proclaim the acceptable year of the Lord's favor."

Gibson gives us a few more flashbacks. We see the Last Supper, where Jesus, at table with his disciples, shares a meal and institutes what Christians call the Eucharist or Holy Communion. He predicts his suffering and death, and tells them to "love one another, as I have loved you." I savored the moment—and that's all it was. Quickly, invariably, the film shifted back to its visual liturgy of agony.

Where is the central message of Jesus—the coming of a new order called the Kingdom of God—which would turn everything about our lives and the world upside down? Where is the whole new way of living he brought to us and told us to follow in a new community that breaks down all our former barriers? Where is the personal, moral, economic, and political transformation that this new king and new kingdom usher in? And why were the religious and political rulers so afraid of it? Those are the questions that never get answered in this movie. We witness a gruesome account of the last twelve hours of Jesus' life; we watch him die a hideously painful death; and then we get a whiff of his resurrection.

But there is not enough of the Kingdom of God here for me. Nothing much more is here than his suffering. We see the suffering, and we may be moved by it. But the film makes it so easy to miss the message. The spiritual connection between the two, suffering and Kingdom, is at the heart of the meaning of Christ's Passion. To focus so exclusively on the suffering may be Gibson's right as a moviemaker. But spiritually, it diminishes the message. It is a mistake.

I did indeed grow up in the evangelical churches, and I still describe my Christian faith as evangelical. I fear that the film's omission of the message of Jesus can further contribute to the most unfortunate kind of evangelical Christology. That Christology goes like this: Jesus was born only to die, only to save us from our sins. The blood sacrifice (which Gibson almost obsessively focuses on in his film) is the key. So sinful is the world that it requires the sacrifice of the very Son of God in order to be redeemed. To such a Christology, the circumstances of Jesus' birth—that he was born to a poor family, from an oppressed race in an age of empire—are irrelevant.

The character of Mary, the mother of Jesus, was central in Gibson's film. Maia Morgenstern's expressions of love, pain, and devotion constituted perhaps the best of the film's acting. Yet the movie has no room for Mary's "Magnificat." "My soul magnifies the Lord," sings Mary in her praise to the God who has blessed her as the mother of the Messiah. "He has shown strength with his arm; he has scattered the proud in the imagination of their hearts. He has brought down the mighty from their thrones, and lifted up the lowly; he has filled the hungry with good things, and sent the rich away empty." What an incendiary prayer! These are not the words of a faith-based social service initiative of the kind favored by the White House. These are the words of social and spiritual revolution. This is the content and consequence of the Kingdom of God. But it is irrelevant backstory for an evangelical Christology that just needed a Savior to be born in order to die for sin.

That Christology turns the next thirty-three years of the life of Christ into a period of almost wasted time—just getting Jesus ready to be the blood sacrifice. He had to put in the time to grow up enough to be killed. In the evangelical church where I grew up, there was real interest in Christ's miracles, but mainly because they helped to establish his divinity. Christ's fellowship with the poor and outcasts, his challenges to the ruling authorities—these were mostly passed over. Nor were his teachings, so formational for the life of the early church, an important part of my evangelical upbringing. In fact, these teachings were relegated to some distant future time. They described not social action now, but ideal circumstances later, in a future "dispensation," when we are all safely in heaven. Frankly, I never got this. After all, why would the peacemakers be blessed once we are all in heaven? That's not where they are needed. We need them now; it's here that they are a blessing.

I never really heard much about the *kingdom* in my evangelical church; everything was about the *atonement*. And that's what I fear in Gibson's film. But the Passion of Christ makes no sense apart from the Kingdom of God. The question, again, is why, for what purpose, was Jesus killed? I asked that question once at a famous evangelical Christian college. The students were all befuddled by the question. Finally, one gave me the stock evangelical answer, "To save us from our sins?" Well, that's fine for a theological answer, for the consequence of the cross of Christ. All Christians believe that the death and resurrection of Jesus Christ is the key to our salvation. But that is not a concrete, social, political, historical answer. Do we really imagine that the Roman ruler, Pontius Pilate, was thinking to himself that he needed to execute Jesus to facilitate Christians' being saved from their sins?

Jesus of Nazareth was sentenced to death and executed as a seditious criminal by the political and religious authorities of his day who believed him to be a threat to their power. Crucifixion was the form of capital punishment Romans used for political criminals. And Jesus, his kingdom, his teaching, his claims to truth, and his identity as the Son of God were all a threat to those powers. They still are. They always were, and they are today, despite the eagerness of political leaders to proclaim their own personal faith. The private piety of many American churches, especially many conservative churches, poses no challenge to power. The truth is that if Jesus had restricted faith in himself and in his message to just the personal religion of his followers, he never would have been crucified. And they would not have been persecuted. He would have been no threat to any religious or political power structure but, rather, a welcome guest at Presidential Prayer Breakfasts. Indeed, if Jesus had stayed out in the countryside and simply instructed his disciples in how to lead a quiet moral life, there would have been no confrontation at all. But Jesus made a decision to go to Jerusalem, to the center of power, and to deliberately *provoke* a confrontation.

The movie flashes back briefly to Palm Sunday, to Jesus' triumphal entry into the city at the beginning of the week that would end in his death. When the crowds placed palm leaves in his path and shouted "Hosanna" to the "King," they knew (and the on-looking officials knew) that they were making a political statement as well as a religious one, especially in that highly charged context of Roman imperialism, at the beginning of a holiday that celebrates redemption and freedom from slavery. Clearly, Jesus was not a violent revolutionary like the so-called Zealot party of his day. But the Kingdom of God that Jesus proclaimed was even more revolutionary.

One simply cannot understand the Passion of Christ without the context of his birth, life, teachings, and confrontation with established powers. Mel Gibson's movie falls far short of conveying that context. And that, I submit, is a big problem with using this movie for "outreach."

JEWS AND CHRISTIANS

A second problem with using such a vivid and dramatic movie for "outreach" when it brings with it so little of the contents and context of the Gospel is the way that the film presents the opposition to Jesus. I am speaking here about *The Passion*'s potential to fuel or to occasion anti-Semitism. One of the ugliest stains in Christian history was the claim that "the Jews killed Jesus." That false accusation of "Christ-killers" led to centuries of anti-Jewish violence, from the beating up of Jewish children after Good Friday Passion plays to supplying justification for—or complacent aquiescence to—the ultimate evil of the Holocaust. In the last half century in particular, both the Roman Catholic and Protestant churches have clearly condemned anti-Semitism as un-Christian.

In the Scriptures, Jesus' confrontation is not with "the Jews," but rather with the religious and political establishments—the Jewish and Roman authorities. Both Pilate and the priests regarded Jesus as dangerous. But the Gospels tell a story of an intra-community conflict occurring among the Jews around Jesus. The opposition to him was led by the high priest Caiaphas, his council, and the angry mob they gathered to help demand Jesus' death. In the movie, as opposed to in the Bible, these characters all come off very very badly: Gibson's chief priests, opulently robed, sneer at

Jesus, while others in the council level vicious verbal and physical attacks. All the noise and polarizing drama might lead viewers to forget that these priests, historically, did not represent all Jews everywhere, but primarily the ruling class of Judea. Native ruling classes cooperate with foreign imperial power. Thus, both in the movie and in the Scriptures, when Pilate asks Caiaphas and his cohorts if Jesus is really their new "king," the priests quickly proclaim their political loyalty to Rome. In both John's Gospel and in the movie, Pilate hears them say: "We have no king but Caesar."

But Jesus also has many Jewish supporters: his own disciples; the crowds that thronged to him throughout his ministry; the pilgrims who greeted him upon his entry into the city for Passover. Even in the Sanhedrin, he had sympathetic supporters like Joseph of Arimathea, and like Nicodemus who, according to John's Gospel, visited Jesus secretly. (Gibson depicts Nicodemus very briefly as protesting the "travesty" of the Sanhedrin's proceedings against Jesus.) Both men, according to the Gospels, went together to Pilate to ask for the body of Jesus. In the film, these men are displaced by Mary, the mother of Jesus, Mary Magdalene, and John the disciple. Other sympathizers along the route to Golgotha—like Simon of Cyrene, attested in the Gospels, and Veronica, a legendary fourteenth-century figure who finds her way into Gibson's Jerusalem—are also, of course, Jews.

Gibson's Caiaphas is indeed especially venal, even taunting Jesus at the cross. This Hollywood high priest certainly provides the driving force for Christ's crucifixion. Gibson's Pilate, by contrast, is a moderate and even considerate figure, compassionately offering Jesus water, anguishing about the situation that Caiaphas has put him in, washing his hands of the affair while acceding to the priests and their mob with obvious regret. This depiction goes well beyond the Gospels' presentation of both men. It also distorts what we know historically. The historical Pilate was a vicious ruler who, several years after Jesus' execution, was recalled to Rome for having used excess force to disperse a Samaritan religious gathering. The most sadistic characters in the film are the Roman soldiers who take sick pleasure and even glee in endlessly flagellating Christ. More likely, the historical Pilate's sensibilities aligned with theirs.

Gibson takes one clause from the Gospel of Matthew about Pilate's wife being warned in a dream that Jesus was innocent, and creates of it a major character, "Claudia." Following one of his extra-biblical sources, the visions of the nineteenth-century nun Anne Catherine Emmerich, Gibson turns Mrs. Pilate into a proto-Christian, fighting for the life of Christ and giving both comfort and linens to his mother, Mary, and Mary Magdalene. Presenting her as a sympathetic ally, and her husband as a conflicted but not horrible man, seems to place even more of the onus for Jesus' suffering, in Gibson's story, on the priests. By contrast, both the Gospel accounts and history would judge that both the Roman governor and the Jewish leadership shared responsibility. The point is that these leaders do not constitute the whole nation, neither in that generation nor, certainly, for all generations thereafter. Any suggestion of that is indeed ugly anti-Semitism.

Stephen Waldman of *BeliefNet* has suggested that, in the controversy over anti-Semitism and *The Passion*, Christians and Jews seem to be talking past each other, much as blacks and whites did in the events surrounding the O. J. Simpson trial. Christian leaders have also voiced legitimate concerns about the impact of the film on Christian-Jewish relations. And some Jews have maintained that they see no anti-Semitism in the film. What remains critically important today is the crucial relationship between Christians and Jews, which must be one of mutual respect, support, and dialogue; forging a common cause for social justice and peace here at home and around the world.

THE VIOLENCE IN *THE PASSION*

The issue of violence in *The Passion of the Christ* has been so controversial that it deserves some comment. First, good Christian orthodoxy makes clear that we are not saved by the sufferings of Christ; we are saved by his death and resurrection. Brian McLaren, a Christian pastor and author, told me that the movie's portrayal of Christ's suffering seemed "so unrealistic" that it stopped affecting him. The film seemed to get seduced by special effects. My father, also an Evangelical pastor, said that while it reminded him of "all that Christ did for us" (a frequent comment I hear from Evangelical friends), it did seem to him a little overdone. McLaren points out that often, the great events of the Passion of Christ are referred to in the Gospels by simple phrases without elaboration and even dependent clauses, such as "They scourged him," or simply "They crucified him," or even "When they crucified him," etc. Less here is more.

The Gospel accounts themselves really do not dwell on the suffering, the beatings, the flagellation, and the details of crucifixion as much as Gibson's *Passion* does. Many of the extra-biblical additions and elaborations come from the various Catholic sources that Gibson relies on heavily, as many reviews have pointed out. The Stations of the Cross, a powerful Catholic devotional and liturgical tradition, figures centrally in *The Passion*. The believer "walks" in Jesus' steps along the Via Dolorosa, whether on pilgrimage in Jerualem or, during Lenten season, around the walls of any Catholic church, where fourteen pictures of Jesus at his different "stations" mark his—and the believer's—progress. This tradition is utterly new to many of the conservative Evangelicals who have been so attracted to this film. Indeed, the movie is really a compilation of the biblical accounts and the Stations of the Cross.

I believe that such sharing and crossing over of traditions is a good thing. I have personally participated in very meaningful marches on Good Fridays that reenact the Stations of the Cross that appear in, indeed organize, the action of the movie. When I walk, I do so to meditate on Christ's suffering as reflected in the injustice and suffering in my own neighborhood and world. Many of Gibson's goriest embellishments on the Stations, however, drew, again, on details provided by Anne Catherine Emmerich. These I did not find helpful.

The moviegoer's response to the R-rated violence in Gibson's film is as much a matter of individual taste and sensibilities as anything else. But there are some deeper issues here. The critical question is: What does the movie say about violence itself, especially in light of Jesus' teachings on the subject? Gibson, to his credit, makes much of Jesus' words in Luke: "Father, forgive them." Yet the troubling scene of the black crow pecking out the eyes of the unrepentant criminal on the cross next to Jesus—another touch from Emmerich—carries a different message: Revenge. So does the severe damage that Gibson's post-crucifixion earthquake does to the Jewish Temple. The Scriptures have no such stories: no punishing crow, and no torn Temple, but a torn "veil" or curtain. The death of Jesus on the cross and the new life of Jesus in the resurrection are the ultimate repudiation of revenge and triumph over violence. The crow, the shattered Temple, the war drums in Gibson's brief resurrection scene, all present the opposite message. But is this really the message of the Gospels, that unjust violence leads, ultimately, to "just" payback?

This is where Mel Gibson's own "theology" of violence seems to come into play. I confess that I loved *Braveheart,* and that I have even seen *The Patriot,* and a couple of his *Lethal Weapon* movies. In all those films, the main character (played by Gibson) or his family are the victims of violence, often unrelenting violence. Gibson regularly plays characters with an incredible capacity to endure seemingly endless abuse and attacks. Remember the succession of bad guys and terrorists in the *Lethal Weapon* series? They beat Gibson to a bloody pulp, again and again, only to have him rise up in the end to overwhelm them with superior force.

What might make for a good action flick does not necessarily make for a good story about Jesus. I was especially troubled when, during the first stage of Jesus' brutal flogging, he rises up on the pedestal to which he is chained to stand almost erect, seemingly in defiance of his persecutors. They have just finished pummeling him with stiff and stinging whips, and might indeed have been finished. But Jesus, pulling himself up from the ground, stands tall over his whipping post, enraging his torturers and inciting them to much more vicious violence. They lash him almost skinless with metal-tipped leather thongs. This is pure Gibson—pulling himself up to take one more punch from the bad guys in *Lethal Weapon*, crying "*Free-DOOOOMMMM*" from his rack of pain in *Braveheart*. In *The Patriot*, Gibson the Avenger is back, mighty and almost mystical, wreaking vengeance on the British for violence against his family in an orgy of blood. That paradigm is a sure seller for Hollywood movies, but it is decidedly not the pattern of the Gospel and the way of Christ. In the cross, the violence of the world is overcome by the power of suffering love. Through the cross, unjust death leads not to payback but to Life. Caught between these two conflicting paradigms, the director of *The Passion* drowns out his brief flashbacks to Jesus' own preaching the Good News of love, forebearance, and forgiveness in what seems like an ocean of Jesus' blood.

PASSION AND OBEDIENCE

In saying that I miss hearing the Gospel in Gibson's movie, that I miss Jesus' core preaching of the Kingdom of God, I diminish in no way at all the centrality and significance of Jesus' suffering. Many critics of *The Passion*— some religiously liberal, some religiously secular—offended by Gibson's graphic depictions of Christ's suffering, have also complained that the film should have focused more on the positive teachings of Jesus. But Jesus Christ was not just a nice guy saying nice things about the way the world should work. His cross and his teachings are one. Christians believe that Jesus was the very incarnation of God, come into the world to bring the "good news" of salvation and the transforming power of the Kingdom. In the cross, Christ confronts the "powers and principalities" of this world with the power of his call to a new order. The resurrection is his vindication, a vindication without revenge. *Christus Victor*.

Having confessed my taste for action movies, I must confess as well (with apologies for what must seem my inconsistency) that I have always been a closet Franciscan, a great admirer of Saint Francis of Assisi. Francis was called to take the message of the Gospel back into the world. His practical spirituality was very focused on the suffering of Christ. Legend has it that Francis's devotion to Christ reached such a level that he came to bear that suffering in his own body. This legend of the stigmata has always moved me deeply—a very unlikely devotion for an Evangelical. Yet Francis's imitation of the suffering of Christ was never removed from his utter immersion in working for God's Kingdom. On the contrary, Francis strove so full-heartedly to live by the teachings of Jesus in the Sermon on the Mount that his emulation of Christ's suffering became just a further example of his obedience to Christ, loving and working for God's creatures. This is the sort of message that I most miss in Mel Gibson's *The Passion of the Christ*.

Francis knew that to follow Jesus was to live in solidarity with the poor, to embrace a life of joyful simplicity instead of materialistic pursuits, to choose the way of the cross as an alternative to violence and war, and to profess allegiance to God and to all of humanity over any nation-state. In the context of those commitments, Francis sought to enter into the suffering of Christ in order to better comprehend and to live out the way of Jesus.

But to focus on the suffering of Christ, apart from an understanding of the teaching of Jesus and his way of the Kingdom, is not only to miss the central point of the Gospels, but to separate personal piety from public discipleship. And that goes right to the issue of using *The Passion* for Christian "outreach." Gibson's movie is causing ordinary people to ponder and discuss the issue of faith, and that is indeed a good thing. Let us hope that those faith conversations take us not just to the gory details of Jesus' suffering but rather to the transformational power of his message for our lives and times.

SUSAN THISTLETHWAITE

❖

MEL MAKES A WAR MOVIE

"Passion among top five highest grossing R-rated movies ever *"*

Entertainment Tonight

Christian churches in the United States are largely responsible for a record turnout for an R-rated movie. The more you contemplate this fact, the more peculiar it seems. The film's R rating comes from its excessive and graphic violence. We need to ask, Why is one of the arguably most violent movies playing in theaters today an icon[1] of conservative Christian faith? And why have so many churches, its violence notwithstanding, embraced it? Perhaps the answer is no more complicated than this: *The Passion* presents Jesus as a hero in a war movie.

THE ROMANCE OF THE FILM: A CLASSIC HERO

The Passion of the Christ establishes itself as a war movie by drawing on the film archetype of the hero. Many modern Hollywood writers and directors

1. Icon is the name of Mel Gibson's production company. An icon is "a representation... of some sacred personage...itself venerated as sacred." *The Random House Dictionary of the English Language,* 1966 unabridged ed. [s.v. "icon"].

have played with the heroic stereotype, shaping it more toward the confused moral reality that we often experience in real life. Sometimes, the best option we have to evil is not good, but simply another (though, hopefully, lesser) evil; sometimes the corrupt battle not the pure, but those who are corrupt in different ways. Clint Eastwood's *Unforgiven* exemplifies this sort of shades-of-gray storytelling, wherein even the hero himself is deeply flawed and thus morally compromised. (Since Eastwood's heroic film persona is so well established, this movie actually gets to tell the hero story and to subvert it at the same time.) Gibson's corpus of films, however, has moved steadily toward the older, clearer, cleaner model: Evil is clearly evil, and good clearly good. No moral relativism compromises the clarity of the struggle. The hero—the stalwart dad of *Ransom*, the stalwart warrior of *Braveheart*—unambiguously claims all of our sympathies.

The films of the last century are a vocabulary in modern culture. They have provided images, stored in our collective cultural unconscious, that we share because we have experienced this visual medium all our lives. Even if you have not seen a particular film, you may have been exposed to it in fleeting images on television as you click your remote (Bogie and Bergman in *Casablanca*). Or you may have seen films that reference other films (*Play It Again, Sam*). Only a few frames suffice, therefore, to convey a visual text to the viewer, one whose language he or she will recognize as familiar.

"Hollywood as a factory of myths adheres rigidly to certain basic generic conventions and rules, and very rarely allows its 'workers' to move outside them. Probably the most 'universal' (locally speaking) of such mythic, generic ground rules is the standard 'good vs. evil' format...without which very few myths, ancient or modern, could even be said to exist."[2] Examples of such formulaic thrillers in the action-film genre are the *Die Hard* series, the

2. Jake Horsley, *The Blood Poets: A Cinema of Savagery 1958–1999*, vol. 2 (Latham, Md: Scarecrow Press, 1999), p. 408.

Lethal Weapon series, the Jack Ryan films (*Patriot Games*, etc.) and "even an above average but formulaic thriller like *Ransom*." All of these films "depend on the unambiguous identification of the good and the evil in the audience-mind, in order to satisfy it and weave its low-grade form of quasi-mythic propaganda." Is there a person who lives in the United States who does not know that Mel Gibson starred in the *Lethal Weapon* series and in *Ransom*?

And now, Gibson has written, produced, directed, and sold *The Passion*. He filmed his story with the actors speaking unfamiliar languages, Aramaic and Latin. Though now subtitled, the film was originally conceived as being shown without them: the acting (and the audience's familiarity with the story) was to carry the movie. This means that, as in a silent movie, the actors' expressions and physical reactions are exaggerated. The film must be read as a series of very powerful tropes, as a sequence of heroic images and tableaux, rather than as a true story, populated by round characters, with a narrative structure.

The Hero, the Snake and the Devil

While many Hollywood films play to the mythic dimensions of good vs. evil, it is not all that often that evil is actually personified. But in the first scene of *The Passion*, Satan appears to Jesus when he prays in the Garden of Gethsemane. As the film opens, a handheld camera leads the viewer around, recalling the vertigo-inducing, destabilized feeling that was so creepy in *The Blair Witch Project*. Gethsemane is more like a smoke-filled, primeval forest than a garden, and blue light, thick fog, and jumpy camera-work cue the viewer that nothing good will happen here. Jesus appears, agonizing in prayer. The camera pans to Jesus' face and we see our next big visual clue: this is a strong, good-looking, American white guy. In the Hollywood visual lexicon, good-looking, American, and white usually code "morally good." Thus, even if we (somehow!) did not know the Christian "backstory," we would know as consumers of Hollywood images that we have just met the movie's hero.

But then, a black-cowled figure appears in front of the prostrate, praying

Jesus. The eyebrowless face under the cowl, deathly pale, is feminized rather than explicitly feminine. (In his interview with ABC's Diane Sawyer, Gibson did refer to Satan as "she," only shifting, when sharply questioned by Sawyer, to the pronouns "he, it.") The horror-movie quality of the film is ratcheted up when a maggot appears in the figure's nose. Down the devil's black, slimy robe the camera glides until our view rests on its hem, and we see a snake slither out from under its (her?) robe. Now we know which garden we are really, religiously in: not Gethsemane, but Eden. In Eden, Satan found its opportunity through a woman and came in the form of a snake. Now the Satan-snake slithers menacingly toward the hero and rears its head as if to strike.

With one strong, decisive movement, Jesus stomps the snake to death. The character of Jesus as mythic good guy is established with astonishing economy. The male is stronger than the female; the hero is stronger than evil. Jesus has come to kill sin.

Bad Guys Wear Black

Innumerable visual clues let the viewer know the identity of the Bad Guys: they are the Jewish leaders, and they really have it in for the hero. Others in this volume will detail the extraordinary decision of Gibson as director to have solely *Jewish* soldiers, dressed like Orcs, coming to arrest Jesus. (Historically, first-century Judea was a Roman police state; and the Gospel of John specifically states that Roman soldiers were sent to Gethsemane.) Gibson's Jewish soldiers immediately engage in brutalizing Jesus, punching him, chaining him, and finally throwing him over a bridge, where he dangles in chains in an almost cruciform position above a stunned Judas. In brief, before the Romans crucify Jesus, the Jews do. This remarkable scene, nowhere in the Gospels, has its movie parallel in other Gibson films. The beating and chaining reminds the viewer of *Lethal Weapon 2*, where Mel Gibson as Sgt. Martin Riggs is tied in chains, suspended midair under a stream of water, and repeatedly tortured.

Caiaphas is hugely overdrawn as an evil figure. His black robes are encrusted with gold (evoking the image of Jews as mercenary moneylenders), his teeth stained, his face cruelly set against the suffering Jesus before him. As he stomped around screaming, he reminded one movie critic of the corrupt union boss Johnny Friendly (Lee J. Cobb) in *On the Waterfront*.[3]

As is the case with most action features, the Bad Guys are not sketched with much subtlety. Caiaphas actually wears a black hat throughout the film. The most striking visual clue to the fact that the Jews are the evildoers, however (as opposed to the ordinary Roman soldiers who are brutal buffoons), is that while the Jewish temple elite, Caiaphas at their head, watch the flogging of Jesus with looks of intense satisfaction on their faces, *the devil figure weaves in and out among them*. Satan has shown up in other movies: he appears, for instance, in *The Devil's Advocate*, where he menaces the lead female character. In *The Passion*, only Judas is menaced by demonic visions. But in the scenes crowded with Jewish priests, Satan weaves in and out among them, watching as they watch Jesus being flogged. They are not disturbed, and Satan himself is serene. The devil does not menace these men; in fact, he seems quite at home, almost indeed like one of them.

The Hero Saves the Girl; or, Magdalene Was Framed

As in other heroic action movies, this hero also saves the girl. In a flashback, a dusty street scene of a hostile crowd appears abruptly. The Jesus figure, his face steely with Clint Eastwood-like resolve, stares down the menacing crowd, and then bends to draw in the dust. Straightening up, Jesus then stands tall as the camera pans up the back of his legs, a direct film reference to *High Noon*, when Gary Cooper faced down evil in the dusty streets of a western town. Stones drop from the hands of the hostile crowd and a haunt-

---

3. John Petrakis, "Tough Guy," *Christian Century* (March 23, 2004), p. 40.

ingly beautiful woman (Monica Bellucci), bruised and cut on her anguished face, crawls in the dust to grasp Jesus' feet.

This is the *Pretty Woman* version of Mary Magdalene, the beautiful redeemed prostitute. Gibson's film contains many outright lies, and this is a big one. Toward the end of the sixth century, Pope Gregory the Great "preached a homily...that established a new Magdalen for western Christendom." The Pope proclaimed, "'We believe that this woman [Mary Magdalene] whom Luke calls a female sinner, whom John calls Mary, is the same Mary from whom Mark says seven demons were cast out.' In other words, Gregory collapsed into one individual the identities of three distinct women described in the gospels."[4] The Pope identified Mary of Magdala, a woman who figures prominently in the crucifixion and resurrection stories, as a whore. There is no textual evidence at all for this identification. The only other time Mary of Magdala is mentioned is in Luke 8:1–2, where she is named among a group of disciples traveling with Jesus, and that is where the reference to her as one from whom "seven devils had come out" appears. Now that everyone has read *The Da Vinci Code*, this gross slander has become much better known. In a more scholarly vein I have written on the calumny of the Church's creation of the Magdalene as repentant prostitute, "It was a way to exclude women from religious leadership in the Jesus movement."[5] In terms of what we actually know from the Gospels about Mary Magdalene, "she was eighty-six, childless, and keen to mother unkempt young men."[6]

The movie industry has picked up where the medieval Church left off. In an essay on Magdalene in five contemporary films, particularly Franco

4. Katherine Ludwig Jensen, *The Making of the Magdalen: Preaching and Popular Devotion in the Later Middle Ages* (Princeton, N.J.: Princeton University Press, 2000), p. 33.

5. Rita Nakashima Brock and Susan Brooks Thistlethwaite, *Casting Stones: Prostitution and Liberation in Asia and the United States* (Minneapolis, Minn.: Fortress Press, 1996), p. 239.

6. E. P. Sanders, *The Historical Figure of Jesus* (London: Penguin Press, 1993), p. 75.

Zeffirelli's *Jesus of Nazareth* (1977) and Martin Scorsese's *The Last Tempta-tion of Christ* (1988), Jane Schaberg observes, "[Each] film's Magdalene is the conflated figure of...the repentant whore."[7]

To establish Jesus' heroic credentials, he saves a beautiful woman from certain death, and from prostitution. She is grateful, as any heroine would be. Throughout *The Passion*, Monica Bellucci casts anguished, swimming eyes on the brutalization of her savior.

The Hero Loves His Mother

By far the most appealing character, perhaps the central character, in *The Passion* is Jesus' mother, Mary (Maia Morgenstern). Mary his mother looks at what is being done to her son with expressive anguish. She also looks often at the jeering crowd with accusation. Mary is pleading, evaluating, judging. As an audience member witnessing this brutality, I felt included in the crowd, included in her accusing look. "Will you sit there and do nothing? What have you done that my son must go through this? What have you done? What have you done? What have you done?" She wipes up his blood and is besmeared with it at the end, having kissed her dying son's feet.[8] Centuries of traditional Mariology are revived in this picture. Mary, immaculately con-ceived, is the only human who really can look upon Jesus' brutalization and crucifixion without guilt. As Jesus is removed from the cross, there is a pause for the tableau of Michelangelo's sculpture the *Pietà*. The mother contem-plates the sacrifice of her son. And she looks directly at the audience, the full culmination of her condemnation in her eyes.

Mothers and sons in wartime is the theme of *Saving Private Ryan*, a recent film that depicts the gruesome, gory, bloody violence of the D-day invasion in World War II. The premise of the film is that Private Ryan's mother is about to

7. Jane Schaberg, "Fast Forwarding to the Magdalene," in *Semeia* 74 (1996), p. 33.

8. Scott Haldeman, "Reflections for Worship/Arts class 9 March," unpublished document.

receive notice that three of her sons have been killed in combat; the fourth, military command discovers, is lost in France. They send a small team to find him and send him home. A letter from Abraham Lincoln is read and it concerns "the solemn pride that must be yours to have laid so costly a sacrifice upon the altar of freedom." And upon the altar of the God who demanded this sacrifice.

The Martial Resurrection

"Do not be afraid" (Matthew 28:10). When the Gospels record Jesus as speaking immediately after the resurrection, his first words are of reassurance. In sharp contrast, we have Gibson's take on the resurrection, perhaps the most offensive scene in *The Passion*. A shaft of light appears on stone, and a fluttering, clearly empty shroud deflates on the tomb's stone slab to the beat of martial drums straight out of the Scottish hills of *Braveheart*. Boom, boom, boom go the drums. A grim and pale-faced Jesus, unscathed despite the lengthy torture inflicted on him, sits up with a look of quiet anger on his face. Like Sylvester Stallone in *Rambo: First Blood*, when the Rambo character has been thrown down a mineshaft that detonates around him, this hero also rises. Out of the mineshaft (Stallone); out of the tomb (James Caviezel). This is war, not peace; confrontation, not concord. We feel less reassured than anxious: What will happen now? The screen goes black.

Modern heroes like Rambo or Rocky take everything their enemies can dish out and they come back off of the ropes. So, too, does Gibson's Jesus. But this martial resurrection makes no sense without the furious brutality of the majority of the rest of the film. When the flogging starts, the Roman soldiers use switches. They beat Jesus, who is manacled to a stone pillar. Jesus slumps to his knees. The Romans stop, panting from the exertion of hitting him. The hero, defiantly, struggles back to his feet. Furious at this show of defiance, the Romans get out the scourges. First gouging a nearby wooden table (so that we can see the damage that they intend to inflict on soft flesh), they fall on Jesus, scourging him in a frenzy, while flecks of his skin and his blood fly back upon their own faces and bodies. Jesus falls to the ground. The torturers then turn him over and scourge his exposed chest as well. They cease only when Jesus is a mass of bleeding flesh surrounded by a spreading pool of blood. The Hollywood action-hero genre trumps the very idea of true Incarnation: No real human being, no matter how strong, could possibly have survived this.

Jesus is forced to stand. He is beaten repeatedly before and after his presentation to the crowd. Thorns gouge his head. He is hit, shoved, and kicked all the way through the city and up the hill to Golgotha. The nails are pounded in. The cross is raised and dropped. His torment is excruciating, and excruciatingly portrayed. And then, after a brief pause, Gibson gives us his martial resurrection.

The attraction of grand myths that explore the battle between good and evil is that they give us a way to grasp some kind of meaning in a violent world. "The potency of myth is that it allows us to make sense of mayhem and violent death."[9] The hero returns to punish evil, and especially those who wronged him. But what works for *High Plains Drifter* betrays the Christian gospel. The subliminal message of the simplistic myth given visual power in Gibson's *Passion* is the opposite of the teaching of Jesus of Nazareth: "Love your enemies and pray for those who persecute you" (Matthew 5:44). The reviewer in *USA Today* got that point: "*The Passion*'s hero is a man who preached love, but Gibson's movie is all about hatred."[10] The Bad Guys better watch out.

THE RUSH OF BATTLE

No one who has reviewed this film, whether they praise or pan it, fails to mention the extraordinary amount of violence. A review in *USA Today* describes the film as "more gory than glory," and notes its "graphic brutality."[11] Violence

9. Chris Hedges, *War is a Force that Gives Us Meaning* (New York: Public Affairs, 2002), p. 23.

10. "The Passion of the Christ," *USA Today* (March 12, 2004), p. 6E.

in the movies is scarcely news. Hollywood has had a long love affair with violence from *Birth of a Nation* to *Natural Born Killers* to *Kill Bill*. Violence in film fulfills many different artistic aims. *Apocalypse Now* was originally considered a major disappointment, compromised in part because of its incoherent violence. With twenty-five years of retrospect, however, its status has climbed to that of a flawed masterpiece.[12] Coppola used violence to express what could not be understood: Vietnam itself. The violence in *Apocalypse Now* to some extent succeeded in breaking through the emotional censorship that Americans had imposed on themselves for the only war this country has "lost."

The violence in the Gibson film seems almost to have the opposite intention. If Coppola used violence to try to break through emotional numbing to induce reflection, Gibson seems to use violence to induce emotional numbing in order to suspend reflection. The rhythmic, monotonous quality to the violence in *The Passion* had me as a viewer simultaneously nauseated and glancing at my watch. During the unrelenting carnage of the flogging scene—the central passage of this movie that drags on, beginning to end, for forty minutes—the mind finally shuts down in defense as emotional grief overwhelms. This kind of violence suspends thought. Period. The film's primary achievement is to take thoughtful reflection out of Christianity, and to replace it with shame, guilt, and repentance. The film labors to *convict* the viewer.

The voyeuristic invitation to the filmgoer as an onlooker to the violence done to Jesus (you are, after all, trapped in your seat and seemingly part of the crowd) is to participate vicariously in his savaging. The viewer is drawn in as complicit in the violence done to Jesus, up to and including his crucifixion and death, when the grieving Mother Mary turns her dazed, tear-filled eyes on us. The film itself establishes no narrative that gives a compelling reason why the Temple leaders and the crowd are so determined to have

11. *Ibid.*

12. Horsley, p. 297

Jesus undergo such savage beating and an even more brutal death. The film does open with a text, the one called the "Suffering Servant" passage from Isaiah 53:5, "He was wounded for our transgressions, bruised for our iniquities...and with his stripes we are healed." But the viewer has to supply the rest of the context, and for Christians watching the film, this is pretty much the celluloid version of Sunday school: "Jesus had to die for us because we are so sinful." As moviegoers have been interviewed immediately upon viewing this film, many report feeling "sadness, shame, and guilt." By having to supply the interpretive context for the hero's shocking suffering and cruel death, the viewer becomes a party to the context. For a mass-market sort of missionizing, this is an effective strategy.

This classic version of "why Jesus had to die" is called "substitutionary atonement." The massive amount of violence in the Gibson version suggests that: 1) Jesus had to endure an awful lot of pain to pull off our salvation; 2) he endured more than any other human being ever could (he should have died at least twelve times during the beatings, floggings, blows and falls); and 3) his suffering was more important than any other suffering ever endured.[13]

The shockingly bloodless crucifixions on either side of Jesus are a striking visual contrast. You are supposed to conclude that no other human being ever suffered as much as Jesus did in the last twelve hours of his life. This claim is itself as unethical as it is mythologizing. It relativizes the suffering of kidnapped Africans, slaves who were often scourged and beaten throughout their lives. It relativizes the suffering of Jews, who endured the years-long torture of starvation, brutalization, and horrific death during the Holocaust. It relativizes the suffering of abused children, who in their innocence and helplessness are often subject to terrifying violence for years. It relativizes the suffering of countless unnamed human beings in the history of the world.

13. My thanks to Dr. JoAnne Terrell, Associate Professor of Christian Ethics and Theology at Chicago Theological Seminary, for these thoughts.

In *The Passion of the Christ*, Gibson's message is: *No one* has ever suffered like this. That is, until the next filmmaker decides to top Gibson and to shoot an even more gory, blood-soaked version.

THE INTERPRETATION WARS: THE (HOLY ROMAN) EMPIRE STRIKES BACK

Gibson has used this genre of film to declare war on the recent move in the last four or five decades within both Catholic and Protestant churches to open theology and biblical interpretation to the modern world. It is the view of fundamentalist Christianity, the perspective Gibson most represents, that Christianity is best understood as a struggle between God and the devil. The "world" is a synonym for the secular temptations of the devil. The interpretive perspective of modern Christianity, the view that history plays a role in the production and interpretation of Scripture and tradition, is viewed by the fundamentalist as nothing short of the work of the devil which must be vigorously fought. A war movie is very appropriate to represent this view.

Clearly Vatican II is in Gibson's rifle sights, especially the document *Nostra Aetate (In Our Time)* that, in the section on the relationship of the Church to non-Christian religions, states, "[Jesus'] passion cannot be blamed upon all the Jews then living, without distinction, nor upon the Jews of today."[14] The interfaith work of Christians and Jews since the Holocaust gets a huge slam from the film. The pastor in Denver who posted a sign outside his church—"Jews killed the Lord Jesus; 1 Thess. 2:14, 15; Settled!"—got one of its messages exactly right.[15]

14. *The Documents of Vatican II*, ed. Walter M. Abbott, trans. Ed. Joseph Gallagher (Chicago: Association Press, 1966), p. 666.

15. "'Jews Killed Jesus' Sign Causing Controversy," TheDenverChannel.com, February 25, 2004; http://www.thedenverchannell.com/news/2875731/detail.html [March 16, 2004]

But there are more targets. Protestant and Catholic work that interprets the Scriptures in their original contexts and Christian doctrines in their social and political origins also take a hit. The targeting of modern biblical interpretation can be best seen in Gibson's insistence that he did not interpret the Scriptures in making his movie; he only filmed what they already contained. In an interview with Bill O'Reilly, Gibson stated, "I think it's meant to just tell the truth. I want to be as truthful as possible."[16] In other interviews Gibson has claimed his film is the most accurate depiction of the death of Christ ever made. "He told one reporter that watching it would be like 'traveling back in time and watching the events unfold exactly as they occurred.'"[17] Well, to quote Pilate here, "What is truth?"

The truth is that since World War II (and even before), scholars, as well as clergy and laypeople, have been studying the Scriptures in their original languages, comparing the different versions of the Gospels, noting internal conflicts, using not only linguistics but cultural anthropology and other fields to try to understand our biblical heritage not only as the source of our faith, but also as historical documents of their own times. That most of this work has been done by persons of deep faith has not allayed the fears of very conservative Christians that the goal of such treatment is to undermine the authority of the Bible itself, to accuse it of somehow being "untrue."[18]

This scholarship is Gibson's target when he presents his latest R-rated film

16. Transcript "Mel Gibson Talks to O'Reilly While Filming 'The Passion,'" FOXNews.com, January 14, 2003; http://www.foxnews.com/story/0,2933,112307,00.html [March 12, 2004].

17. Peter T. Chattaway, "Comment: Mel Gibson's Jesus Movie Sparks Controversy," CanadianChristianity.com, March 6, 2004; http://www.canadianchristianity.com/ cgibin/na.cgi?nationalupdates/030730comment [March 12, 2004].

18. For example, see Peter Gomes, *The Good Book: Reading the Bible with Mind and Heart* (San Francisco: HarperSanFrancisco, 1996); Cain Hope Felder, ed., *Stony the*

as "The Truth." It is with no surprise that we recognize that this is the same scholarship that has been brought to bear in analyzing this movie's wild inaccuracies, inventions, and historical mistakes. The "true believer" who accepts Gibson's invitation to conflate Icon Productions with Christianity sees such criticisms of the movie as further testimony to the unfaithfulness of contemporary theological scholarship to the Bible.

The Passion of the Christ, its slick state-of-the-art cinematography notwithstanding, actually presents the face of a militant Christian fundamentalism, a "dangerous messianic brand of religion...of those who believe that they understand and can act for God."[19] Gibson has claimed that the "Holy Ghost was working through me on this film, and I was just directing traffic."[20] His moral certitude about his movie—which is, after all, just his interpretation of the biblical story, and not the story (much less the Bible) itself—recalls the mind-set of those in a state of war. It is a throwback to the muscular Christianity of the Crusades. When the Crusaders captured Jerusalem in 1096, they killed so many inhabitants in their zeal—Muslims, Jews, and Eastern Christians—that the city was "awash in a sea of blood." In their own eyes, the Crusaders saw their actions as the instruments of God's just judgment "on the Muslim 'infidels,' who deserved to die for their rejection of

Road we Trod: African American Biblical Interpretation (Minneapolis, Minn.: Fortress Press, 1991); Elisabeth Schussler Fiorenza, *Bread Not Stone: The Challenge of Feminist Biblical Interpretation* (Boston: Beacon Press, 1984); John E. Stambaugh and David L. Balch, *The New Testament in its Social Environment* (Philadelphia: Westminster Press, 1996); R. S. Sugirtharajah, *Asian Biblical Hermeneutics and Postcolonialism: Contesting the Interpretations* (Maryknoll, N.Y.: Orbis Books, 1998); Ken Stone, ed., *Queer Commentary and the Hebrew Bible* (New York: Sheffield Academic Press, 2001).

19. Hedges, p. 147.

20. Gary Younge, "Bloodthirsty or a Classic? Gibson's Film of Christ's Last Days Alarms Jewish Groups," *Guardian Unlimited* August 4, 2003; http://www.guardian.co.uk/international/story/0,3604,1011784,00.html [March 12, 2004].

Christ and their 'desecration' of the Holy City."[21] The serious alienation between Christianity and Islam created by this massacre continues to this day, fuel for tremendous violence. Millions throughout history—Christian minorities, Jews, native populations resistant to missionizing—have paid with their lives for what their persecutors deemed was their "rejection of Christ."

It is within this context of religiously inspired brutality that Mel Gibson's film must be evaluated. Gibson certainly sees himself as a crusader for True Christianity. Anyone who criticizes him "attacks" him; anyone who dares to question him questions the Bible. Can the world really afford this brand of religion anymore? It has betrayed what is best in Christianity. And it is just too bloody dangerous.

THE THEOLOGICAL CONSEQUENCES: GOD ABUSES HIS OWN CHILD
Classical Christian theology, as represented in a document such as the sixteenth-century *Heidelberg Catechism*, maintains that humans "daily increase our guilt" and that we cannot, by our own efforts, save ourselves. Salvation can only be accomplished by the Lord Jesus Christ, the incarnate God who "by the power of his Godhead" was able to "bear, in his manhood, the burden of God's wrath, and so obtain for and restore to us righteousness and life."[22]

Humans have sinned and incurred God's wrath. God's wrath is mighty. Somebody had to pay and pay large for the whole sum of human rebellion against God. That somebody in the classical Christian theological paradigm

---

21. Charles Bellinger, *The Genealogy of Violence: Reflections on Creation, Freedom and Evil* (Oxford University Press, 2001), p. 99.

22. *The Creeds of Christendom, with a History and Critical Notes,* Philip Schaff, ed., rev. David S. Schaff (Grand Rapids, MI: Baker, 1996): 3:311–313.

is Jesus of Nazareth. This paradigm is also central to the Gibson portrayal of Jesus' Passion.

What is so graphically displayed in this film—perhaps as never before— is what wrath-of-God theology looks like when taken to its logical extreme. As you view Gibson's movie, as you watch the blood flow, the blows fall and the hammers pound the nails into flesh, keep in mind that in the theology undergirding this film, *God is the author of this violence*. Gibson's God the Father wills Gibson's Jesus, the Son, to undergo this sickening suffering as an atoning sacrifice to Himself, to pay for the sins of the world.

The world is a violent place. There is no denying this fact, and the related fact that, often, this violence is of human origin. Christian theology makes sense of such apparently senseless acts of violence and gives them meaning. How different would Christianity be if, let us say, its central message was the legend that Jesus survived the cross, married, settled down, raised kids, and lived to a ripe old age as an esteemed teacher whose central message was "Love one another"? The Christian religion would certainly have been different. It might not have spoken quite as powerfully to the brokenness that is at the heart of the human condition. But it might not have perpetrated the Crusades, the Inquisition, the Holocaust. My point is not to play "what if," but to question a view of the atonement for human sin that has accompanied, century after century, a Christian replication of sacrificial violence on the lives of those unable to defend themselves from it. Is this merely coinciden- tal, is it a profound misunderstanding, or is it a judgment on a doctrine that must be abandoned for Christians to be able to live in peace with themselves and with their neighbors of other religions?

Many contemporary theologians have questioned the classical view of the atonement, that "God sent Jesus to die for our sins," precisely because it is, as has been famously argued, "Divine Child Abuse." The theology that claims "Christ suffered in obedience to his Father's will" is exactly the problem.

"This 'divine child abuse' is paraded as salvific."[23] What father demands the suffering of his child?

Theologies of the cross need not reify violence. The suffering of God on the cross can be a way to understand the full measure of what it means that "God is with us." God is with us even in the most painful suffering of our lives. A student in a theology class once told me that she was raped at a dump. Told by her attacker not to move, she lay on the trash, bleeding, fearing she would be killed. She said that, at that moment, in her terror, she had a vision of Christ on the cross saying to her, "You don't have to explain to me how you feel."

God's presence in Jesus of Nazareth has a word for suffering humanity. That word is not condemnation: "Look what you did. Look what I am suffering because of you." That word is, "You are not alone. I am with you." That is a message that Mel Gibson's movie does not portray.

Actual Child Abuse

Often in cases of actual child abuse, the abusive parent insists that he or she acted for the child's own good.[24] If nothing else convinces you that violence is at the heart of this movie, attend a showing of *The Passion* and watch the droves of parents bringing their children in. Then sit and listen to children crying, even screaming as the scourge falls on Jesus' back, the nails are driven into his hands.

I have seen this film twice now. Once I went with a group of Christians and Jews to a pre-release screening—all grown-ups, a fact I did not suffi-

---

23. Joanne Carlson Brown, "Divine Child Abuse," *Daughters of Sarah*, Summer 1992, p. 24.

24. Alice Miller, *For Your Own Good. Hidden Cruelty in Child Rearing and the Roots of Violence*, trans. Hildegarde and Hunter Hannun (New York: Farrar, Straus & Giroux, 1983).

ciently appreciate at the time. To write this book chapter, I went again, this time to an early show, once the film was in theaters. I was astonished that fully one-third of the audience was children—many under the age of twelve—accompanied by their parents. Some children looked to be as young as five or six. I had prepared myself, I thought, for another round of the violence in the film. But I was not prepared for the children's crying. I was not prepared for the children's screaming.

Stephen King, whom all of us would trust to know horror when he sees it, was horrified when he saw, in the theater, the number of children taken by parents to see the film. One mom, he wrote, had three children, two of whom looked about six. This mom bustled into the film late, talking on her cell phone. "The theater manager, she told her friend, had had the nerve to suggest to her that the level of violence in *The Passion* wouldn't be good for children as young as hers. 'I told him,' Mom said, 'that if it gets too bloody, they can just close their eyes.'" King focused on another little girl whom he names "Alicia." "Alicia hid her face for fifteen minutes...but that left another fifty minutes of punishment, torture, cruelty, and death still to go. And was I ashamed to be in that theater..."[25]

The wonderful King James translation of the Bible has Jesus say, "Suffer the little children to come unto me." That text in its archaic use of the word "suffer" took on a whole new meaning for me last week. This is a film that is inflicting abuse on the young children dragged to see it. They will never be free of these brutal images of scourging, of beating, of hammering. Their screaming in fright should tell you something. This is not a film about the Prince of Peace. This is not a film about forgiveness, tolerance, mercy; about God so loving the world that God does not leave us to suffer in it alone. The film's publicists and apologists have insisted that this *is* the film's message. But the children know better.

25. Stephen King, "The Passion of Alicia," *Entertainment Weekly*, March 19, 2004, p. 72.

This is a film of conscious self-righteousness that judges and condemns. It punishes and it incites. With all the power of the Hollywood craft, this film betrays the very message of forgiveness that is at the heart of Jesus' teaching. Twenty-three seconds of a flashback to the Sermon on the Mount is not enough for the director to claim his movie is about love and forgiveness. It is not.

I can forgive Mel Gibson for inflicting this lie on me. I cannot forgive the conspiracy of rectitude that has inflicted this lie on the children.

MARY C. BOYS, S.N.M.J.

❖

SEEING DIFFERENT MOVIES,
TALKING PAST EACH OTHER

A Holocaust survivor whom I know called in great distress a couple of weeks ago. The controversy over *The Passion of the Christ* had evoked memories buried for many years. Experiences from her Polish childhood had returned in the form of nightmares, her dreams now dominated by Catholic boys emerging from church on Good Friday and Easter Sunday ready to stone any Jews they encountered. Even Jews of another generation who have had little or no experience of anti-Semitism in North America express apprehension about the controversy. A usually sanguine rabbinic student whom I know well told me after seeing the film that for the first time in her life she was fearful of being identified as a Jew in that theater.

The film has aroused contrasting responses from many Christians captivated by its powerful portrait of what Jesus suffered on their behalf. Some sob throughout the viewing, others drop to their knees in prayer. For months many prominent Christian clergy across a range of denominations have been exhorting their adherents to see the film, offering fulsome praise for its religious message. A young gay man—whom many of the film's enthusiasts would condemn as a sinner—wrote me about how his emotions began to churn as he watched what happened to the Jesus of the film: "I could relate to Jesus. I know too well what it is like to be hated by religious leaders and to be thought of as a threat to society."

Other Christians abhor the violence of the film, and question the simplistic moral dualism that Gibson has portrayed. A number of theologians and biblical scholars—among whom I am one—call attention to the ways in which Gibson, going well beyond any scriptural warrant, has intensified Jewish responsibility for the death of Jesus. This depiction, we fear, might make the film into an occasion for anti-Semitism, particularly in Europe and in South America. The film's effects in non-Christian nations also bear thinking about. When Pope John Paul II visited Syria on May 8–9, 2001, Syrian president Bashar al-Assad welcomed him with a speech that included an attack on Jews as those "who try to kill the principles of all religions with the same mentality with which they betrayed Jesus Christ." Will Arab and Muslim nations use Gibson's emphasis on Jewish complicity to further inflame Middle East tensions?

TALKING PAST EACH OTHER: CHRISTIANS AND JEWS

Stories about Jesus' death, particularly as preserved in the Passion narratives of the four accounts in the Gospel, lie at the heart of Christian identity. They offer an encounter with the way that Jesus experienced the human condition, including betrayals by those closest to him, his own fear of death, uncertainty about God's will, and the endurance of terrible suffering and an ignominious death.

The death-resurrection of Jesus lies at the heart of the church's liturgical life and spirituality, its creeds and its doctrines. The Gospel accounts have evoked centuries of reflection, given rise to powerful rituals, inspired beautiful art and music, stimulated tomes of theology, and sustained persons through times of horrifying suffering. They symbolize much of what is sacred in Christianity.

They are also stories with a shadow side. We know from history that mis-interpretations of the Passion narratives have rationalized hostility to and violence against Jews. As Gerard Sloyan, a respected New Testament scholar (and Catholic priest) writes in *The Crucifixion of Jesus: History, Myth, Faith*: "The chief actual sufferers from Jesus' death by crucifixion have been, para-doxically, not Christians but Jesus' fellow Jews."

Yet most Christians have little awareness of this. Despite many pro-nouncements from a range of Christian churches that "the Jews" do not bear responsibility for the death of Jesus, large sectors of the Christian populace seem unaware of this teaching and uninformed of its biblical and theological warrants. Jews, who have so consistently borne the brunt of the hostility and violence that the interpretations of the death of Jesus rationalized, may understandably regard the churches' efforts with wariness. Nor in most cases have Jews had opportunity to learn in a positive way about the significance of Jesus' death for Christian life.

So Jews and Christians talk past each other on a topic that has been a source of bitter division for centuries, led to violence against Jews, and com-promised the integrity of Christian proclamation of the Gospel.

TALKING PAST EACH OTHER: CHRISTIANS AND CHRISTIANS

As if all this were not enough, Christians talk past one another, both across denominational lines and, just as often, within denominational boundaries. The controversy that the film has engendered reveals substantial differences between Christians over how to interpret the death-resurrection of Jesus, and particularly over how to read Scripture.

Two different approaches to reading the Bible seem to be at play in the controversy over the film. The first approach, evident in Gibson's own com-ments, regards Biblical texts as making "plain sense." To read Scripture is to discover God's word; no further knowledge or thought is requisite. Gibson thinks that he is merely "telling it as it is," since, as he told Diane Sawyer in an ABC interview broadcast on February 16, 2004, "I know how it went down." As he said in another interview on Eternal Word Television Network, the Gospels are eyewitness accounts. (Here he even goes beyond church tradition, which holds Mark as a secondhand account, and Luke as a third-hand account: Peter supposedly confided his memories to Mark; Paul—not among the original twelve—to Luke.) With his frequent references to the Holy Ghost as the movie's real director, Gibson offers a "blessed assurance" that his film is the most authentic presentation ever of the way the Passion and death of Jesus actually happened.

So it is not surprising that many filmgoers, often only vaguely familiar with these Biblical texts, hear Gibson's assurances and conclude that *The Passion of the Christ* accurately dramatizes not only Scripture, but also true history. They equate Scripture with history. As one of my many e-mail critics puts it, "The film presents just what the New Testament says, so if you condemn the film, you are condemning the New Testament." Facts are facts, Scripture is Scripture, history is history, and all three are the same. Another e-mail has it: "It's clear from history: the Jews condemned Jesus. We cannot change history, the Jews were much more culpable for killing Jesus than the Romans.... I certainly do not want anti-Semitism to occur, but you cannot change the facts of what occurred at that time in history." Yet these same fans are untroubled by (or unaware of) all of Gibson's extra-biblical embellishments, many drawn either from the early nineteenth-century mystic Anne Catherine Emmerich, or from Gibson's own imagination.

A second approach regards Scripture as God's word *in human language*. Since human experience mediates divine revelation, knowing the literary style and historical context of Biblical writings is crucial to discerning their multiple meanings. The term "critical" is often associated with methods that enable readers to interpret Biblical texts in their ancient contexts. "Critical," however, refers not to one's attitude toward the content or status of the

Bible, but to ways of thinking that enable us to recognize the assumptions and bias that we moderns might impose upon these ancient texts. "Critical scholarship" means *self*-critical scholarship.

Gibson voiced his contempt for this approach to Scripture in an article in the September 15, 2003, *New Yorker*, in which he remarks to author Peter Boyer, "Just get an academic on board if you want to pervert something." Gibson's derision notwithstanding, this approach is restricted neither to the many academics who practice it, nor to the many thinking believers who embrace it. It also happens to represent official Roman Catholic principles of Biblical interpretation.

Although Catholic approaches to Scripture have developed over time, one long-standing principle is that biblical interpretation is a communal rather than an individual endeavor. For Catholics, any individual's (or group's) understanding of Scripture is to be regarded from within the living tradition of the Church—a principle associated particularly with the Council of Trent (1545–63). To that end, the Vatican has in recent times appointed the Pontifical Biblical Commission, an international body of scholars, to guide reflection on Scripture. In one of its most extensive publications, a 1993 document entitled "The Interpretation of the Bible in the Church," this commission instructed: "Holy Scripture, inasmuch as it is the 'word of God in human language,' has been composed by human authors in all its various parts and in all the sources that lie behind them." Therefore, "its proper understanding not only admits the use of [a contextual] method, but actually requires it." Contextual (i.e., "critical") approaches do not threaten faith. Rather, they offer ways of exploring Scripture in greater depth. As the commission says, "Because sound interpretation requires a lived affinity with what is studied and with the light of the Holy Spirit, full participation in the life and faith of the believing community and personal prayer are necessary."

Of course, the Pontifical Biblical Commission is neither the last word nor the only word of instruction on how to read the Bible. On the specific question of how to read the Biblical accounts of Christ's Passion, the Church also has the guidance from the Second Vatican Council. *Nostra Aetate*, the council's declaration in 1965, teaches specifically that collective blame cannot be imputed to the Jews as a people "for what happened in Christ's passion." Over the years, various Vatican commissions and national conferences of bishops have built upon this point. In their 1988 monograph *God's Mercy Endures Forever*, the American bishops wrote, "It is necessary to remember that the passion narratives do not offer eyewitness accounts or a modern transcript of historical events." Similarly, in their 1988 *Criteria for the Evaluation of Dramatizations of the Passion* (also available in Spanish), the bishops noted the complexity and richness of first-century Judaism. Thus, they conclude, dramatic presentations of the Passion "should strive to reflect this spiritual vitality, avoiding any implication that Jesus' death was a result of religious antagonism between a stereotyped 'Judaism' and Christian doctrine." The bishops, further, call for depictions of the Passion to "conform to the highest possible standards of biblical interpetation and theological sensitivity."

Recommendations about more historically accurate and theologically judicious interpretations of the Passion narratives have thus become a central element of Catholic teaching. Mindful of the confusion and controversy that Gibson's film evoked, the Secretariat for Ecumenical and Interreligious Affairs of the United States Conference of Catholic Bishops issued a publication, *The Bible, the Jews and the Death of Jesus: A Collection of Catholic Documents*, just prior to the film's opening.

In light of these resources emanating from the "living tradition of the church," it would seem that Catholics would regard Gibson's interpretation of the Passion with, at minimum, reserve, and his exalted claims to divine inspiration with skepticism.

Quite the contrary. Many Catholics have rapturously embraced Gibson's film, making it their own religious cause célèbre. Why is it that Gibson's interpretation of the Passion seems to be championed by many Catholics, some of whom object vociferously to any criticism of the film? Even more perplexing is the number of Catholic hierarchs who respond to Gibson with either praise or timidity, even though he rejects the institutional Church, the teachings of the Second Vatican Council, and the legitimacy of recent popes. Equally baffling is the reverence of the Catholic League which, despite its self-description as "the nation's largest Catholic civil rights organization," has neither official standing nor widespread support. It calls Gibson "Saint Mel," while it assails Catholic scholars and clergy critical of the film as "elitists" and as "dissident theologians, nuns, and priests," excoriating them as "maligners of Mel."

Something more than "talking past each other" is occurring here. We seem to be witnessing a very complex moment in which cultural, ecclesial, and inter-religious opinions clash in a public forum better suited to superficial sound bites than to serious dialogue. It has been an ugly and dispiriting controversy.

THE CLASH OF PERSPECTIVES: AN ANALYSIS

Since I am among the critics—and thus among the criticized—I cannot wrap myself in the mantle of neutrality. Neither do I claim certitude about the analysis that follows, which is best understood as my own attempt to make sense of the controversy and its implications. Before I begin, however, we would do well to sort out several discrete factors that have affected the course of the controversy. Three of the most important are the element of public celebrity, the country's cultural divide, and the current political climate within the Catholic Church. A word on each.

We live in a celebrity culture. Would-be candidates for political office announce their entry into a gubernatorial race on Jay Leno; politicians seek the endorsement (and money) of Hollywood stars. Indeed, by virtue of little more than their celebrity, Hollywood stars can themselves become powerful political figures. The defining characteristic of these celebrities is their fame, which provides them with a large public stage on which to perform, off-screen as well as on, before many star-struck fans. Further, in the case of Mel Gibson, fans perceived (and were encouraged to perceive) that anyone who questioned the film was personally attacking this celebrity, whose (well-publicized) religious conversion had rescued him from depression and addiction. Here, then, was a celebrity who had dared to challenge Hollywood's preoccupation with sex (though not with violence), and who had the courage to give public witness to his religious convictions. As one e-mailer wrote to me: "Can't you see how counter-cultural, what a thorough rejection of materialism, what a faith-motivated effort this is?" Another, calling attention to films with "graphic displays of degenerate sex, senseless violence, and anti-Christian messages coming out of Hollywood on a daily basis," questioned how I could "choose to attack a devout Catholic's masterwork?" He added, "I can only wonder at how many pieces of silver were your consulting fees." (For the record, the scholars who wrote the report evaluated the script in confidence, and received no financial compensation whatsoever.)

As these e-mails reveal, we scholars had inadvertently wandered into a cultural divide; and to Gibson fans, our report seemed entirely on the wrong side of that divide. One e-mail correspondent wrote that she welcomed such a film after "all the negative movies and Broadway plays about Christ in recent years." She continued: "The godless, secular media (and Jewish Hollywood moguls) make films that trash Christianity/Catholicism, and now, finally we have a film about all Jesus Christ suffered and you have the audacity to criticize?" Another e-mailer, having denounced my "poor dark, sinful, tortured soul," assured me the film wasn't "anti-semetic" [*sic*], and then added: "I am sure the elite Hollywood Jews will go on making big bucks on raunchy, crass, sex filled, violent, anti-Christian movies. Ask yourself what happens when haters of Christians and Christianity see these movies."

A common note sounded in these numerous e-mails condemning the scholars' report, or my own comments in subsequent interviews, is outrage. Outrage at what their authors perceive to be assaults against a Christianity under siege from a "godless" culture. Who are the "godless" who mount such attacks? Not simply persons who reject religion; not only those who are themselves Christian. Rather, the outraged relegated those of us with public, explicit religious commitments to the lowest circle of hell reserved for the godless: To point out the problems in Gibson's project was to "attack" it—an act that, in their eyes, was tantamount to attacking the Gospels, and even Christianity itself. For Gibson's furious fans, criticism of the film made one a heretic.

Some portrayed us as rejecting the New Testament or belief in Jesus. Phil Brennan wrote in a column in an online journal, *NewsMax.com:* "An arrogant gang of so-called scholars and journalists is conducting a very public crucifixion of Mel Gibson for daring to make his new film, 'The Passion of the Christ,' and it's about time that the motives behind their attempt to destroy him were examined." According to Brennan, "This group of Catholic and Jewish revisionists doesn't think very highly of the New Testament, which the Roman Catholic Church for 2,000 years has insisted was inspired by the Holy Spirit and is therefore, as other Christian churches agree, unerrant [*sic*]." In a similar vein, an e-mail critic commented, "I bet that if it where [*sic*] up to you and the ADL [Anti-Defamation League] you would have all the New Testament Bibles destroyed."

Others questioned our personal religious commitments, again confusing faith in Jesus with enthusiasm for Gibson's movie. One person wrote me, "Where did your love for the Lord go…? Why have you turned on Jesus in derision and in denigration?" This same writer offered counsel: "Go back to your roots, find your Christ again. He's still waiting to forgive you and accept you. It's not too late. Use your talent and notoriety to bring others to Him, not to take them away or confuse them, or to sow division among them." He also instructed, "Forget all of this nonsense which we call 'scholarly.' Open your heart." These disparaging remarks evoke the controversy over the nature of the "learned ministry" during the First Great Awakening

(1730–1760), when Gilbert Tennent berated "Pharisee-Teachers...[who were] blind as moles and as dead as stones, without any spiritual taste and relish." Anti-intellectualism has long afflicted American religiosity.

At times the not-so-subtle anti-Semitism of my e-mail correspondents surfaced in even more despicable ways. "Last time I checked," one person wrote, "the Jews at that time, and at that place WERE the antagonists. They are the ones who WANTED Christ to die. It's amazing you never see Germans complain of their constant negative portrayal in the media concerning the Nazis, yet you can't even make ONE movie that is true to the Bible." The writer continued, citing Matthew 27:25, the cry of the people, "His blood be upon us and our children." Several other e-mailers likewise suggested an analogy with modern Germans, thereby implicitly equating first-century Jews with Nazis.

Others were even more direct, as the e-mail that concludes: "Frauds like you always side with enemies of the Church. Historically, there is no greater enemy of the church than Judaism, which renounces our Lord and Savior, Jesus Christ and says some horrific things about him in the Jew Talmud." This same writer suggests: "If you're so willing to side with our enemies, maybe you shouldn't be a Catholic anymore. Short of that, how about shutting your big mouth?" His judgments and tone are mirrored in the letter of another correspondent, who ended his message, "Praying for the conversion of the 'Perfidious' Jews (and their pseudo-Catholic allies), I remain sincerely yours in Our Lord Jesus Christ."

These e-mails are the religious equivalent of road rage. That sort of anger will not be assuaged by discussion of the principles of biblical interpretation or by reading *The Bible, the Jews and the Death of Jesus*. Their indignant self-righteousness and dualistic rendering of good and evil echo in other cultural controversies, whether over the monument to the Ten Commandments in an Alabama courtroom or over the civil rights of gays and lesbians. Gibson made his own contribution to the theologized rhetoric of this particular controversy, calling his critics "dupes or forces of Satan."

But what about the Church's official voice in all this? Surely, we scholars naively thought when we assembled our report last April, our bishops will draw upon their own instruction, and the substantial tradition of Catholic biblical interpretation, to counter Gibson's claims that his film was the most authentic interpretation of the Gospels ever rendered. Surely, we less naively hoped as the controversy widened, our bishops will caution those who outright reject such principles and call attention to the determination voiced in 1998 in the Vatican's statement *We Remember: A Reflection on the Shoah*. That document called on Catholics to turn "past sins into a firm resolve to build a new future" because the "spoiled seeds of anti-Judaism and anti-Semitism must never again be allowed to take root in any human heart."

Perhaps this will yet happen. As things stand at present, however, the official voices of Catholicism also clash. The bishops themselves are talking past each other, as their statements seem to fall into three categories: enthusiastic approval, conflict avoidance, and (mostly cautious) criticism.

TALKING PAST EACH OTHER: THE CATHOLIC HIERARCHY

Some church leaders have been effusive in their praise for Gibson. The president of the Catholic Bishops Conference of the Philippines, Archbishop Fernando Capalla, not only endorsed the film but considered it a "must see" for Christians and Muslims. His fellow bishop, Ramon Arguelles, reported that before the bishops came to the theater for the screening that Icon Productions had considerately arranged for them, "We were saying that Mel Gibson may be the best evangelizer of our times." Arguelles expanded his praise: "So far the best evangelizer of our time is Mother Teresa. Now, they say, Gibson may beat out Mother Teresa." (I find this appalling.) Joseph Devine, president of National Communications Commission of the bishops of Scotland, is promoting the movie as "a profoundly religious film, the most authentic depiction of the Passion ever committed to film." Among Vatican officials, Darío Cardinal Castrillón Hoyos remarked, "I am ready to exchange all of my homilies on the passion of Jesus for just one scene from Mel Gibson's film." Archbishop John Foley, an American who heads the Vatican's social communications office, also voiced effusive praise.

In Baltimore, William Cardinal Keeler's more measured response steered around the controversy. Keeler's Ash Wednesday (February 25, 2004) statement reported that "most who have viewed the film have been struck by its power and force. They tell me they have been drawn into the warmth of the Lord's all-embracing love, even as they are helped to understand the enormity of his sufferings and final anguish." Others, the cardinal recognized, are less positive. "Some others are troubled by the use of material not present in the Gospels, especially when they recall a period of history in which Jews suffered persecution at Christian hands in the context of the ancient passion plays." Although Cardinal Keeler then mentioned the release of relevant Catholic documents, *The Bible, the Jews and the Death of Jesus*, his concluding word ("Pray that this movie will help draw people closer to the Lord of all mercies") seemed a strangely laudatory endorsement from the Episcopal Moderator for Catholic-Jewish Relations for the U.S. Conference of Catholic Bishops.

Other prelates, in contrast, offered a more critical perspective. Cardinal Jean-Marie Lustiger, Archbishop of Paris, said that he had "extreme reservations about the theatrical performance of the Passion, and even more so about electronic and film versions." A week before the film opened, Bishop Patrick J. McGrath of San Jose, California, implicitly addressed any who might follow Gibson's claim about knowing "what went down." He wrote in the *Mercury News:* "While primary source material of the film is attributed to the four Gospels, these sacred books are not historical accounts of the historical events that they narrate. They are theological reflections upon the events that form the core of Christian faith and belief." McGrath made mention of "periods of Christian persecution of Jews, and the direct effects of this persecution still touch us today."

Similarly, Archbishop Daniel Pilarczyk of Cincinnati released a statement on Ash Wednesday to the official archdiocesan paper, *The Catholic Telegraph*. Noting that the violence and brutality would likely deter him from seeing the film, Pilarczyk offered two considerations. "No matter what the filmmaker intended, the film is not a full and faithful presentation of the four Gospel narratives of the passion of our Lord." Rather, Gibson's film "is an individual artist's interpretation and must be viewed as such." Second, Pilarczyk exhorted, "the film must not be allowed to justify any resurgence of the anti-Semitism that most religious communities have worked so hard to leave behind." His candor resulted in some twenty persons immediately canceling their subscriptions to the archdiocesan paper. Evidently, these Catholics would rather get their religious instruction from Hollywood than from their own archbishop.

Richard Sklba, auxiliary bishop of Milwaukee, contributed a column regarding the "potentially anti-Semitic undertow" to that city's *Catholic Herald*. One of the very few to note explicitly the criteria developed by the Holy See (Vatican) and the United States bishops regarding presentations of the Passion, Sklba, a New Testament scholar, indicated his intention to offer his own reflections after he had viewed the film and "studied its message." For the present, however, Sklba said, "We cannot remain silent if any presentation of the Lord's Passion undercuts true Catholic teaching or implies a possible return to the errors of the past. Respect for ourselves and for our Jewish neighbors demands nothing less."

OFFICIAL CATHOLIC RESPONSE: AN ANALYSIS

To outsiders who see the official Church as always "on message," the varied responses of the bishops comes as quite a shock. Insiders will be less surprised, since the Catholic Church is less monolithic than it appears. Nevertheless, the controversy over the film reveals the contentious atmosphere at the twilight of John Paul II's long papacy, and in particular, the ascendancy of the neoconservative and traditionalist program with which Gibson himself is also associated. It exposes the fact that the principles of Catholic biblical interpretation are ill-understood—and not simply by many laypeople. The controversy also provides a clue to the multiple cultures that thrive under the big tent of Catholicism.

Illness and age have reduced Pope John Paul II, once a man of enormous physical and intellectual vigor, to a fragile figure. To whatever degree he can exercise leadership now, he is less forceful, and thus less effective, than when he was younger. A power vacuum has formed, and contesting ideologies stand poised to fill it. At stake is the interpretation of the Second Vatican Council (1962–65), which conservatives now challenge as having led the Church along errant paths by reconciling it with modernity. A vociferous, loosely allied group of "traditionalists," often associated with international organizations such as the Legionaries of Christ and Opus Dei, seeks a return to a Church of an earlier era—typically, the Church of the sixteenth century after the Council of Trent. So they are especially critical of modern developments, such as a vernacular liturgy, use of "critical" biblical methods, and ecumenical and inter-religious initiatives. The Latin Mass in the style of Trent (the sixteenth-century "Tridentine Mass") often serves as their chief rallying cry.

Sociologist Michael Cuneo, constructing a typology of such thinking in his 1997 book *The Smoke of Satan,* distinguishes "conservatives," "mystical Marianists and apocalypticists," and "traditionalists" (or "separatists"). The conservatives recognize the legitimacy of Vatican II, but reject interpretations that regard the council as "revolutionary." Instead, they emphasize traditional piety and morality, giving great weight to the authority of the papacy. The Marianists and apocalypticists reflect a Catholic premillennial outlook. Devotion to Mary, especially in terms of messages she has given in various apparitions, offers such people hope of survival in a godless world.

The traditionalist or separatist groups reject the authority of the papacy after Vatican II, accusing later popes of teaching false doctrine. Some, following the lead of Francis Schuckardt, hold to *sedevacantism:* the chair (i.e., papacy) is vacant. In Schuckardt's logic, the papacy exists to preserve eternally valid and unchanging Catholic doctrine. If that teaching changes, then the popes who preside over such changes must be false. It follows also that the traditionalists completely reject the teachings of Vatican II, since those teachings changed doctrine in a number of areas—including the Church's understanding of the role of the Jews in the death of Jesus. In essence, these separatists are Catholic fundamentalists who see themselves as zealously protecting "the truth."

The most influential thinker whom many of these traditionalists draw upon is Irish priest Denis Fahey, particularly his 1935 *The Mystical Body of Christ in the Modern World*. Fahey's anti-Semitic views, incidentally, influenced the infamous Fr. Charles Coughlin, the "radio priest" and rabid anti-Semite whose radio broadcasts in Detroit attracted millions of listeners across the midwest in the 1940s. Hutton Gibson, Mel's father, is a widely published and active spokesperson for the separatist point of view.

The younger Gibson seems to fall under the traditionalist or separatist rubric. He has given over five million dollars to fund his own church on sixteen acres in Agouna Hills, California, that has no connection to the Archdiocese of Los Angeles. He rejects the legitimacy of recent popes—though his production company, Icon, apparently had no qualms in seeking the endorsement of Pope John Paul II. He derides any interpretation of the Bible that differs from his own. Yet, as anomalous as it may appear, Gibson has his protectors in Rome and his champions at home, especially the Catholic League. Gibson seems to have become the patron saint of disaffected Catholics, the celebrity with the star power, and sheer volume of cash, to mainstream their agenda before the whole world.

Thus, to challenge Gibson's interpretation of the Gospels willy-nilly involves taking on his champions—and, like Gibson, they can be fierce in their zealotry. Theirs is a "take-no-prisoners" approach to religion. Woe to those they denounce! No wonder most bishops ducked the conflict.

Although this separatist Catholicism rejects biblical interpretation as it has developed over the past sixty years, within the Church, such modes of studying Scripture are generally not contested. To the contrary: The work of Catholic biblical scholars permeates the curriculum of seminaries and Catholic schools. It provides the material for religious education textbooks, and is widely accessible in books, videos, and online resources. It has enriched biblical research and teaching throughout the world, for Catholics and non-Catholics alike.

Yet, as many a sermon reveals, attentive study of Scripture—exegesis—has yet to take hold in the Church's pastoral life. Too often what has been learned in classrooms has been left there. Nor is this simply a matter of in-depth knowledge of biblical texts: Many people seem to lack a larger interpretive framework—the sort offered by the Pontifical Biblical Commission, for example—and so have only a cursory grasp of the important issues addressed in collections such as *The Bible, the Jews and the Death of Jesus*. And while the antipathy that once existed between Jews and Catholics has largely disappeared on the North American scene, most Catholics, including many priests and bishops, have at best a cursory knowledge of Judaism and only superficial relationships with serious Jews. Were there more deep friendships, they would have been better able to hear Jewish fears, and slower to dismiss them by saying of the film, as many have, "I didn't see any anti-Semitism." Perhaps, too, this episcopal timidity about speaking up for the principles of Catholic scriptural interpretation is the fallout from the sexual abuse crisis, which seems to so consume the energies of bishops that ecumenical and inter-religious concerns, by comparison, command far less attention.

Cultural perspectives also shape Catholic responses. The enthusiastic endorsement of the Philippine bishops, for instance, may in large measure be explained by the dramatic way in which Filipino culture dramatizes the Passion. This is the case in Latino/a cultures as well, since their popular religiosity emphasizes enactments of the Passion. In fact, a poll summarized by the *L.A. Weekly* reveals that Latinos are going in droves to *The Passion of the Christ*; some 91 percent of those exiting the theater report they would "definitely recommend" it. It is unsurprising that Gibson's interpretation, with its flamboyant violence, speaks to their piety in ways that other, more restrained interpretations may not. But it becomes all the more difficult to root out the anti-Judaism that so often accompanies simplistic renditions of the Gospel accounts.

A CRISIS IN THE CHURCH OR TEACHABLE MOMENT?

From my own perspective, the controversy over *The Passion of the Christ* represents both a crisis and a teachable moment. As a lifelong practicing Catholic, and a member of a women's religious order for nearly thirty-nine years (a.k.a. "a nun"), I have seldom felt so let down by the failure of so many Church leaders to live up to the Church's own deep traditions. As a woman of the Church, I am chagrined by the inability of my own community to dialogue within its own ranks. As one with years of experience in Catholic-Jewish dialogue, I am mortified by the insensitivity of so many Catholics, clergy and lay, to Jewish fears. Yet, as a teacher and scholar, I am hopeful. Many organizations, institutions, and communities are using this controversy to stimulate dialogue, education, shared Scriptural study, and mutual respect. May such occasions help us to talk *with* each other, not past each other; and may they help us also to listen to each other and to hear each other. It is up to us to work to ensure that our sacred story is never again marred by being put to sacrilegious uses.

ADELE REINHARTZ

❖

JESUS OF HOLLYWOOD

On Ash Wednesday, Hurricane Mel descended upon our global community, leaving a swath of violence and destruction in its wake. Why and how this particular film came to preoccupy so many of us for so many months is still a mystery to me, for it is by no means the first film ever to treat the last twelve hours of Jesus' life. In the century or more since the birth of cinema, Jesus' betrayal, trials, condemnation, and death have been brought to life on the screen in well over a hundred films.

These cinematic treatments range from the bloody to the sanitized, from the graphic to the refined, from the boring to the riveting. The earliest known Jesus movie, *The Passion Play at Oberammergau* (1898), covered this same sequence of events. (Contrary to its name, the film was actually staged and shot on the rooftop of the Grand Central Palace in New York, not at Oberammergau in Germany.) Since then, the Passion has appeared on its own in other films devoted primarily to Jesus' last hours (*Golgotha*, 1935; *Jesus Christ Superstar*, 1973), as a play within a film in movies about the staging of a Passion play (*He Who Must Die*, 1957; *Jesus of Montreal*, 1989), as a sidebar in fictional features (*Ben Hur*, 1959; *Monty Python's Life of Brian*, 1979), and as the climax of Jesus' life in numerous full-length Jesus "bio/pics" (*The Greatest Story Ever Told*, 1965; *Jesus of Nazareth*, 1977).

Nor does Gibson's film mark the first occasion that Jewish and other public leaders have raised their voices in protest against the potential anti-Semitism of a film rendition of Jesus' Passion. In 1916, B'nai B'rith complained about the portrayal of the priests and Pharisees in D. W. Griffith's *Intolerance*. According to Cecil B. DeMille's autobiography, "certain Jewish groups" expressed concerns about his silent film *The King of Kings* (1927); he responded by making some changes to the final version. In September 2003, a headline in *The Canadian Jewish News* declared that the recently released film, *The Gospel of John* (2003), "stands to revive the deicide charge"; and in a later issue Paul Shaviv, a Toronto Jewish educator, expressed outrage at the ways in which this film portrays the Pharisees and priests. Shaviv darkly warned Jews not to be in the vicinity when viewers exit the theaters after watching this movie.

Whether or not one sees such reactions as justified or hysterical, there is one good reason that any Jesus movie can arouse fears of anti-Semitism: the prominent role that the Gospel accounts of Jesus' Passion give to the Jewish leadership and the Jewish crowds. Although crucifixion was well known to be a Roman mode of execution, the Gospels are unanimous in their attempt to thrust the moral responsibility for Jesus's death upon Jerusalem's Jews. All four Gospels portray Pilate as extremely reluctant to condemn Jesus (Matthew 27:24; Mark 15:14; Luke 23:14; John 18:38), and all depict "the Jews" as calling for Jesus' crucifixion (Mark 15:11–13; Luke 23:18–23; John 18:6, 15). Luke's Pilate tries to evade responsibility by sending Jesus off to Herod, on the grounds that the Galilean subject should be tried by the Galilean ruler (23:6–11); John's Pilate drags the hearing out at length, in order to provide as many opportunities as possible for the Jews to agree to Jesus' release. When the Jews nonetheless cry out for Jesus' death, Pilate loses patience: "Take him yourselves and crucify him, for I find no crime in him." The Jews then insist: "'We have a law, and by that law he ought to die, because he has made himself the Son of God'" (John 19:6–7; cf. 18:30–31). Matthew's Pilate, famously, washes his hands of the whole affair:

> So when Pilate saw that he was gaining nothing, but rather that a riot was begin-
> ning, he took water and washed his hands before the crowd, saying, "I am inno-
> cent of this man's blood; see to it yourselves." And all the people answered, "His
> blood be on us and on our children!" Then he released for them Barabbas, and
> having scourged Jesus, delivered him to be crucified (Matthew 27:24–27).

At first glance, then, Gibson's claim that he has merely represented a histori-cally-accurate and authentic film of the events of Jesus' Passion might seem to be well-founded. But New Testament scholars, the vast majority of them Christian, have long understood that the Gospels are not literal, historical accounts of everything that Jesus said and did. The evangelists did not set out dispassionately to tell the objective facts of how Jesus met his death. Rather, they sought to express their own faithful understanding of Jesus' sig-nificance for humankind, to persuade their readers, provide comfort and guidance to their communities, and to explain why many, indeed most Jews did not accept that Jesus was the Messiah and the Son of God. The evangel-ists (themselves probably Jews) also tried to forge an identity based on Jew-ish texts and values, but distinct from Jewish authority structures. For these reasons, the prominence of the Jewish authorities in the Gospels' various ver-sions of the Passion may or may not reflect the actual historical events, but they certainly express nascent Christianity's ambivalent relationships to more mainstream Jews and Judaism. It is highly unlikely that the authors of the Gospels had any inkling of the tremendous and disastrous impact that their Passion accounts have had on centuries of Jewish-Christian relations, or that they would have condoned the violence that has occurred in Jesus' name.

Filmmakers, however, are in a different position. Hollywood has always had an acute anxiety about authenticity. Not surprisingly, most Jesus movies explicitly claim to tell the true story of Jesus, even as they clearly do not fall into the documentary genre. But by fidelity to "truth" or "history," these filmmakers generally mean faithfulness to Scripture; they do not query, as scholars do, the relationship between Gospel and history. Yet their approaches to Scripture do not occur in a vacuum. Rather, they are mediated by their own beliefs, by what they may—or may not—have learned in Sunday school, by public displays at Christmas and Easter time, and by Western art, music and drama, including the ongoing Passion play tradition, and, of course, by other Jesus movies. Jesus filmmakers also take their potential audience and other marketing considerations into account. And of course they must grapple with the question: What to do about Caiaphas and the other Jews who appear in their Gospel sources?

Fundamentally, filmmakers have two options. They can follow the Gospels' lead in placing primary moral responsibility upon the Jews, thereby leaving themselves open, as Mel Gibson has discovered, to charges of aiding and abetting anti-Semitism. Or they can diverge from the Gospels to focus on Pilate's culpability, thereby forgoing or at least undermining a claim to Scriptural fidelity. The option of taking the Gospel line is illustrated by the little-known German silent movie *Der Galiläer* (1917). Outside the Temple, Caiaphas whips a huge Jewish crowd into a bloodthirsty frenzy. The crowd rushes to Pilate's palace screaming (silently!) for Jesus' death. Pilate, filled with compassion, offers to release him, but the crowd demands Barabbas instead and then takes Jesus's blood upon themselves, not once, as in Matthew, but twice. The film is not merely faithful to the words of Scripture, it magnifies the elements upon which the deicide charge is based.

The second option, to focus on Pilate, appears most clearly in films that do not set out to be faithful to Scripture at all. Denys Arcand's *Jesus of Montreal*, for example, is a film about the making of a Passion play. The priest of St. Joseph's Oratory in Montreal commissions a young actor, Daniel Coulombe, to refresh the Passion play that has been performed for decades on the church grounds. After considerable research and many rehearsals, Daniel stages the play for the benefit of a rapt audience on Mount Royal, and for us viewers.

In Daniel's Passion play, Caiaphas and Pilate are both present at Jesus's trial but the key player is clearly Pilate. Pilate interviews Jesus—Is he a member of a sect, or perhaps a poet?—and mocks Jesus' emphasis on love: "Isn't that a bit optimistic as a doctrine? You wouldn't last a week in Rome." He declares Jesus harmless, and hands the file to Caiaphas, who has been lurking in the background, prayer shawl draped over his head. Pilate expresses his disdain for priests who, he says, are either idiots or profiteers. But Caiaphas reminds Pilate of the political realities: "The priests support Rome. You wouldn't want rumors spread. Tiberius is suspicious. We want to help you govern, but one must set an example. He attracts crowds, he has disciples. He performs miracles. He's caused riots in the Temple. Crucify him." Caiaphas smiles superciliously and walks away as he advises Pilate, "It is better to sacrifice one man from time to time" (cf. John 11:50; 18:14).

Pilate returns to Jesus and informs him calmly of what will now transpire: "My soldiers will take you. They're brutes, of course. We don't get the elite. You'll be whipped, then crucified. It won't be pleasant. You're not Roman, but try to be brave. Who knows, I may be doing you a favor. A philosopher said the freedom to kill oneself during hardship is the greatest gift man has. In a few hours you'll cross the Styx river of Death whence no one has returned, except Orpheus, it is said. Perhaps your kingdom lies on the far shore. Or maybe Jupiter Capitolinus awaits you, or Athena, or the god of the Germans or the Franks. There are so many gods. Perhaps the river has no other shore... You at least will know. Courage." He then orders the soldiers: "Take him away."

On the face of it, this scene, like the Gospels, implies that Pilate does not particularly desire Jesus' death, but that he gives in to Caiaphas' demands for political reasons. But if we view this scene in the context of the film as a whole, a different interpretation emerges. Like all other aspects of Daniel's Passion play, the trial is allegorical, pointing beyond the details of the Passion narratives to a devastating critique of contemporary Quebecois society. Pilate's attitude toward the priests is not in fact directed at the high priesthood in first-century Judea, but at what the movie consistently portrays as the corrupt and hypocritical Catholic priesthood in late-twentieth-century Quebec.

Martin Scorsese's *The Last Temptation of Christ* (1988) also takes liberties with the Gospels. As he informs his viewers in the scrolling text that opens the film, *Last Temptation* is an adaptation not of the New Testament, but of Nikos Kazantzakis's famous novel. Like Arcand's Pilate, Scorsese's Roman governor is momentarily amused by the opportunity for conversation with this "king of the Jews." When Jesus refuses to perform tricks on Pilate's demand—a demand that Luke associates with Herod (Luke 22:8)—Pilate dismisses Jesus as "just another Jewish politician." He admonishes Jesus: "It is one thing to change the way people live. You want to change the way they think and feel....Killing or loving, it is all the same. We don't want them changed. You do understand what has to happen. We have a space for you up on Golgotha. Three thousand skulls up there, more." As Pilate walks away, he tells Jesus, "I do wish you people would go out and count them sometime. Maybe you'd learn a lesson. No, probably not." Caiaphas is nowhere in sight; Pilate is calm, polite, aloof, and alone. The Roman governor neither knows nor cares whether Jesus is a thorn in the side of the Jewish authorities. For him, Jesus is just another Jewish troublemaker, and he applies the usual remedy: crucifixion. In this film, then, no Jews are involved in Jesus' condemnation, hence there is no question of any Jewish responsibility.

Most Jesus movies fall somewhere along the spectrum between fidelity to Scripture and complete freedom from Scripture's constraints, and between exaggerating the Jewish role or omitting it altogether. While most do assign to Jews a substantial role in the events leading to Jesus' execution, they also adopt a variety of techniques that are intended, in principle at least, to nuance or soften the Jews' role, and thereby to deflect potential charges of anti-Semitism.

Cecil B. DeMille's *The King of Kings* consistently portrays Caiaphas as a money-hungry power monger, but it does clear the Jewish crowds of major moral responsibility. When Pilate asks: "Shall I crucify your king?" it is Caiaphas, not the crowd (as it is in John 19:15) who declares, "We have no King but Caesar." After Pilate washes his hands of the affair, it is the high priest and not the crowd who proclaims a version of Matthew 27:25: "If thou, imperial Pilate, wouldst wash thy hands of this man's death, let it be upon me and me alone!" The contrast between Pilate and Caiaphas is nowhere more apparent than in their behavior in the final frames of the scene. Pilate pronounces himself "innocent of the blood of this just man; see ye to it" and then stalks off to sob alone in his throne room. Caiaphas, self-satisfied, smirks, arms folded, savoring his victory. By reassigning to Caiaphas the lines that Matthew attributes to the Jewish crowd as a whole, DeMille reconfigures the trial scene to place blame squarely—and solely—upon the high priest.

George Stevens's *The Greatest Story Ever Told* (1965), on the other hand, simply omits the most problematic elements. Like Scorsese (and like the Gospel of Luke!) he writes Caiaphas out of the trial scene and omits the crowd's declaration of responsibility in Matthew 27:25. Pilate washes his hands but does not declare himself "innocent of this man's blood." Instead the film offers a voice-over that recites from the Apostles' Creed: "Suffered under Pontius Pilate, was crucified, dead and buried...." The omissions and the voice-over point to Pilate as the major culprit in Jesus' suffering and death.

Pier Paolo Pasolini's *The Gospel According to Saint Matthew* (1966) offers a more subtle approach. This film takes every word of its dialogue from the first Gospel, though it rearranges some scenes and omits many portions of the text. The visual elements of the film, however, tell a contemporary tale. In the trial scene, the camera places the viewer among the crowd that has gathered at the Temple compound to witness the trials before the high priest and Pilate. We crane our necks to see above the heads of those in front of us; we can distinguish the players but we do not view them very clearly. The effect is to lump the Jewish and Roman authorities together and to create a gap between the governing elites and the crowd of commoners. This visual gap symbolizes the chasm between these two groups in the social, political, economic, and ideological arenas. By situating the viewers among the crowd that perceives the proceedings only from afar, Pasolini also engages our support for opposition to hierarchy and political authority. We watch helplessly as a gross injustice is being done. We hear Pilate declare himself innocent of Jesus' blood, and we hear a lone and disembodied voice cry out: "His blood be on us and on our children!" The speaker, whoever he might be, does not, however, represent either the watching crowd or any faction among them. Like Arcand, Pasolini would have us view this scene not as a faithful rendition of history and/or Scripture, but as an allegory of contemporary society. The opposition between political and religious authorities on the one hand, and the people on the other, reflects Pasolini's own Marxism and his critique of the Italian social and political institutions of his time.

If the cinematic tactics of DeMille, Stevens, and Pasolini do not entirely exonerate the Jews or their leadership, neither do they emphasize Jewish guilt. Other films, however, are less successful in their efforts to do the same. Franco Zeffirelli's six-and-a-half-hour marathon, *Jesus of Nazareth* (1977), creates a fictional character, Zerah the scribe, who does the dirty work that other films ascribe to Caiaphas, including the hiring of Judas to betray Jesus. This move is intended to deflect the charge of anti-Semitism, though it is not at all clear how inventing a guilty Jew accomplishes this goal.

John Heyman's *Jesus* (1979), a film created and used primarily for evangelical purposes, also sends a contradictory message. *Jesus* claims to be based entirely on the Gospel of Luke. Although the film strays from the third Gospel upon occasion, its rendition of the trial before Pilate follows Luke very closely, including Pilate's attempt to have Herod take care of the matter. A voice-over introduction to this segment declares solemnly: "And they took him before Pontius Pilate, the most vicious of all Roman procurators, alone responsible for the crucifixion of thousands." While this comment would seem to prepare us for holding Pilate morally responsible, the other details of the scene work against this view. Indeed, the reluctance that Pilate expresses in Luke is accentuated by the final detail of the scene, in which Pilate grudgingly tosses the crucifixion order down from his balcony to the pavement below.

A sincere attempt at softening the Jews' role is also made by the 2003 film *The Gospel of John*. This film is tied even more closely to its Biblical source text than are either Pasolini's or Heyman's movies. In fact, not a single word, aside from the occasional "he said," is omitted from the Good News Bible translation; the entire text, including the lengthy account of Jesus' trial before Pilate, is included in the film. Any modification to the portrayal of the Jews in the trial scene must therefore come, as in the Pasolini film, from elements other than the dialogue. In this regard, the film makes some attempts to deflect attention from the Jews. Caiaphas is present, but he is not singled out as the sole or principal culprit, nor does he confer directly with Pilate, as do his counterparts in the films of DeMille and Arcand. Still, there is palpable antagonism between the two leaders, and the crowd is unmistakably Jewish, as the men's fringed garments make obvious. (In this film, as in most others of this genre, Jesus does not wear fringed garments, nor does he regularly cover his head. Even films that attempt in some way to convey Jesus' Jewishness visually distinguish Jesus from his Jewish opponents by means of their clothing.) The dark colors worn by some members of the Jewish crowd convey a rather sinister impression, as does the zeal with which some clamor for Jesus' death. At least the crowd is relatively small in size, perhaps in order to convey the idea that it was not all or even most of those Jews present in Jerusalem who pressed for Jesus' death.

The production team and the academic professionals involved with this film recognized the dilemma created by the use of the Gospel of John as the script for the movie, particularly in the Passion scenes. Because this film undertook to reproduce faithfully virtually every word in the Good News Bible translation of the Gospel of John, it was not possible to omit dialogue or to reassign it to other characters. Under this constraint, the academic advisory committee composed a brief text that scrolled at the very beginning of the film. This text places the trial scene and other parts of the Passion narrative into a broader historical context. It reads as follows:

> The Gospel of John was written two generations after the crucifixion of Jesus Christ. It is set in a time when the Roman Empire controlled Jerusalem. Although crucifixion was the preferred method of Roman punishment, it was not one sanctioned by Jewish law. Jesus and all his early followers were Jewish. The Gospel presents a period of unprecedented polemic and antagonism between the emerging church and the religious establishment of the Jewish people. This film is a faithful representation of that Gospel.

These lines situate the entire Gospel story within the context of Roman imperialism and colonization, explicitly hold the Romans responsible for Jesus' crucifixion, and gesture valiantly toward the polemical nature of the Gospel's narrative and rhetoric. In declaring its goal of "faithfully" representing the Gospel, the film is explicitly *not* claiming to be an accurate rendition of the historical events. Its viewers are not meant to see the Gospel's often negative representation of the Jews and Judaism as a statement of what Jews are really like. As a member of the advisory committee, I endorsed this text as the only means of "damage control" possible under the circumstances. Yet I doubt that a few lines scrolled during the opening seconds of a long film can have much impact upon the viewer's interpretation of and response to a set of scenes that occur near the end of the film nearly three hours later.

Where does Mel Gibson fit in? On the continuum between films that explicitly claim fidelity to Scripture and those that explicitly do not, *The Passion of the Christ* is clearly in the former camp. In his famous ABC interview with Diane Sawyer, Gibson repeatedly states that his movie bases itself squarely on the Gospels. While he does not deny that his film, and his own religiosity, are influenced by the writings of nineteenth-century visionary Anne Catherine Emmerich, he insists: "I didn't do a book on Anne Catherine Emmerich's Passion. . . . I did a book [*sic*] according to the Gospels." Gibson, like DeMille and others, draws no distinction between the Gospels and history. He views the Bible as literally, historically true, in every respect. "You either accept the whole thing or don't accept it at all," he tells Diane Sawyer.

Gibson's *Passion* does indeed draw elements from all four Gospels, just as many of his predecessors' did. Like all Jesus films, it also embellishes these accounts. The movie contains many visual elements, characters, lines of dialogue, and scenes that have no foundation whatsoever in the Gospels. Some of these, like the story of Veronica on the road to Golgotha, wiping Jesus' face with her veil, derive from later Catholic tradition; some, such as the details of how Jesus is nailed onto the cross, draw on the visions of Anne Catherine Emmerich; others, like the flashbacks to the domestic life of Mary and Jesus as a child and young man, evidently come from Gibson's own imagination. Some details even pay homage to earlier Jesus movies. Gibson's Pilate, and the Roman centurion who is moved to faith at the foot of the cross, look suspiciously like their counterparts in Stevens's *The Greatest Story Ever Told*. And by having Caiaphas show up at the crufixion, Gibson's film also reproduces a detail otherwise found most famously in DeMille's *The King of Kings*, but missing from the Gospels themselves. (Luke, uniquely, has Jewish leaders mock Jesus at the cross, but the evangelist does not single out Caiaphas.)

In all of these respects, Gibson's movie falls squarely within the norms and conventions of the Jesus film genre in that it takes the outline and some details primarily from the Gospels, and adds elements from later Christian tradition, individual imagination, and popular culture. Thus, in Gibson's version of the trial before Pilate, the Roman governor attempts to please the crowd, as in Mark. He washes his hands of Jesus' blood, as in Matthew. He sends Jesus off to Herod Agrippa, as in Luke. And he dithers at length before finally ordering Jesus's execution, as in John. Like his counterparts in DeMille's *The King of Kings* and in the epics from the 1950s and later, Gibson's Pilate is a compassionate man who tries hard to avoid executing Jesus. It is the Jewish crowds, and above all Caiaphas and his crew, who orchestrate Jesus' extreme suffering and his death, even if it is the Romans who inflict the most savage blows, extract the most blood, and nail him to the cross. Gibson defends himself against the charge of anti-Semitism by explaining to Diane Sawyer: "He was born into Judea, into the House of David, he was a child of Israel among other children of Israel. The Jewish Sanhedrin and those who[m] they held sway over and the Romans were the material agents of his demise. Critics who have a problem with me don't really have a problem with me, they have a problem with the four Gospels."

Fair enough. As we have seen, the Gospels are hardly reticent in blaming the Jewish authorities and the frenzied crowds for Jesus' death. Yet what is troubling about Gibson's film is not this basic element of the plot, but the ways in which Gibson, much like the 1917 film *Der Galiläer*, in fact exaggerates the Jews' role, going far beyond what the Gospels present. *The Passion*, like this silent film, accentuates the role of Caiaphas and his fellow Jewish leaders. Caiaphas is a bloodthirsty, scheming, vicious villain who will do everything in his power to persuade the suave, compassionate Pilate to order Jesus' crucifixion. Richly clothed, Caiaphas is not only physically ugly, but morally ugly too: ugly in his hate for Jesus, ugly in his disdain for truth, justice or God. The scene in which he pays Judas echoes the stereotypical association of Jews with money that is present in medieval anti-Semitism and finds its way into DeMille's portrayal of Caiaphas as well. The Jewish crowds are huge, as in almost all of the Jesus movies. True, there are occasional voices that speak in Jesus' favor, but the crowd easily overwhelms them.

More disturbing than this play upon traditional anti-Semitic clichés is

Gibson's pervasive association of the Jews with Satan. The film sets the particular events that constitute Jesus' passion into a larger prophetic framework. This context is announced in its very first frames, which scroll a version of the Suffering Servant text in Isaiah 53: "He was despised and rejected by men, a man of sorrows, and familiar with suffering. Like one from whom men hide their faces he was despised, and we esteemed him not. Surely he took up our infirmities and carried our sorrows, yet we considered him stricken by God, smitten by him, and afflicted." An on-screen note dates the quotation to 700 BC.

The quotation evokes the ancient Christian belief that Isaiah prophesied the coming, the suffering, and the death of Jesus. This claim anchors and provides a rationale for the relentless violence to which the film subjects both Jesus and the viewer. Initially, the action focuses on Jesus' psychological and emotional suffering, as he struggles to come to terms with the fate that God has in store. With his arrest, the suffering becomes physical. We see and hear every lash and blow that the Jews and the Romans inflict upon Jesus. By the time Jesus is brutally nailed onto the cross, he is drenched in blood from head to toe, one eye is swollen shut and the other is bloodshot. The details of this violence far exceed the literary depictions in the Gospels. They are the expression of Gibson's own imagination—on view in many of his other movies—fueled in this instance by Emmerich's lurid visions.

To the suffering servant, Gibson adds another traditional element, hints of which can also be found in the Gospels and which is amplified considerably in Emmerich's writings—namely, the idea that God and Satan are locked in a cosmic battle. The death of God's son on the cross, an event that should have signaled God's defeat, is God's victory over Satan once and for all. In the Gospels, this cosmic theme exists in an uneasy paradox with the very human story of a man who is preyed upon and wrongfully executed by the political powers of his day. The film intensifies this paradox by accentuating the cosmic, historical, and physical aspects of Jesus' Passion. The cosmic element of this battle is signaled by the periodic appearance of an androgynous figure, with female features, shaved eyebrows and a deep, masculine voice. The historical and physical aspects, as we have seen, are tied closely to the Jews.

Gibson's *Passion* identifies the Jews as the instruments of Satan, the material agents, as Gibson explained to Sawyer, who initiate the events that lead to Jesus' death. This role is displayed graphically in a scene in which Jewish children themselves become demons. After Judas realizes the true import of his own actions in betraying Jesus, he is stricken with remorse. As he sits dejectedly, he is approached by two young Jewish boys wearing skullcaps. Before our very eyes, these boys morph into devil-children, disfigured, ugly, and vicious; they multiply in number as they pursue Judas to the outskirts of the city, where he eventually commits suicide. This image is echoed later on in the film, when the Satan figure is holding a demon-child who turns around and smiles wickedly at the camera in a perversion of the Madonna and Child image. No doubt these images are meant to be symbolic; the transformation of Jewish children into demons is apparently a figment of Judas' guilty and tortured mind. But how chilling that this film, knowingly or not, plays upon the age-old trope of Jews as the children of the devil, a motif that has its source in John 8:44, in which Jesus declares that the Jews who do not believe in him have the devil as their father.

In his defense against charges of anti-Semitism, Gibson points to the fact that he removed the English subtitle for Matthew 27:25 ("Let his blood be on us and on our children") and that in this regard the film should not be seen as focusing specifically on Jewish responsibility. Perhaps so. But with or without this line, the exaggerated Jewish villainy is overwhelmingly clear. And the line is still present in Aramaic on the sound track, hence available to any viewer who knows a Semitic language. Given the worldwide distribution of the film, the absence of this line from the subtitles may or may not have the desired effect, depending on the languages known by the diverse members of its global audience.

Does Gibson's film, do all these films, foment anti-Semitism? If this question means: Do Jesus movies intend to stir up hostile feelings toward Jews that under certain conditions might lead to physical violence? the answer is no. Each film has its own theme and emphasis, but it is doubtful that any of them, Gibson's film included, deliberately set out to provoke anti-Semitism. But if the real question is, Can these films help to perpetuate certain beliefs and stereotypes that have been implicated in anti-Semitism? then the answer must be yes. This is particularly true in the case of films such as Gibson's that explicitly claim to be telling a story that is faithful both to Scripture and to history.

Whatever filmmakers' intentions might be, they cannot exert complete control of the message that people will take away from their movies. Viewers who enter the theater with no prior hatred of Jews will not exit two hours later as anti-Semites. But those who enter with blatant or latent anti-Semitic feelings or opinions will find plenty of reinforcement in Gibson's movie. I do not anticipate any anti-Semitic incidents at the local cineplex as viewers of Gibson's melodrama leave the theater. But I regret that this film, like many of its predecessors, has added to the visual library of images through which Jews are portrayed as conniving, bloodthirsty Christ-killers.

Is Gibson's *The Passion of the Christ*, then, anti-Semitic? This is a difficult question to answer. But at the very least, *The Passion* is morally careless. And now it, too—its fervent storytelling, its violent imagery, its narrative excesses—is upon us and our children.

EUGENE KORN

JOHN T. PAWLIKOWSKI, O.S.M.

❖

COMMITMENT TO COMMUNITY

INTERFAITH RELATIONS AND FAITHFUL WITNESS

THE OLD AND THE NEW

The story of the crucifixion and resurrection of Jesus is central to Christianity. Through both sermons and reading the Gospels in worship service, Christians have always heard the Passion narrative proclaimed and taught. However, in the thirteenth century the Church developed a new, popular way to broadcast its ancient message of Christ's Passion: through public *dramatizations*. These productions became a regular feature of the Lenten season, the period of forty days between Ash Wednesday and Easter. The plays were meant to stimulate penitence on the part of the faithful, to encourage them to reflect on their sins, for which Christ died.

These dramas retold the Gospel accounts of Jesus' death with this pastoral goal of repentance, and this distinct theological message of sin, suffering, and atonement. Entertaining as well as educational, these plays achieved heightened effect by drawing the moral contrast between good and evil as sharply as possible. The characters that carried this message were scripted from the Gospel accounts. Thus Jesus and his followers represented the forces of good. The forces of evil, depicted as the absolute moral and theological opposite of Jesus, were represented by Satan, the Jewish religious authorities, and the Jewish people. These dark forces collectively embodied the opponents of Jesus and, thus, of the Church. As these Passion plays developed, the characterizations grew more extreme. Ultimately, "the Jews" in these plays were often portrayed as subhuman agents of evil, intimately allied with Satan.

The lament of Mary from the thirteenth-century lyrics that later became Carl Orff's *Carmina Burana* gives us the measure of how far these retellings of the Gospel accounts dramatically exaggerated the role and characterization of "the Jews." Mary cries out, "Oh the crime of this hateful race, the animal-like hands of those crucifying you...this barbarous people...oh, blind deplorable race!... He who is innocent is condemned by a damnable people, fulfilling what is necessary...Men of blood rage against the Lord of salvation."

Telling the Passion story in this popular way with this negative stereotyping of "the Jews" as the villains often incited Christians to angry violence against real Jews. In 1539, Roman municipal authorities were forced to cancel that year's performance because in years prior the Passion plays provoked Christian audiences to sack the nearby Jewish ghetto. The Church itself recognized the Passion play's violent potential, and tried to control it. Bishops in the medieval and early modern period frequently advised local Jewish communities to avoid appearing in public during Good Friday and Holy Week, to avert possible attacks. This past is not so distant: Many American Jews today have European grandparents who were forced to hide during Holy Week for fear of Christian violence, and even Jews in the United States in our generation have themselves been taunted as "Christ-killers."

It is no exaggeration to state that from the Middle Ages through the mid-twentieth century, this theological focus on Christ's suffering, combined with readings of the Passion that portrayed the Jews as Christ's ultimate enemies who were responsible for his suffering, provoked and sustained hostility against European Jews. Pilate's role in the Passion had less dramatic traction, because the Roman culture that Pilate represented had long ago embraced Christianity. "Romans" were now Christians; but "the Jews" were still Jews. Because they refused to convert to Christianity, Jews in later generations were regarded as "rejecting" Christ just as emphatically as had their ancient ancestors, whose villainy was so baroquely depicted in these Passion plays at Easter season. Thus, though the pastoral goal of these plays turned on the message that Christ died for the sins of humanity, the dramatic message of these plays was that the Jews had killed Jesus. Christian hostility toward Jews rested on this theological foundation of deicide, "God-killing." Passion plays were the most visible, and popular, representation of these teachings.

Theological anti-Judaism did not create Nazism, nor did it directly cause the Holocaust. Although Hitler, Himmler, Hess and other high Nazi officials were baptized Catholics, they were not Christians in any meaningful sense. But centuries of Church teachings had conditioned Christian believers, both ecclesiastical and lay, to see their Jewish *contemporaries* as complicit in the death of Christ. When bad things happened to Jews, it seemed deserving; when Christians did bad things to Jews, it was often understood in a context of avenging the wrong that Jews supposedly did to Christ. Once the Nazi-initiated extermination of Jews began, the majority of Europe's Christian population tolerated this genocide, sometimes condoning and committing the murders themselves. Most of the people who operated the crematoria of Birkenau and many of those who helped implement the Final Solution were believing Christians. Theological anti-Judaism had prepared the ground for political anti-Semitism.

In the wake of this mass murder, Christian theologians began to reflect on the role that the anti-Jewish elements of their teaching had played in the extermination of European Jewry. Serious self-reflection spurred churches

to reformulate Christian teachings about Jews and Judaism. The most significant Catholic theological breakthrough occurred at the Second Vatican
Council in 1965, with the promulgation of *Nostra Aetate*. Significantly, the
first order of business was to reject the charge of deicide, for that doctrine
had provided the theological foundation for a millennium of anti-Judaism.
The council also explicitly deplored any expression of anti-Semitism by any
persons for any reason. Protestant churches likewise repudiated the toxic tradition of theological anti-Judaism. And in 1988, Pope John Paul II stated that
anti-Semitism is a sin against God and humanity.

This remarkable theological change has led to a continuing process of reconciliation between Christians and Jews throughout the world. New Christian theology maintains that affirming the truth of Christianity does not entail
the denigration of Judaism; believing the message of one faith community to
be true does not require that the other be false. This purging of anti-Semitism
and anti-Judaism from Church doctrine has, in turn, encouraged many Jews
to commit without fear to a new relationship with Christians. Christians and
Jews have entered a fruitful partnership, constructively speaking with and listening to each other on issues of moral, social, and religious importance.

Eugene Korn

JEWS IN SEARCH OF TRUST AND GOD: THE DIALOGUE WITH CHRISTIANS
At the dawn of the twenty-first century, the Jewish people find themselves in
a new, yet old, existential situation. Time has begun to heal the trauma, dislo-
cation, and terrible losses of sixty years ago—the genocide in Europe as well
as the mass expulsions of Jews from Arab lands where they had lived for centuries. In the pluralistic democracy of America, Jews are full citizens. With
the birth of the State of Israel, Jews once again have a commonwealth in
their native land for the first time since the first century AD. As a result of
these developments, modern Jews generally feel less vulnerable to the anti-

Semitic hatreds of the past. Yet problems remain. As the only democracy and the only non-Muslim nation in the Middle East, Israel remains in a protracted struggle for acceptance. Long-standing and virulent anti-Semitism in Arab countries continues to foster terrorism against Jews in Israel and worldwide. And the unexpected resurgence of anti-Semitism in Europe has darkened Jewish hopes and sharpened age-old Jewish fears and insecurity.

A key to the future of the Jewish people is its relationship with Christians and Christianity. Although churches have lost much of their temporal power in the modern era, America and Europe remain largely Christian cultures, formed by Christian ideas and ideals. And since radical militant Islam has now targeted Western democracies as well as Israel and the Jewish people, the Jewish alliance with Christian neighbors is as natural as it is necessary. Moreover, both communities are threatened by another less brutal but more subtle danger: the powerful cultural effect of materialism and secularism. All these considerations raise a fundamental question: Can Jews and Christians face the future as allies and strengthen each other in the common struggle against intolerance, hatred and materialism?

The many centuries of Christian hostility toward Jews were expressed both theologically and socially. As a result of Christian acceptance of pluralistic society and the remarkable transformation of Christian teachings today about Jews and Judaism, this hostility has greatly diminished. Sister Mary Boys has described the sources of this change as "the six R's": (1) repudiation of anti-Semitism; (2) rejection of the charge of deicide; (3) repentance after the *Shoah;* (4) review of teaching about Jews and Judaism; (5) recognition of Israel; and (6) rethinking of converting Jews. These profound theological changes, together with Pope John Paul II's powerful gestures of reconciliation in Rome and in Jerusalem, have moved Jews to dream of a peaceful future in partnership with Christians and the Church.

Since both Christianity and Judaism are centrally *religious* traditions, serious Christian-Jewish relations cannot be confined to secular politics, social ethics, and pragmatic survival strategies. Interfaith relationships need a religious component if Jews and Christians are to understand each other profoundly. Jews must find a way to discuss Scripture, God, covenant, Israel, and religious practice with Christians, and to find a basis in their own tradition for respecting and appreciating the traditions of others. Jews need to find a way to proceed theologically that "makes room" for the validity of Christianity, just as Christianity has begun to do for Judaism. Christian-Jewish reconciliation, in brief, cannot do without religious dialogue. Dialogue does not suppress difference. On the contrary, it respects difference and draws strength from it.

Jews have always been in a religious minority. In the centuries after Constantine, however, the Christian majority culture turned actively hostile. The threat of violence, exile, and forced conversion, and the eventual physical separation from their non-Jewish neighbors because they were herded into ghettoes, caused Jewish communities to turn inward. Their separateness forced on them, Jews also maintained it themselves, in part through careful avoidance of intimate interactions with others. Jews were unable to exercise equal influence on the direction of these relationships, so they often concluded that distance was the safer policy.

Though the Enlightenment broke down the ghetto for European Jews, the Final Solutions of the last century demonstrated how fragile the Jews' integration had actually been. Even after the Holocaust, anti-Semitism has been given a new legitimacy, cloaked in the rhetoric of anti-Zionism. Often the benevolent interest that some churches show toward Jews has turned out to be a function of those communities' concern to "save" Jews by converting them. Trusting outsiders, for good historical reasons, has been hard to do. And without trust, interfaith relations are hard to sustain.

If trust is one sine qua non of interfaith relations, a second is respect. When people believe that their way is the only right way and only good way, talking with others from different communities can too easily turn into an exercise in evangelization ("My way is the only way, and I care about your well-being, so you must come and join my group or you are damned!") or contempt ("Why would you want to stay with something like *that*, when you could have something like *this*?"). In this area, traditional Judaism has a substantial advantage. Its internal ancient teaching has roots to support a commitment to religious pluralism. These roots are found in the rabbinic doctrine of the Noahide Covenant.

Jewish theology and law maintain that Jews are bound to God by a covenant of 613 commandments (*mitzvot*). God and Gentiles have a separate sacred covenant that consists of seven *mitzvot*, known in rabbinic parlance as "the Noahide commandments." The scriptural basis for this covenant is in Genesis, when God makes his will known to Noah after the Flood (Genesis 9:1–17). The Noahide Covenant prohibits six types of behavior: murder, theft, sexual immorality, idolatry, eating the limb of a live animal (a paradigm for cruelty and devaluation of life), and blasphemy against the one God of the universe. The seventh commandment is positive: human societies are enjoined to establish courts of law to justly enforce these six prohibitions. Most important for interfaith relations, each covenant is valid for its respective adherents. Gentiles are not expected to convert to the Jewish covenant. The Noahide Covenant gives Gentiles an independent way of life and an authentic religious path. Judaism teaches that God considers faithful Gentiles, their lifestyle, and their worship to be sacred. According to rabbinic teaching, non-Jews who faithfully keep the Noahide commandments are more beloved by God than Jews who violate the fundamentals of their covenant of Torah. Ancient and medieval rabbis paid Gentiles the ultimate theological compliment, teaching that "righteous gentiles have a share in the world to come." Judaism never taught *extra ecclesiam nulla salus* ("outside the Church there is no salvation"). This concept of covenantal pluralism lays the groundwork for respecting most sacred traditions outside of Judaism.

Yet the relationship between Judaism and Christianity is unique, and far more profound than those between Judaism and other religions. Christianity and Judaism are much more like each other than either is like, say, Buddhism, or Confucianism, or Hinduism. For whatever divine reasons, God has thrown Jews and Christians together in a long and tortured history. He has given both peoples a shared sacred text, the Hebrew Scriptures—or more accurately, "Shared Scriptures." Both communities believe in the One Creator of the universe. Both traditions emphasize social and ethical commitments as the way to express love of God. Finally, both communities share a messianic vision of human history. Even if the particular details of the messianic process and of the agents of that redemption differ, both Jews and Christians are challenged by their religious traditions to improve the world. We both work toward the same goal of making the God of Abraham known in the world, and we both strive, in the words of Genesis, "to be a blessing for all the nations of the earth." Within Judaism, these convictions about Christianity's unique status are indisputable. Even Maimonides, who was the greatest Jewish thinker of the last two thousand years and the harshest critic of Trinitarian theology, acknowledged that Christianity is a positive historical force in spreading the messianic idea in human history.

Whereas fifty years ago interfaith cooperation was championed primarily by liberals of tepid religious commitment and minimalist theological conviction, today it is people seeking God in their experience and transcendent meaning in their ethics who benefit most from this alliance. Despite their profound theological differences, faithful Jews and faithful Christians stand together in Western culture in asserting a set of core values.

Post-modern culture has spawned a pervasive value orientation whose foundations contain the seeds from which destructive forces can grow again. Hedonism drives much of contemporary ethos. Violence saturates our media, and now appears too often as just another legitimate form of entertainment—even, in the instance of certain R-rated movies, as a legitimate means of religious instruction! Such attitudes contribute to the erosion of

COMMITMENT TO COMMUNITY 189

moral discipline and the numbing of conscience. But both moral discipline and conscience are essential to securing the values of human welfare and dignity. In our utilitarian culture, human life has lost intrinsic value. The poor, the young, the ill get ignored; the old, disregarded. Human life can be measured and quantified, like a commodity that is cost-justified and sometimes discarded. This moral philosophy denies the cardinal principle of Jewish and Christian ethics: that all persons are created in God's image, which means that every human life has infinite sacred value.

Relativism is one of the most widely accepted theories in our time. Moral objectivity and moral absolutes have come under ferocious attack, and are now on the cultural defensive. Absent firm principles, we lack a bar by which human actions are measured, and sometimes this means that there is no bar at all for serious moral judgment. Finally, fanaticism has become a potent force both in world politics and in the religious identity of many believers. It denies religious freedom and diversity, and we now live with the experience of massive slaughter committed in the name of faith. All this frightens, for the Holocaust taught us that when ethical values do not assume primary importance in human action, radical evil results.

In his essay "No Religion Is an Island," Rabbi Abraham Joshua Heschel taught prophetically that Judaism and Christianity should be allies against these contemporary cultural threats. In our modern and post-modern context, religious Jews and Christians share a common mandate to make the world a better place, a world where all persons are precious because they are created in God's image, where moral values are real and not illusions, where there is a spiritual center to the universe, and where there is meaning to every human life.

For both spiritual and practical reasons, therefore, Jews and Christians share urgent common tasks. We need to explore together how we can live out our religious values in a secular world. We need to recognize the riches of our shared Scripture, to understand the meaning of sacred covenants for modern life. We need to find ways to introduce spiritual values into political, social, and national life. We must strive to understand each other and to learn how to value each other's community as a way to enhance knowledge of ourselves.

Can Jews and Christians succeed in seeing the image of God in the face of each other? The foundation for doing so has been laid. Through dialogue, both communities have begun to overcome the heritage of hostility that defined our past, and to develop the mutual trust that brings with it the security to be partners for a better future together. This can only be done when Christians no longer see Jews as enemies of God, or Judaism as theologically obsolete, and when Jews no longer see Christians as implacable enemies of Jewish physical and spiritual survival.

John Pawlikowski

RESPECTING PERSONHOOD AND DEEPENING UNDERSTANDING:
THE CONTEMPORARY JEWISH-CHRISTIAN ENCOUNTER

The Christian understanding of Judaism, and thus of the nature of the Christian-Jewish relationship, was profoundly transformed in the 1960s. In major part this was the result of the declaration by the Second Vatican Council in the Catholic Church that Jews were to be seen as continuing in the covenant with God after the coming of Christ and that Jews were not to be held collectively responsible then or now for Jesus' death. This change in the Church's perspective on the Jewish people represented one of the most radical turns in ordinary Catholic teaching at the council. Many Protestant denominations also issued major statements at this time that closely parallel, and even go beyond, the declaration from Vatican II.

Given the long history of anti-Judaism in Christianity, the turnabout in Christian teaching over the past four decades is amazing. It has been brought about by several factors. Textbook studies in the late fifties and early sixties

by Protestants and Catholics revealed that this long history of negative por-
trayals of Jews still exercised an influence. The results of the Catholic textbook studies done at St. Louis University were particularly influential in providing scientific support for the effort at the Second Vatican Council to repu-
diate this "against the Jews" tradition. In the last fifty years, many Catholic
textbooks have been revised accordingly. This work needs to continue.

The American experience likewise had an impact on the change in Christ-
ian attitudes toward Jews and Judaism. There was a certain sense of tolerance that became accepted in America both by Catholics and Protestants.
While theologically they often held the same views regarding Jews as their
European counterparts, they did not generally translate these attitudes into
social legislation in the same way as was true in Europe. This was because
American society and culture was always more pluralistic from its origins.
And in the first part of the twentieth century a strong coalition developed
among Catholic, Protestant, and Jewish leaders to support social change for
the workers in America. This experience of working across religious lines for
social justice left many Christian leaders with a positive attitude toward interreligious relations. This was certainly true in the Catholic community. Hence
it is no accident that the American Catholic bishops at Vatican II provided
strong support for the passage of the declaration on the Jewish people as well
as for the parallel document on religious liberty.

The experience of religious pluralism in this country was defended over the
course of American history by Catholics such as Charles Carroll, a signer of
the Declaration of Independence, by the bishops assembled at the Council of
Baltimore in 1837, and by Cardinal Gibbons of Baltimore when the Vatican was
casting questioning eyes on the American church regarding religious toleration.
This tradition contributed to the strong support given to the declaration of
Vatican II on the Jews by American Catholic bishops. And the joint effort of
Catholics and Jews to improve the lot of the working class during the thirties
and forties provided a human face for interreligious understanding. Jews were

no longer theological stereotypes but human persons who shared the same sometimes unjust conditions of American society. Theology did not change immediately. But eventually the strength of the positive human encounters prevailed. This new personal framework certainly aided the process that occurred at Vatican II and through important Protestant declarations.

Two other documents from Vatican II, on the Church in the Modern World and on Religious Liberty, both strongly supported by the American bishops, reflect the American ethos. These argued for the basic dignity of every human person expressed in the freedom of conscience, even to the point of protecting the right not to believe. These documents hold human dignity, not right belief, as the fundamental cornerstone of any just society.

What became important in the Christian-Jewish relationship was the commitment to respect the personhood of the other. Discussions about religious differences continue. But such differences would not impede the development of a profound appreciation for each other as faithful religious communities. A growing recognition, highlighted in the 1974 Vatican statement for the tenth anniversary of the original conciliar declaration, emphasized that Christians must come to know Jews as they define themselves, not as Christian tradition had stereotyped them. This statement had at its roots the recognition that such stereotyping over the centuries had led to the eventual dehumanization of Jews in Christian societies.

Such stereotyping regrettably has been returned to Christian consciousness with *The Passion of the Christ*. The sinister appearance of nearly all the identifiable Jews in the film, their visual association with Satan, their depiction as an evil cabal bent on having Jesus executed come what may, and the destruction of the Temple with its underlying theology of the end of Judaism as a religion, are all classical anti-Jewish stereotypes that *The Passion of the Christ* has brought to the forefront.

Mel Gibson is a creative maker of films. He could have substantially advanced the radical change in understanding the Jewish-Christian relationship that has developed since Vatican II. But his conservative anti–Vatican II theological agenda prevented that. Instead he has added new stimulus to the old anti-Jewish stereotyping that could cause a resurgence of concrete anti-Semitism at some point. The general spirit of religious toleration in America will likely prevent that here. But there are some genuine questions how the film may play in other parts of the world. For forty years many in the religious community, particularly Christian educators, have worked tirelessly through textbook revisions and teacher training institutes to eradicate the remaining seeds of anti-Semitism from the Christian churches. The question before us now is, Will this come to a halt after the Gibson film? Gibson is marketing the film as a resource for Christian education. If he is successful in this regard, he may help to undermine everything that has been accomplished thus far.

This will be the most urgent challenge facing the Christian churches after *The Passion of the Christ* ends its run in commercial theaters. I believe it is incumbent upon Church leaders to make clear to teachers that the Gibson film cannot replace or undo the forty years of change. Gibson's image of Jesus' relationship with Judaism cannot be allowed to replace the new understanding so well articulated by Cardinal Carlo Martini, the recently retired archbishop of Milan and a biblical scholar in his own right. Martini has written that Jesus was fully Jewish and that we cannot understand the meaning of his message without appreciating its profound rootage in the Judaism of the time. This same perspective can be found in the 1985 Vatican "Notes on Teaching and Preaching about Jews and Judaism." These are not newfangled ideas, as Gibson has termed them, but the stuff of contemporary Christian teaching today.

The remarkable change in the Christian-Jewish relationship has the possibility of becoming a model for fundamental changes in the relationship among all religious groups. If we can turn around this historically contentious relationship, we may have the possibility of a model for eradicating violence from the expression of religion as such. And religion cannot be a constructive force in global society unless it first purifies itself of its violent past, and in some cases, of its violent present as well. That is why the gesture of Pope John Paul II asking forgiveness from Jews, on the first Sunday of Lent in 2000 and subsequently during his historic visit to Jerusalem, was such an important symbolic gesture. It helped to begin to heal the wounds of previous hostility and to generate a new sense of trust. Gibson's film has eroded some of that trust. There is a growing feeling that the Christian churches have insufficiently reacted to his evident reintroduction of classical anti-Judaic stereotypes.

Some have said that Jews and Christians view *The Passion of the Christ* with different glasses. In one sense that is true. The late Fr. Edward Flannery once remarked that Jews know best those pages of Christian history which the best Christians have frequently thrown out of their textbooks. The history of anti-Semitism is Christian history. Christians must acquire a new pair of glasses to see this along with Jews. I have been utterly amazed and disheartened by how many Christians, including pastors and those in the Church hierarchy, show not even the slightest public awareness of this history. We cannot change this painful history. But we can take responsibility for it, as Pope John Paul II did in 2000 and as Gibson has not done in 2004.

Even if there is no immediate threat to Jewish life and property as a result of Gibson's movie, this lack of trust may undermine the personal relationship painstakingly built up over the years. The loss of such trust would be most painful and distressing.

THE FUTURE OF JEWISH-CHRISTIAN RELATIONS

It is the new Christian teachings regarding Jews and Judaism that have made possible the continuing journey of reconciliation between the two great religious traditions. Christians can tell the story of Christianity without denigrating Judaism, without implying that the Church has superseded the synagogue; they can affirm their own faith while acknowledging the continuing spiritual vitality of Jews. And Jews can relate to faithful Christians in full dignity and freedom.

The Gibson film has produced a defining moment in contemporary Christian-Jewish relations. Will the constructive process now be halted? The answer largely rests with the Christian churches. They should reaffirm their commitment not only by issuing statements and monographs, as important as these are, but also by concrete programming with Christian laity and clergy. One evident conclusion from the experience of *The Passion of the Christ* is how little the previous episcopal documents and the new biblical scholarship have in fact penetrated to the people in the pew, and even perhaps to the clergy that speaks to them. Christian leaders need to aggressively commit their churches to full-scale implementation of their own teaching. If this occurs, then the problems associated with Gibson's film may prove to be a blessing in disguise.

But there is a necessary role for Jews as well. They must be open to renewed dialogue with Christians, to share their pain about Hollywood's reintroduction of these old defamations of their heritage and personhood. But they also need to learn far more about Christians' understanding of salvation in and through Christ. Such dialogue occurs in some places. Christian and Jewish leaders need to encourage it everywhere, so that members of the two faith communities may indeed become a blessing to each other.

The Passion of the Christ reverted to the old, discredited interpretations of the Passion narrative. Its satanic image of Jews, its toxic evocation of deicide, and its implied supersessionist triumph of Christianity over Judaism, undermines the basis for honest Jewish-Christian dialogue and for respectful Jewish-Christian relations. Should Gibson's atavistic interpretation capture the hearts of Christians and the thinking of future Christian theologians, continuing reconciliation will be difficult.

In March 2000 when Pope John Paul II visited the *Yad VaShem* Memorial in Jerusalem, he repeated the moving prayer of the Vatican document, "We Remember":

> Let us build a new future in which there will be no more anti-Jewish feeling among Christians, or anti-Christian feeling among Jews, but rather the mutual respect of those who adore the one Creator and Lord, and look to Abraham as our common father in faith.

The challenge before faithful Christians and faithful Jews is to choose life over death, good over evil. Whether the Pope's lofty summons exercises more influence on our future than does Mel Gibson's dark vision of Jewish-Christian conflict and opposition is up to us.

AMY-JILL LEVINE

❖

FIRST TAKE THE LOG
OUT OF YOUR OWN EYE

DIFFERENT VIEWPOINTS, DIFFERENT MOVIES

Mel Gibson's *The Passion of the Christ* is, to some viewers, the most biblically faithful and historically accurate film about Jesus ever made. Others find that the film grossly distorts both the events of the past and the scriptural record of those events. To some, the film communicates the life-transforming balm of Christian love; to others, it conveys the toxic poison of anti-Semitism. In effect, the film has become a flashpoint in the U.S. culture wars. The problem in this war, as in most, is that those on one side of the ideological divide either do not or cannot see the contested issues from the perspective of the other. As a result, different people watching the same movie take away different messages. They do not see the same film. And they do not understand why their particular experience is not universally shared.

Different presuppositions, different experiences, and different memories all contribute to complicating the issue. Many American Christians do not know that Jews today are still accused of being "Christ-killers." Many are unfamiliar with the West's tragic history of depicting Jews as ugly, greedy, murderous, and in league with Satan. Many would be shocked to learn that the Gospels they regard as exemplars of grace and compassion often sound to Jewish ears—and even to the occasional liberal Christian—as denunciations of Jewish tradition and belief. Conversely, many Jews do not appreciate the depth of love and compassion that Christians find in the story of Jesus' death. Many Jews are unaware that most Christians do not understand their Scriptures or their theology in an anti-Jewish way. And many Jews do not realize that even those Christians who seek to convince them that Jesus is their Lord and Savior do so out of love for the Jew, G-d's "chosen people," and not out of hatred for Judaism.

Different communities read Scripture differently too. On this issue, divisions exist within single religious groups as well as across them. Some believers, whether Jewish or Christian, regard the Scriptures of their community as inerrant, inspired if not dictated by the Spirit of G-d, and the primary guide for life. Others, whether Jewish or Christian, see the same texts as the products of human hands and hearts; while they treasure the texts as both inspirational and instructional, they do not ground their beliefs in claims that the texts are historically precise or, in some empirical or scientific way, "true." Thus, the liberal Christian finds a kindred spirit in the liberal Jew, and conservative Christians find their comrades primarily in the Orthodox Jewish community.

These divisions reflect broader cultural alliances. For example, liberals, whether Jewish or Christian, in general support full religious as well as civic enfranchisement for gays. They often support the erasure of gender roles in worship; they often are pro-choice. Conservatives in both traditions, in general, regard homosexual practice as sinful, support a "separate but (sort of) equal" liturgical structure, and subject any consideration of reproductive rights to their interpretation of the laws of Scripture. Again, these parties do not understand each other. Those closer to the conservative end of the spectrum tend to accuse liberals of lacking respect for the biblical authority of

God's Word and of substituting their own values for those given on Mt. Sinai or at the Sermon on the Mount. Those who see Scripture as God speaking through humans may well regard the conservative position as a principled refusal to think long and hard about difficult issues. My point here is that no one outside a given group seems to understand "the other" group as that group understands itself.

How then, with so many different and contesting points of view, can any of us see what our neighbors see when we all look at *The Passion*? Perhaps the time has come to follow the suggestion from the Gospel of Matthew (7:3–5; cf. Luke 6:42): Before we remove the speck from our neighbor's eye, let's work on removing the log from our own. As with debates on gay rights, gender roles, and abortion, each side is doing the best it can to frame a faithful, moral, just, and honest response. The sides will not come to agreement, but they need not talk past each other or substitute ad hominem invective for considered discussion. And to understand what the other side is saying, each must first listen in order to hear, instead of assuming that they already know all they need to know.

"SALVATION IS FROM THE JEWS" (JOHN 4:22)

Those who find no anti-Semitism in *The Passion* begin by stating that, according to Christian thought, it was divine design, not Jewish enmity, that ultimately led to Jesus' death. They would never state that "the Jews" killed Jesus. To the contrary, Jesus was handed over by G-d the Father, and he died of his own free will. He took his place on the cross because of human sin. As the old hymn goes, "'Tis I, Lord Jesus, I it was who denied thee. I who crucified thee." Or, as Acts 4:27–28 puts it, insisting on universal responsibility coupled with divine decree, "both Herod and Pontius Pilate, with the Gentiles and the people of Israel, gathered together against your [G-d's] holy child Jesus, whom you anointed, to do whatever your hand and your plan had predetermined to take place." When the Virgin Mary (played by the Jewish Maia Morgenstern), holds the body of her dead son and stares directly into the camera, she indicts everyone.

Mr. Gibson himself testified to this theological vision by publicizing the fact that he filmed his own hand driving the first nail into Jesus' palm. He has also recounted continuously, in the months leading up to the release of the film and subsequently, that *The Passion* is a project of faith. His conviction that Jesus died for him pulled him out of his own suicidal despair, and the film, as he saw it, is his gift to the world, given in gratitude to G-d.

The movie offers additional scenes that undercut any suggestion that "the Jews" bear particular responsibility for Jesus' death. It clearly portrays sympathetic Jewish characters, such as Nicodemus, who protest loudly that the Sanhedrin trial of Jesus is a sham; and Veronica, who wipes Jesus' face along the long road to Golgotha. Of course, Jesus is Jewish, as is Mary, his mother, Mary Magdalene, John the beloved disciple, and Simon of Cyrene, who helps carry the cross. The brutes in this movie are the majority of Roman soldiers who, when scourging Jesus, evidently enjoy their task. When they force Simon of Cyrene—who is wearing a kippa— to help Jesus, the Romans refer to him derisively as "Jew." And it is the Roman soldiers who actually perform the act of crucifying Jesus in a scene where, were crucifixion not barbaric enough, they increase Jesus' suffering by wrenching his shoulder out of its socket to conform his arm to the cross.

Some viewers have even insisted that they see the film as showing enormous respect for Judaism, since the story refers positively to sacred texts and beloved themes from Judaism. The epigraph that opens the movie derives from Scripture held sacred by the synagogue as well as the church, namely, the Book of Isaiah. In a direct citation of the first question recited by the youngest person at every Jewish Passover meal, the Virgin Mary, sensing that Jesus has been arrested, asks, "Why is this night different from all other nights?" The line establishes, eloquently, Mary's own Judaism just as it connects the death of Jesus to the Passover. Even the choice of using Aramaic and Hebrew for the dialogue have been seen as indicating respect for Judaism, for these two languages are still heard in synagogue worship.

How viewers understand the New Testament also affects their assessment of the movie. Christians who regard the authors of the Gospels as divinely inspired will conclude that the Gospels cannot be anti-Semitic: the categories are mutually exclusive. Anti-Semitism is a sin, and sinful statements have no place in Holy Writ. When the Gospels do mention that some Jews were involved in Jesus' death—Annas and Caiaphas, the Sanhedrin and the Jerusalem crowds—they are not being anti-Semitic. They are simply reporting what the faithful regard as fact. And thus, when the movie depicts some Jews seeking Jesus' execution, it is not anti-Semitic either. It is, rather, biblically as well as historically faithful.

So too, when Paul, who is as Jewish as the Anti-Defamation League's Abraham Foxman, observes that the fledgling church in Thessalonica "suffered the same things from [its] own compatriots as they [i.e., the churches of Christ Jesus that are in Judea] did from the Jews *who killed both the Lord Jesus and the prophets...*" (1 Thessalonians 2:14–16a), he is not being anti-Semitic. He is, in this view, simply stating fact. Indeed, several Jewish commentators have noted that the Talmud, although offering quite a different account of the trial and execution of Jesus, does state that Jews sought his death. Surely, then—so this first group of viewers concludes—if Jews themselves say that they executed Jesus, the point cannot be an anti-Semitic one. Comments from other Jews today cohere with this view: Michael Medved, David Horowitz, and Daniel Lapin, among others, celebrated Gibson's production as profoundly spiritual and visually arresting. Maia Morgenstern, the actress who played the movie's Virgin Mary and the granddaughter of a Jew murdered by the Nazis, saw the film as an indictment not of Jews but of the evils of a totalitarian political system.

Finally, those who see no evidence of anti-Semitism in Gibson's film tend to be those who make no immediate connection, or any connection at all, between the Jews of the early first century as depicted in the Gospels and the Jews of today. Most Christians, when contemplating the suffering and death of Jesus, do not equate Caiaphas with Mrs. Goldberg down the street any more than Jews, when celebrating the Passover and detailing the persecution of Israel by ancient Egyptians, equate "Pharaoh who knew not Joseph" (Exodus 1:8) with Omar Sharif.

Gibson, according to his supporters, has finally portrayed crucifixion in all its horror. Jesus does not look like Max von Sydow; he does not look as if he's posing for a shampoo commercial. Gibson's Jesus is an Aramaic-speaking Jew from Galilee; he is the Man of Sorrows, and the movie's audience, by watching him suffer, participates in his sufferings. The viewer follows the cinematic Stations of the Cross, and "by his wounds they are healed" (see 1 Peter 2:24). That such a blessing could be seen as anti-Semitic is, to this group, literally unthinkable. To the contrary, by honoring Jewish texts, traditions, and language, and by portraying a Jewish Jesus, the movie states dramatically what the Gospel of John forthrightly teaches: "Salvation is from the Jews."

"THEN JESUS SAID TO THE JEWS . . . 'YOU ARE FROM YOUR FATHER THE DEVIL'" (JOHN 8:31, 44)

While large segments of the American public celebrate *The Passion*, numerous other viewers, of all religious persuasions and none, find it profoundly anti-Semitic. Just as knowledge of Christian theology leads the majority of Evangelical and Catholic viewers to overlook or see through any possible anti-Semitic implication in the film, so knowledge of the history of Christian anti-Semitism leads others to conclude that *The Passion* is both a symptom of and a contribution to an old and hideous problem. Like the reasons for seeing the film as blameless, so the reasons for seeing the film as anti-Semitic are cumulative.

To be sure, Christian theology insists that humanity bears the responsibility for crucifying Jesus, but history and theology do not always march hand in hand. Centuries of Christian history witness the charge that the Jews—not just the ones in Jerusalem on that one fateful day, but all Jews in all places at all times—bear particular responsibility for Jesus' death. Passion plays and sermons often reinforced this view, and Jews knew to keep indoors during Holy Week lest the faithful, inspired by what they saw and heard, decided to avenge their Lord by executing his presumed executioners. Otherwise put, Good Friday was never a good Friday for the Jews. Given this history, many Jews as well as Christians treat the Passion story with trepidation. And given the way the film was marketed, these viewers had good reason to worry. The hand that struck the first nail also struck deep concern in those attuned to Jewish-Christian relations.

Even before the film was released, concern that it would recapitulate these old Christian canards crystallized. These concerns stemmed from Gibson's dependence on Anne Catherine Emmerich for much of his script, and were further roused by his production decisions and his screening strategies. By his acts of both commission and omission, Gibson made people worried.

Emmerich's visions, which provided Gibson with much of his material, were hardly a high point in interfaith dialogue. She claimed that "Jews... strangled Christian children and used their blood for all sorts of suspicious and diabolical practices." (Emmerich would have been no fan of multicultur-alism either, convinced as she was that Noah's son Ham was the progenitor of "the black, idolatrous, stupid nations" of the world.) Following Emmerich's *Dolorous Passion* closely, Gibson's script described Jesus' cross as being built on the night of Passover in Jerusalem's temple. (To grasp how offensive this image is to Jews, think of the analogous, and equally false, idea that the ovens of Auschwitz were literally built in local churches.) Both Emmerich and Gibson had Jewish guards arresting and abusing Jesus. Both placed Jesus' Sanhedrin trial at night, and again in the Temple. Both had huge crowds of Jews baying for Jesus' death. In a line straight out of Emmerich, Gibson's Pontius

Pilate asks Caiaphas, once Jesus is before him, whether the Jews normally half-kill their prisoners before trial. And so on. (The list is dolorous itself.) Eventually, several of these unfortunate scenes were dropped from the final cut of the film. Alas, an even larger number of them remained.

Emmerich found Pilate a sympathetic figure. Her Pilate, and, thus, Gibson's, is an honorable man, and his wife is saintly. This revised Roman executes Jesus reluctantly and under duress, forced by his fear that Caiaphas will start a revolt if he, Pilate, does not comply. The scene is flat-out contrary to the Gospels. In John 11:47b–48, the chief priests and the Pharisees confer about Jesus (who is not present) and the council notes: "This man is performing signs. If we let him go on like this, everyone will believe in him, and the *Romans* will come and destroy both our place [i.e., the Temple] and our nation" (emphasis added). Caiaphas replies, "You do not understand that it is better for you that one man die for the people than to have the whole nation destroyed" (11:50). In other words, according to the Gospel of John—which, when he chooses, Gibson follows closely—Caiaphas recognizes that Jesus' popularity might create the circumstances for a revolt. The evangelist's high priest is the one who seeks to stop a riot, not start one. Here, history and Gospel agree against Emmerich and Gibson: contemporaneous Jewish, Greek, and even Christian (see Luke 13:1–2) sources picture Pilate as an insensitive political opportunist, a lout, and a murderer.

Besides the script itself, in the view of our second group, the costuming and the score of Gibson's movie also serve both to divorce Jesus and his followers from Judaism and to identify Jews in particular with evil. The Virgin Mary and Mary Magdalene are robed like Dominican nuns. Those Jews sympathetic to Jesus, and Jesus himself, in the visual codes of the movie are stripped of their Jewish identity. Missing from Jesus' garments, for example, are his fringes (*tzitzit*), those signs that G-d in the Book of Numbers (15:37–41) commanded Jewish men to wear "so that... you will remember all the commandments of the Lord and do them..." (We might think of these as the ancient Jewish versions of WWJD bracelets.) Nor can we conclude that Jesus has Torah inscribed on his heart and therefore doesn't need the visual aid, for the Gospels themselves specifically mention that Jesus wore *tzitzit*/fringes (see Matthew 9:20; 14:36; Mark 6:56; Luke 8:44). Missing as well from Jesus' wardrobe is the Jewish male head covering, the *kippa*. These are in fact a much later convention, but Gibson uses them in his film to indicate Jewish ethnicity for other characters. Simon of Cyrene, for example, dragooned by the Roman soldiers into helping Jesus carry his cross, does wear this head covering. By the time they arrive at Golgotha, however, Simon is both bareheaded and genuinely sympathetic to Jesus. The visual cue that Simon is a Jew disappears. Seen theologically, the scene implies that Simon has ceded his Jewish identity and become "Christian." The only "Jews" who remain are the high priest and his ilk.

This visual coding also marks the children who torment Judas and eventually hound him to his death. Their head coverings indicate that the children are Jewish, and their makeup as well as their actions indicate that they are demonic. Some viewers connect these children with John 8:44, where Jesus says to "the Jews": "You are from your father the devil, and you choose to do your father's desires. He was a murderer from the beginning and does not stand in the truth...." The demon-child held by Satan, and the frequent merging of Satan with the crowds of Jews, confirms this connection of cinematic image and biblical text. Completing the visual cues, even physical appearance separates characters into good and evil. Pilate and his wife are physically attractive, as are all the proto-Christian characters: Jesus and Mary Magdalene (played by the two best-looking actors in this or any other group), the Virgin Mary, John, Simon of Cyrene. (Some of this is just pure Hollywood idiom, of course, especially in action movies, where the Good are often and not coincidentally also the Beautiful.) The "Jews" who are left, working the side of evil, sorely need both dental work and rhinoplasty. They compound their unattractiveness by using extreme hand motions and body language. (With the high priest in particular, the term "ham it up" comes, inappropriately, to mind).

Just in case visual clues did not serve to divide the characters into good (Christians, who perhaps once were Jews) and evil (Jews who stay Jews), the score conducts its own casting. As musicologist Michael Marissen points out, the proto-Christians are accompanied by perfect fifths, that is, lush, harmonious, classical "European" sounds; the Jews are accompanied by augmented seconds, familiar from klezmer music or *Fiddler on the Roof*. Audiences attuned to such cues thus both see and hear that humanity is divided into two opposing groups, and "the Jews" are on the ugly, minor-key, losing side.

Presentations of the nasty, over-the-top Caiaphas and his degenerate Temple minions (minyan?) confirm Judaism's moral degeneracy. First, the high priest, on a waddling donkey no less, makes a special trip to Golgotha to taunt Jesus. (Historically, this would have been impossible: the high priest would not set foot in a graveyard, which is basically what Golgotha was; nor does any of the Gospels place him there.) Stationed at the cross, Caiaphas is so wicked that he is even condemned by one of the two thieves crucified with Jesus. According to the Gospels, the curtain of the Temple tears in two around the time of Jesus' death (Matthew 27:51; Mark 15:38; Luke 23:45; John lacks this detail). In the movie, the entire building is torn. Thus Judaism's holiest place is shaken to its foundations. In terms of visual symbols, Judaism dies with Jesus, but it will not be resurrected in this film.

Even if we could bracket out these matters of Gibson's sources, script, costuming, score, and staging, concerns about the movie's effect on Jewish-Christian relations, and about its contribution to the American culture wars, still remain. Had Gibson done any sort of historical work before appropriating Emmerich's nineteenth-century visions for his supposedly first-century story; or if he had not done historical work, but had screened his film for "liberals" also, rather than just to those predisposed toward his own theology; or if he had not opened his screenings, but only engaged in conversation with the scholars who provided him with a confidential report on the script; or had he continued to ignore the scholars' report, but not chosen to include selections of the Gospels' historically most anti-Jewish lines and scenes, *dayenu* (as Jews say at Passover in recounting the grace shown by the divine): It would have been enough. But he did none of those things.

Perhaps even more disturbing, Gibson publicly vacillated on including Matthew 27:25, the cry of "all the people" (or, in the movie, the high priest), that Jesus' "blood be on our heads and on our children." Now you see it (in the subtitles), now you don't. Actually, now you only hear it. The back-and-forth kept attention focused on him, but it also only increased anxiety. The script that I saw lacked the line; the early summer screenings contained it; Gibson removed the line in late summer, then reinserted it sometime in early 2004; and then he decided for the release to retain the line but eliminate the subtitle. For viewers familiar with the controversy, the unsubtitled Aramaic came through clear as day.

Or, finally, had Gibson not originally marketed his movie as "historically accurate," "like traveling back in time and watching the events unfold exactly as occurred," again, he could have avoided much controversy—had that, indeed, been what he had wanted to do. Viewers can choose to accept one man's interpretation. But Gibson claimed to tell it as it really was, which made the movie a sort of documentary. When confronted with his historical howlers, he said it was just a movie, not a documentary. And when people said, Well, even if it's just a movie, you still have mistakes here, here and here, Gibson claimed that his critics had problems not with his film, but with the Gospels. How one felt about the movie became a test for how one felt about Christianity.

The Passion, which seemed like such a great blessing to one sort of viewer, seemed to others—those concerned with community relations, with historical scholarship, with Christian anti-Semitism—as more like a curse.

"DO UNTO OTHERS . . ." (MATTHEW 7:12; CF. TOBIT 4:15; SIRACH 31:15; BABYLONIAN TALMUD, SANHEDRIN 31A)

How can we have conversation, so that those who see such different films can learn to look through each other's eyes? Jews need to be aware of how precious the story of Jesus' Passion is to our Christian neighbors; Christians need to be aware of the long, ongoing, painful way the story of Jesus' death has been used to harm Jews. Liberals need to recognize that conservatives are not knee-jerk reactionaries who turn off their brain when they read the Bible; conservatives need to recognize that critical scholarship demonstrates disrespect neither toward Scripture nor toward Christianity. The person with the other view of things is not, ipso facto, the Anti-Christ.

One way to break out of our communication impasse is to reformulate our questions. Rather than ask, "Who killed Jesus?" we might inquire, "Why did Jesus die?" Rather than ask, "What do the Jews think?" or, worse, "Why do Christians think that Jews are going to hell?" we might recollect that neither "Jews" nor "Christians" conform to a single party line. Conversation should begin not with the group, but with the individual: "What do you (singular) think?" And, since of course it helps to base opinion on something, we would all do well to study the history of the period. At the very least, we should know that the Gospels offer accounts that, while similar, are also different. We should try to understand why these Gospel accounts differ. Those who care to know about the life and times of Jesus should also know what sources are available to them to provide a fuller sense of Jesus' context. Those who wonder why most Jews chose not to accept the proclamation that Jesus was the Messiah might try to find out what the Jewish definitions of "messiah" are.

A third step involves taking some moral responsibility for our rhetoric and for our reactions. Sappy as it may sound, we really are all our brothers' (and sisters') keepers. Frank Rich, writing in the *New York Times* about what he found to be the anti-Jewish aspects in the movie, observed: "In those early screenings that Gibson famously threw for conservative politicos in Washington last summer and autumn, not a person in attendance, from Robert Novak to Peggy Noonan, seems to have recognized these obvious stereotypes, let alone spoken up about them in their profuse encomiums to the film...." As we've seen, what is obvious to one group is invisible to another. But we can turn Rich's point around, as well. For example, the best-seller *The DaVinci Code* is loaded with anti-Catholic stereotypes: How many liberals have protested?

This concern for preventing any teaching of contempt becomes particularly acute in the international context. Although Western European audiences embraced the movie with much less passion than did those in the United States—in Germany, *Brother Bear* had a stronger opening—it has been a major draw in Poland, where concerns about anti-Semitism remain strong. PLO Chairman Yasir Arafat has pronounced on the film's "historical accuracy." (This statement shows Arafat's command of Western media-speak more than his knowledge of New Testament history; and the Koran, after all, holds that Jesus did not even die in Jerusalem.) In the U.S. and in Canada (for example, in Denver, Kansas City, Toronto, and Montreal), Jewish synagogues and buildings have been defaced and damaged and graves have been desecrated, while a church active in interfaith relations was likewise vandalized with anti-Semitic graffiti, all in the wake of screenings of *The Passion.*[1] Where are those conservatives, who disdained any thought of the film's encouraging anti-Semitism? Will Americans both liberal and conservative speak out, if the film encourages anti-Semitism abroad? Will Icon? When do people assume responsibility for their choices?

1. "Swastikas sprayed on Denver synagogue," *The Denver Post*, March 7, 2004; "Toronto Police probing anti-Semitic hate crimes," *Canadian Jewish Congress,* March 16, 2004; "Anti-Semitic Vandals strike again," *Canadian Jewish Congress* ,March 21, 2004; "Fire guts Jewish school's library," *Globe and Mail,* April 5, 2004; "Hate crime: 'Passion' seems to inspire anti-Semitic graffiti," *Kansas City Jewish Chronicle,* March 5, 2004

Regarding the movie, and religion, and the various other conflicted sites in the culture wars, we will not reach consensus. That will have to wait for the messiah to come or (depending again on your point of view) come back. Our task now is to try to see through each other's eyes, while recognizing that neither side can see the full picture. But we're all in this culture together, and we are all responsible for it.

DEBORAH CALDWELL

❖

SELLING *PASSION*

Last May, A. Larry Ross got a call from a friend who owns a Hollywood production company. Would Ross—president of a Dallas-based Christian public relations and marketing firm—be interested in looking at a rough cut of Mel Gibson's new film about Jesus' trial and crucifixion?

Ross flew to California to meet Gibson and to view *The Passion of the Christ*, then still in pieces and without subtitles. Even at that rough stage, it was generating a lot of buzz.

News about the controversial movie had already been bubbling for a couple of months. Since January, Gibson had been on the chat-show circuit. At one point, talking with Bill O'Reilly, he referred darkly to "forces out there" trying to undercut his work. Later, articles appeared in the *Wall Street Journal* and *New York Times*, both of which repeated Gibson's assertions of historical accuracy. A group of New Testament professors, Catholic and Jewish, then reviewed the script, reading to determine the accuracy of Gibson's presentation of history and the Gospels. Alarmed by what they saw, the scholars, working with Gibson's knowledge, sent him a confidential report suggesting major revisions. In response, he threatened lawsuits. Gibson's lawyers accused the scholars of knowingly working with a stolen script and of attacking his film. The professors' involvement, however, seemed to help Icon to crystallize its strategy for deflecting criticism. That is, imply that critics were actually aggressors: secular left-leaning liberals or overly sensitive Jews with an axe to grind.

The scholarly debate quickly morphed to media juggernaut. Initially, Ross was hired to deal with crisis communication. "We were working to reframe the picture about the issues and show that it was a film meant to inspire, not to offend," says Ross, a cheerful man with a booming made-for-TV voice. By the middle of the summer, the academic controversy had turned to public curiosity, and Ross began helping with media relations.

A marketing veteran, Ross has served for twenty-three years as the Rev. Billy Graham's media director. He is also an expert at presenting popular culture to an Evangelical audience. In 1998, he worked with producer Jeffrey Katzenberg in marketing *Prince of Egypt*—an animated film about Moses' life story—to Evangelicals. In 2002, he worked with Big Idea Productions to roll out *Jonah: A Veggie Tale Movie* to Evangelicals.

So Ross was prepared to offer Mel Gibson some advice. "I told him about a public relations axiom: the largest number of people focused on the smallest point of agreement is where you get your greatest impact."

Gather the vast conservative American Christian audience—Evangelicals, conservative Catholics, charismatics, and others—around one idea, Ross counseled. Gibson knew exactly the idea he wanted to convey. Ross recalls: "Without hesitation, he said, 'Christ died for our sins.'"

The advice from Ross was but one small element in a brilliantly executed marketing strategy that helped Icon Productions catapult *The Passion of the Christ* to almost miraculous commercial success. By last December, the tale of the film's controversy was added to lists of the year's "most interesting" news stories. In the weeks leading to its opening, *Newsweek* ran a February 16 cover story entitled "Who Killed Jesus?" and called *The Passion of the Christ* a "powerful but troubling new movie." ABC's Diane Sawyer interviewed Mel Gibson on national prime-time television.

Finally, on February 25, 2004, the movie opened on 4,643 screens in 3,006 theaters nationwide with $10 million in advance ticket sales. To nearly everyone's surprise, *The Passion of the Christ* is now the biggest top-grossing R-rated film ever, earning more than $300 million within the first month of its release in the United States, a feat that has propelled it into the all-time top-ten domestic box-office hits.

Many observers have given Evangelical Christians the lion's share of the credit for its success. But why did they respond so positively? It turns out there are multiple complicated reasons: the aforementioned brilliant marketing plan, several infusions of juicy controversy, the media bandwagon, and the culture wars. Yet there are some simple reasons, too.

"This movie was about the death and resurrection of Jesus and that's the center of what Evangelical Christians are about," says Christian Smith, a University of North Carolina sociology professor and an expert on Evangelicals in America. "Here the story is being taken seriously, it's well done by movie standards, and it's being put on the screen, not as a historical artifact but from a faith point of view. The movie really affirms something that is core to their identities in a public way."

That sense of public affirmation explains another source of Evangelical enthusiasm for Gibson's movie. "I think Evangelicals feel generally excluded from Hollywood and generally that their values are totally ignored or lampooned and misrepresented," says Smith. "This film takes them seriously and affirms them."

The Evangelicals' feeling of exclusion—and by extension their sense that "Christian values" are also underappreciated and excluded—undergirds the structure of America's current culture war. The movie served as a lightning rod for many of those conflicts. What resulted was a perfect storm over pluralism, free speech, and family values. These issues are always filtered through American politics, which in turn filters them back through religion. For instance, after the 2000 presidential election, pollsters discovered the "worship gap": if you went to church more than once a week, you were likely to support President George Bush by a two-to-one margin. If you never went, you supported Al Gore by the same margin. So if a Mel Gibson movie about Jesus appealed mostly to Republican church attenders as a useful tool in the battle against generally Democratic academics and activists, then those Republican church attenders were going to support the film, no matter what.

Not surprisingly, some people took up arms on the front lines of the battle. Some of the war music that they marched to replayed themes from other, older, darker conflicts. During the months before the film opened and for weeks afterward, a Web site called www.SupportMelGibson.com had as its homepage headline: "Why Do Jewish Leaders Want to Censor Mel Gibson?" in gigantic black letters. The Web site's author wrote his answer: "In the current controversy, Mel Gibson is David against the Goliath of the anti-Christian Hollywood establishment and politically powerful Jewish leaders." The text moved effortlessly from Jewish Hollywood to Jewish conspiracies and thence to a vision of the battle over religious truth, with Jews representing the Dark Side: "Because of near-dictatorial control over the spiritual lives of Jews, Jewish leaders are able to spread lies and disinformation about Christianity in the Jewish community, depriving individual Jews of the opportunity to escape the legalism and corrupt power structures of a faith that denies the divinity of Christ."

Another Web site, www.SeeThePassion.com, sponsored by a group called Women Influencing the Nation, had this to say on its homepage: "This extraordinary movie and its producer, Mel Gibson, are under intense, public attack from all the worst elements of the major news media and the entertainment industry. Powerful forces in Hollywood, New York City, and Washington D.C. are trying to prevent this movie from getting in our local theaters!

This battle has become a focal point for the culture war which will determine the future of our country and the world."

The film was so polarizing, so important to Evangelicals, that the culture war between them and the "secular elites" trumped the (much more ancient) theological battle between Catholics and Protestants. Gibson, a traditionalist Catholic who belongs to an ultra-conservative splinter group, managed to woo and win over Evangelicals—an estimated one-fourth of the U.S. population—to his very Catholic movie.

"Gibson changed the Catholic version of the Passion into something more recognized by Evangelical Protestants because of how [visually] literalist it is—it shows the victimization of a human body," says Richard Wightman Fox, author of the book *Jesus in America*. "What interests me the most about that is the literalism—the implication that he can *give you* the suffering. That goes down more easily with people who tend toward verbal literalism."

Icon's marketers first cultivated their built-in Christian audience with many dozens of private screenings for Evangelical leaders nationwide, followed by professional promotional materials targeted to pastors.

But Icon's brilliant and well-organized marketing strategy also got an unforeseen boost from the culture war—not so much because liberals started out *actually* attacking the film, but because conservative Christians assumed that they were, and that they would. As a result, conservatives spent a lot of time in adrenaline-rush counterattack mode. The scholars, Abraham Foxman of the Anti-Defamation League, and even *New York Times* columnist Frank Rich seemed almost to blunder, unknowing, into this other reality. During the months of Icon's priming the evangelical pump, these "liberals" loudly criticized *The Passion* for its potential anti-Semitism and for its violence. Their criticism played right into Gibson's positioning: both he and his film stood for Christianity, the Gospels, and family values.

"The church was an active ingredient in the movie's success because people got their friends and families excited about it—and then Abe Foxman did the rest," says Doug Martinez, chief operating officer of Outreach, Inc., the Vista, California-based ministry that produced much of the Christian marketing materials. Outreach's mission is to offer advice to churches trying to attract more members—particularly people who never go to church. But Martinez believes the film's success went beyond mere marketing. The controversy itself was part of God's plan, he says. "God knew what he was up to when he picked Mel Gibson to make this film."

The ground was laid months before. One of the earliest private screenings was in Colorado Springs, a picture postcard city that is home to dozens of Evangelical organizations, including Focus on the Family, the International Bible Society, Fellowship of Christian Athletes, Christian Booksellers Association, Concerned Women of America, Intervarsity Christian Fellowship, and Youth for Christ. In June 2003, Gibson asked some of the city's top Christian leaders to screen the film at Focus headquarters. Later, Gibson held a press conference and described his now-well-known faith journey. "I fell to my knees, and God saved me. The wounds of Jesus healed my wounds," he said that day, according to news reports. Gibson also repeated his by-then oft-quoted sound bite, that the Holy Spirit was the actual director of his movie, and that he had merely been "directing traffic." He also suggested that atheists and Muslims had converted to Christianity on the set. Christian leaders were apparently wowed by Gibson and thrilled with *The Passion*.

"I can honestly say, without hyperbole, that *The Passion* ranks with the most moving artistic experiences I have ever had," the Rev. Ted Haggard, president of the National Association of Evangelicals and pastor of the 10,000-member New Life Church in Colorado Springs, wrote in an essay on Beliefnet (www.beliefnet.com). "It is a brilliant film—a compelling vision of Jesus' ministry, a challenging depiction of the violence of Roman crucifixion, and most important, a heart-rending portrayal of sacrificial love."

And so it went. For the next few months, conservative Christian leaders around the country—even including some Catholic bishops such as Arch-bishop Charles Chaput of Denver—screened the film, listened to Gibson's testimony, and then defended the movie against perceived liberal bias.

Darrell Bock was one of the Christian leaders who saw an early screening. A well-known Bible scholar and theologian at the conservative Dallas Theo-logical Seminary, Bock was invited to an August screening with about forty other people. He happened to see it on a Dallas afternoon just a few hours after Gibson had screened it in Houston to Protestant and Catholic leaders, plus a regional representative of the Jewish Anti-Defamation League.

The Houston screening got far more coverage, but the Dallas event was naturally quite charged. Bock's assignment was to assess the film in light of the Catholic and Jewish scholars' earlier spring report—and then write an official response to them. "I went into the film in the mood to make a judg-ment with regard to anti-Semitism, biblical issues, and fiction. I was well-pre-pared," Bock recalls.

As he watched the film, he instantly could see scenes that referred to par-ticular biblical passages. "This was an incredibly authentic portrayal of what went on," Bock says. Because of his academic expertise, Bock knew how horrifying crucifixion was, including the bloody scourging that led to hang-ing on a cross. Gibson's interpretation of that violence did not offend him.

He could also tell which parts of the film were not in the Bible. Bock now says that the film isn't precisely biblically based. For instance, he wasn't thrilled that the movie depicts Jesus being dragged through a crowd to be tried, because the Gospels don't include that. And he thought the scene, toward the end, of the bird pecking out the bad thief's eye was over the top.

Yet when the screening was over, the first thing Bock said to Gibson was: "I think this film speaks for itself. I don't think you'll have to defend it."

The discussion afterward, he says, worked like a focus group, with Gibson asking the assembled pastors, conservative Protestant and Catholic scholars, and messianic Jewish leaders to assess whether the film was fundamentally

Catholic, or fundamentally biblical. "We decided it was fundamentally bibli-cal with Catholic overtones," Bock says.

"This is where Evangelicals have given Gibson the benefit of the doubt," he continues. "You know he had to fill in the gaps. So we asked, what is the character of those additions, and do they comport with the general direction of the script or not? I think we gave Mel a pass on the Mary perspective. But what struck me was not the fretting over who, historically, did what to Jesus, but the extent of Jesus' suffering and the idea that he did this 'for me.' That is what most people are connecting to when they see the film."

Ultimately, Bock sent off a slew of research to Ross, who wrote a memo for Icon based on Bock's research. One of Bock's points was that people out-side the Christian loop weren't, in actual fact, complaining about the accu-racy of the film; they were instead complaining about the content of the Gospels, which contain the uncomfortable fact that Jesus was executed by the Romans at the behest of the Jewish high priests.

Evangelicals know the Bible cold. Their culture is all about the Biblical text. When a problem or issue is on the table in Evangelical churches, it is very common for someone to suggest: "Let's go to the Word," which means "Open your Bible." Evangelicals read directly from their Bibles during weekly Sunday school, Bible studies, and sermons. They attend church, par-ticularly in the South, twice on Sunday and on Wednesday night. In heavily Protestant regions of the country, it is still common for public schools not to schedule activities or even give homework on Wednesday nights, because that is "church night."

So it's not surprising they would love a movie about their most important Bible story. But it is perhaps surprising, given how much Bible reading goes on in vast swaths of America, that Evangelicals did not protest the film's Catholic architecture: Gibson's movie is an animated version of the Stations of the Cross. And it's also interesting that they gave a free pass to Gibson on the many non-biblical scenes in the movie, since for Evangelicals the entire basis of the culture war over gay rights, abortion, and other issues is their contention that the words of the Bible are absolutely authoritative. Thus, the Bible condemns homosexuality with a passage in the Book of Leviticus and the words of St. Paul; abortion is forbidden in the Ten Commandments, and so on. Yet much of Gibson's Bible story is not in the Bible at all. Nor did Evangelicals protest its violence—equally surprising, since many Evangelical churches strongly discourage members from seeing any movie with an R rating.

The upshot is a paradox: for Evangelicals, the movie was not literally "true" to the Bible; but it was "true enough" to support their cause. Yet it was also, as Fox points out, literally "true" in its vivid violence, but not "too true" so that it would have been wrong for an Evangelical to buy a ticket and watch.

Even Evangelicals agree that their support stemmed in part from political issues. "They saw it as a way to make a statement about their support for the biblical portrayal of the death of Jesus, and that got wrapped up in the culture wars," says Bock.

It didn't hurt that Gibson was such a compelling figure. Bock says that midway through the discussion in Dallas that August afternoon, as he did all over the country, Gibson gave his personal testimony. He talked about how he was on the edge of suicide and that thinking about how Jesus suffered for him gave him the calling to do the film. "There's no doubt there's a star element to this, but Evangelicals don't embrace someone just because he's a star," says Bock. "They embraced him because he was a Hollywood star willing to put his faith on the line. They supported the kind of testimony this movie represented."

Later, Icon and Outreach began taking the film to somewhat larger, folksier screenings. And after each of the perhaps thirty screenings—including a few that attracted three thousand people at huge, well-known Evangelical churches—the audience was offered an opportunity to buy some of Outreach's beautifully produced promotional material: door hangers, invitation cards, banners, bulletin inserts, signs, Bible excerpts, and study guides. The company also produced 250,000 DVDs about the movie that were mailed to ministers nationwide.

Meanwhile, the company invited Evangelical pastor-celebrities to Santa Monica to screen the film. They included the Rev. Rick Warren, the widely admired best-selling author of *The Purpose-Driven Life* and pastor of 10,000-member Saddleback Church in California; and Lee Strobel, best-selling author of *The Case for Christ*, and former teaching pastor at the 30,000-member Willow Creek Community Church in Illinois.

On its Web site, www.thepassionoutreach.com, Outreach offered a detailed timeline for using the movie as a tool for evangelism. The timeline starts in December 2003, when churches were instructed to pull together their "Passion Outreach Team" and begin planning for a week of *Passion* events in February and March.

Early January has this directive: "Place your order for *The Passion of the Christ* Outreach materials." The prices were expensive, but not outrageous: $29.24 for two hundred door hangers, $24.61 for two hundred postcards, $49.50 for fifty New International Version New Testaments, $19 for one hundred booklets to hand out near movie theaters.

By late January, pastors coming to the Web site were instructed to "show *The Passion of the Christ* DVD trailer to your congregation during your weekend services" and to "train your members to invite their friends, both to the movie and to the follow-up sermon series."

By February, the instructions became more specific. Churches were to hang "*The Passion of the Christ* Outreach banners" in front of their buildings, mail their "ImpactCard invitations" to the community, and hand out door hangers to members for use in inviting neighbors to the movie and *Passion*-related events at church.

The company's Web site included endorsements from prominent Evangelicals, including Billy Graham, James Dobson, Jerry Falwell, and Southern Baptist Convention president Jack Graham.

There were also thirteen ideas for *Passion* outreach, including showing the DVD trailer during Sunday services in order to drum up interest, distributing Bibles and invitations to the movie to "unchurched" colleagues and friends, and using Outreach resources to preach a sermon series on *The Passion*. Perhaps the most interesting idea was this: "Carefully choose a neighborhood you believe God wants you to reach. With multiple prayer teams, walk every street and pray for every house, asking that God would reach each person with the message of the cross through exposure to *The Passion of the Christ.*"

But the most effective idea was for churches to buy out entire theaters, then at the end of the movie have volunteers extend an invitation to visit the sponsoring church afterward. Both ideas, of course, drove up the film's revenues.

Among the churches that used many of these suggestions was Rick Warren's Saddleback Church in California, which bought 18,000 tickets for more than forty screens. McLean Bible Church in Virginia rented ten movie theaters to show *The Passion* on forty screens over four nights—a total of 11,300 advance purchase tickets. After each showing, one of the church's pastors gave a five-minute talk explaining how to become a Christian and inviting people to a Bible study called "Personalizing The Passion."

Arch Bonnema, owner of a small financial planning agency in Plano, Texas, says that he had the same inspiration. Bonnema, a member of the 23,000-member Prestonwood Baptist Church, saw the film with a group of pastors in December 2003.

"I've been a Christian all my life, but I never knew the full impact of the sacrifice Jesus made until I saw this," Bonnema says. "He could have quit. He's God. But he didn't."

Bonnema saw in *The Passion* a film that "could get the church back on its feet and excited about its purpose." So he called a local twenty-screen multiplex and bought all 6,000 seats to the first showing of the film—6:30 a.m. on February 25, 2004. The cost was $42,000. He distributed 3,000 tickets to his church, and 1,000 to Dallas Theological Seminary. With 2,000 remaining, he sent e-mail to six friends in Dallas, asking them if they wanted some of the tickets. Within three days, he had 23,000 requests for tickets.

Bonnema's story was picked up by Dallas media. Those stories were noticed around the nation. Soon Christians from everywhere were calling him, saying, "If you can do it, so can we."

At 5:30 a.m. on the day of the film's opening—an uncharacteristically cold thirty-four-degree Texas day complete with a downpour—1,000 people showed up to get in line, many in their Sunday best. Of the 6,000 seats Bonnema bought, just 80 went empty.

Bonnema calls the movie the "biggest evangelism tool of this century." But he believes its greatest audience *won't* be non-Christians. "The biggest impact for this film is people who already love Jesus, and who walk out of the film and say, 'Man, I have to be more involved.'"

And not everyone was even following Outreach's made-for-churches script. The movie also attracted commercial fans. For example, during NASCAR's Daytona 500 on February 15, Interstate Batteries chairman Norm Miller arranged to have his Chevrolet driven by Bobby Labonte painted to promote *The Passion*.

Bob Siemon Designs produced jewelry, including The Passion Nail™ pendants—$2\frac{5}{8}$-inch pewter nails on leather necklaces retailing for $16.99. The company also created The Passion Nail™ Key Ring featuring a $1\frac{7}{8}$-inch nail with Isaiah 53:5 inscribed on the side on a stainless-steel ring.

There were also T-shirts (screen-printed with a crown of thorns: $18); a sound track ($11.98); a book depicting the Passion and Death of Jesus in color photographs taken during the filming ($24.99); lapel pins ($2.49); and a leather Bible case with a nail zipper pull ($59.99).

Another Web site, www.passioncommercial.com, offers for sale to churches cable commercials ($995 for an exclusive license allowing use of the commercials in a congregation's coverage area through May 10, 2006). One, entitled "Uneven Exchange," shows domestic violence, people abusing drugs and alcohol, and a gun being fired—all interspersed with bloody scenes from the movie. "The good news is that Jesus died for it, so we don't have to die from it," the announcer says.

The American Tract Society, which often creates pamphlets pegged to movies like *Finding Nemo* and *The Lord of the Rings*, released two *Passion*-related tracts, one called "The Passion—Who Crucified Jesus?" According to the tract, "The culprit is God," whose love for humanity caused him to sacrifice his son. "People will react to this movie's deep and moving experience with Jesus," says promotional info for the tract. "Many will be wondering how to know the Lord! Millions of people will be seeing this movie and some will be discovering Jesus for the first time."

And then there is the fan site. The official international fan sites, www.Passion-Movie.com and www.Passion-Movie.net, feature areas where visitors can specify if they want to see the movie in their region. Fans in the United States, Canada, and Britain can order tickets online, chat on message boards, and buy framed artwork ($111.95 for a canvas of the "Cross at Sunset").

Why did the film—indeed the mere idea of the film—affect so many Evangelical Christians so deeply? A. Larry Ross theorizes that Gibson came across as a sincere Christian during the many months of pastors' screenings the film star attended. Always, at the end of the screenings, Gibson would give a testimony of his faith journey, the telling of which inevitably impressed Protestant ministers for whom a personal faith journey is a critical piece of Christian belief.

"I found him to be a man of deep spiritual conviction," Ross says. "He never tried to defend himself or answer his critics. I was humbled watching his response."

But Christian Smith of the University of North Carolina says Gibson's effect on the ministers may have been more about quirks of human nature: "Evangelicals have a side that really craves respect, and this was something they could say they're a part of." And Smith points out something that not everyone realizes: "Part of being an Evangelical in this country, part of the culture, is feeling embattled. They're engaged with the culture, but they're embattled. Mainline Protestants are engaged but not embattled. Fundamentalists are embattled but not engaged."

That's for the best for Evangelicals, Smith says. "If the day came when Evangelicals consider themselves powerful and mainstream, that would hurt them." And so, the months of early screenings, the appearances at pastors' conferences, the respectful attention Evangelicals received—they all combined to intoxicate those "embattled" conservative Christians.

Darrell Bock was one of those Christians, and he had a similar take on the film's appeal. "This was a chance to carry your placard for Jesus, and say to everyone, 'This is our story. We want you to understand and appreciate our story,'" Bock says. "And they did, and they have."

REPORT OF THE AD HOC SCHOLARS GROUP

❖

REVIEWING THE SCRIPT OF *THE PASSION*

Introductory Note

In May 2003, a group of four Catholic and three Jewish scholars, convened by specialists at the Secretariat for Ecumenical and Interreligious Affairs of the U.S. Conference of Catholic Bishops and the Anti-Defamation League, submitted to Mel Gibson a confidential analysis of a shooting script of a film then called *The Passion*. Their work had been agreed to by Mr. Gibson, though he did not directly provide the script. Although the report has been circulated among some people to whom Mr. Gibson showed prerelease versions of the movie, the scholars group has not made its report public. Now that the film has opened, the group makes its report available for those who might be interested in comparing its findings to the finished film as just released. Except for some added or dropped scenes, the final version of the film is, in most places, close or even identical to the script that the group read.

Mr. Mel Gibson
Icon Producctions
808 Wilshire Blvd, 4th Flr
Santa Monica, CA 90401

Dear Mr. Gibson,

Enclosed please find the report of the group of Catholic and Jewish scholars that has carefully reviewed the script of "The Passion."

The report recommends serious re-thinking of the film. It is important to note that the New Testament scholarship represented so ably here by each of the scholars was mandated for the Church by Pope Pius XII in his famous 1943 encyclical, *Divino Afflante Spiritu*. Some recommendations may have become moot by changes made during filming. We welcome these and believe that further significant changes will be necessary if this film is to avoid the tragic errors of past Passion Plays. In telling the story of the love and suffering of Jesus, and its good news for humanity, it is imperative not to depict Jews as a people who sought the death of Jesus. Such depictions resulted in hatred and violence toward Jews, and diverted Christians from the true meaning of Christ's sacrifice for the sins of all humanity.

The Catholic scholars understand the core truth of their faith as stated by the Roman Catechism of the Council of Trent: "We must regard as guilty all those who continue to relapse into their sins. Since our sins made the Lord Christ suffer the torment of the cross, those who plunge themselves into disorders and crimes crucify the Son of God anew in their hearts (for he is in them) and hold him up to contempt. And it can be seen that our crime in this case is greater in us than in the Jews. As for them, according to the witness of the Apostle, 'None of the rulers of this age understood this; for if they had, they would not have crucified the Lord of glory.' We, however, profess to know him. And when we deny him by our deeds, we in some way seem to lay violent hands on him." (Roman Catechism I, 5, 11; cf. Hebrews 6:6; 1 Corinthians 2:8).

They also believe that the definitive statement of the Catholic faith and the Catholic understanding of the historical (as distinct from theological) responsibility for the death of Jesus lies in our ancient Creed, which states, most simply that Jesus "suffered and died under Pontius Pilate," and mentions no role at all for the Jews. This was written when the Church was finally free of Roman persecution. Likewise Pope John Paul II meditated on the First Station of the Cross in 1998, saying, "Oh no, not the Jewish people, crucified by us [Christians] for so long, not the crowd which will always prefer Barabbas because he repays evil with evil, not them, but all of us, each one of us, because we are all murderers of love." Catholics today must carry on this central tradition in our own time. The group regards this matter with utmost gravity. Your production schedule lends additional urgency. We look forward to your response at the earliest possible moment and to cooperating with you to resolve the issues raised in the report.

Most Sincerely,

Dr. Eugene J. Fisher, Associate Director
Secretariat for Ecumenical and Interreligious Affairs
U.S. Conference of Catholic Bishops
Washington, D.C.

Rabbi Eugene Korn
Director of Interfaith Affairs
Anti-Defamation League

Dr. Mary C. Boys, SNJM
Skinner & McAlpin Professor of Practical Theology
Union Theological Seminary, New York

Dr. Michael J. Cook
Sol & Arlene Bronstein Professor of Judeo-Christian Studies
Hebrew Union College, Cincinnati

Dr. Philip A. Cunningham
Executive Director, Adjunct Professor of Theology
Center for Christian-Jewish Learning at Boston College

Dr. Eugene J. Fisher
Associate Director, Ecumenical and Interreligious Affairs
United States Conference of Catholic Bishops

Dr. Paula Fredriksen
Aurelio Professor of Scripture
Boston University

Rev. Dr. Lawrence E. Frizzell
Director, Institute of Judeo-Christian Studies
Seton Hall University, East Orange

Rabbi Dr. Eugene Korn
Director, Office of Interfaith Affairs
Anti-Defamation League, New York

Dr. Amy-Jill Levine
Carpenter Professor of New Testament Studies
Vanderbilt University, Nashville

Dr. John T. Pawlikowski, OSM
Prof. of Social Ethics, Catholic-Jewish Studies Director
Catholic Theological Union, Chicago

I. INTRODUCTION

The ad hoc group of Catholic and Jewish scholars was assembled by Dr. Eugene Fisher of the U.S. Conference of Catholic Bishops and Rabbi Dr. Eugene Korn of the Anti-Defamation League in order to assess and offer recommendations on the script of *The Passion*. We do so readily since the relationship between Jews and Christians is a central concern to each of us.

We begin this task with an awareness of the tragic impact of Christian "Passion plays" on Jews over the centuries. We know that their dramatic presentation of Jews as "Christ-killers" triggered pogroms against Jews over the centuries and contributed to the environment that made the Shoah possible. Given this history and the power of film to shape minds and hearts, both Catholics and Jews in the ad hoc group are gravely concerned about the potential dangers of presenting a passion play in movie theatres.

The Catholic members of the ad hoc group are all part of an appointed advisory committee that offers counsel to the U.S. bishops on developments in Catholic-Jewish relations. They are all committed to the process of Catholic-Jewish rapprochement launched by the Second Vatican Council. This process includes:

- Numerous Catholic magisterial statements mandating Catholic-Jewish reconciliation and reversing centuries of teaching contempt for Jews and Judaism.
- Pope John Paul II repeatedly praying for God's forgiveness for the sins that Christians have committed against Jews over the past millennium and publicly committing the Catholic Church, at Jerusalem's Western Wall, to "genuine fellowship with the People of the Covenant."

The Jewish members of the ad hoc group (and their children) know personally the effects of being called "Christ-killers." They recently have received anxious inquires about *The Passion* from the wider Jewish community, fearing an upsurge in this particularly hurtful accusation.

All the members of the ad hoc group have witnessed a dramatic increase in anti-Semitism worldwide as a result of the Israeli-Palestinian conflict and other international disputes. They have observed an increase in attacks against Jews living nowhere near the sites of conflict, especially in Europe. They have seen the age-old canard of "Christ-killers" propagated widely over Internet Web sites and airwaves in the Islamic world.

After recent press reports, ad hoc group members were understandably concerned that a graphic movie presentation of the crucifixion could reawaken the very anti-Semitic attitudes that we have devoted our careers to combating. For Jews, this intensifies fears and insecurities. For Catholics, it threatens to reverse the building of a new relationship with Jews and impede acceptance of correct Church teachings regarding the Passion, Judaism, and the Jewish people.

We therefore welcome the opportunity to offer our observations and expertise. We will provide critiques and constructive suggestions for improving the film so as to produce genuine religious inspiration for viewers, while avoiding the prejudice and hatred against the Jewish people that so frequently accompanied Passion plays historically.

II. SUMMARY OF THE GROUP'S RESPONSES
Members of the Ad Hoc Scholars Group concluded unanimously that:

A. *A film based on the present version of the script of* The Passion *would promote anti-Semitic sentiments. (See Appendices 3–4 for details.)*

- Caiaphas is the moving force behind all events, whereas Pilate is effectively powerless. The high priests are shown delighting in the physical abuse inflicted upon Jesus, while Pilate is shocked by it. Caiaphas' machinations will too easily be seen as epitomizing "Jewish" wickedness.

- The Temple—and by extension Judaism—is presented as a locus of evil: Jesus' unusually large cross is manufactured there and Jesus is physically abused there at night before a violent mob of Jews. This torment is said to occur adjacent to the Holy of Holies, a locale seemingly targeted by dramatic earth tremors when Jesus dies. Collectively, these elements uniformly project a negative view of Judaism and the Jewish people.
- A Jewish mob is shown in ever-increasing size and ferocity. The mob is plainly identified as representing the Jewish people as a whole, portraying them as "bloodthirsty," "frenzied," and "predatory." The Roman soldiers who flay Jesus are depicted as urged on by demonic forces, while Jews need no such supernatural stimulation for their wickedness. The few Jewish characters sympathetic to Jesus do not offset the disproportionately numerous hostile Jews.
- Jewish figures are particularly associated with evil uses of money. The high priest, for example, is careful to signal an underling to collect up the "blood money" that a distraught Judas has flung at his "opulent robes." While it is true that the priestly elites were rich, the script also shows them using their wealth to corrupt a large number of ordinary Jews, something for which there is scant historical or biblical evidence.

B. *The present script contains significant historical errors.*
Recent press reports have described the film's producers as "striving for a perfect reproduction of the Passion—from the ancient languages spoken at the time of Jesus right down to his bloody wounds" [*National Catholic Register*, Web edition, March 16–22, 2003]. Unless this interest in historical accuracy is restricted to depictions of physical injuries, we do not understand how Latin could be spoken instead of Greek, or how the major errors listed below could be tolerated:

- The script fundamentally misconceives the relationship between the prefect, Pontius Pilate, and the Temple authorities led by Caiaphas. Caiaphas served at Rome's pleasure. Yet the script shows him bullying Pontius Pilate with an amazing control of the Jewish mob. Pilate even states he fears Caiaphas is plotting a revolt. This is a total reversal of the historical reality of Judea under Roman rule. (See Appendix 1.)

- The script's sympathetic depiction of Pilate is uninformed by historical sources of information about him. (See Appendix 5.)
- The physical layout of the Temple presupposed in the script does not correspond with archaeological facts. There was no "Great Hall" in proximity to the Holy of Holies where a Sanhedrin and a large Jewish crowd could assemble for a nighttime trial of Jesus. The Temple precincts were locked and guarded at night, making the free flow of people in and out virtually impossible. There were no pillars near the Holy of Holies. (See Appendix 1.)
- In the time of Jesus, Romans crucified those Jews they suspected of sedition routinely. Golgotha was an execution site with vertical posts of about six feet in height permanently mounted in the earth. There is no historical basis for a "15 feet x 8 feet" cross for Jesus and absolutely no evidence that crosses of any kind were built by Jews in the Temple.
- The script overlooks the implication that these events occurred around Passover. Jesus is shown slaying the Passover lamb in a private room, instead of making the offering in the Temple with the rest of his people. It also fails to see the difficulty in having large numbers of Jewish leaders and people conspiring and meeting and moving in and out of the Temple on the first night of Passover when they had many other religious duties.

c. *Dramatically, as the script stands, Jesus' opponents are one-dimensional "bad guys."*

The motives of the principal characters—Caiaphas, Annas, Pilate, and even Jesus—are unexplained. The reasons for some of the brutality inflicted on

Jesus are unexplained, indeed sometimes it is literally because "the devil made me do it." Such poor character development is not true-to-life. The drama and pathos seems almost entirely driven by violence.

D. *The portrayal of the person and mission of Jesus is partial and skewed.*

- The film fixes our gaze on a tortured creature. The cross is so much the focus that the significance of Jesus' life is obscured. The script takes us back to the High Middle Ages in its fascination with the pain of Jesus. Indeed, the film takes every opportunity to embellish the violence of the Passion, thereby increasing the likelihood of an audience to be filled with outrage at those who perpetrated such a horrendous crime.

- Thus, viewers learn virtually nothing about the ministry of Jesus, of his preaching and teaching about God's reign, his distinctive table companionship, his mediation of God's gracious mercy. Instead, we are presented only with a body to be tormented, one who literally embraces his cross and removes his own clothes for scourging.

- The script's brutality—including unattested added elements such as the placement of the cross facedown with Jesus attached in order to bend back the protruding nail points—was overwhelming. Without some understanding of the meaning of Jesus' entire life, the inventive cruelty produces a theology of pain: the more Jesus is tortured the greater is his love and, by implication, the more the Father's desires are being obeyed.

E. *The present script uses or ignores New Testament texts without regard for Catholic principles of Biblical interpretation.*

- The script seems unaware that when the Gospels were written, decades after the events they portray, the evangelists to varying degrees wanted to avoid Roman persecutions. In diverse ways they downplayed the histori-

cal fact that their Lord had been crucified for sedition by order of a
Roman prefect. Thus, Luke portrays Pilate declaring Jesus innocent three
times; Matthew shows Pilate washing his hands of the affair; and John has
Pilate shuttling inside and outside the praetorium, physically demonstrat-
ing his indecisiveness. The script simply treats each of these distinctive
strategies as historical facts. It then uses all three techniques, thereby
adding a cumulative power to the evangelists' individual efforts to shift
responsibility from Pilate onto Jewish figures.

• Similarly, disputes decades after the crucifixion between the evangelists'
churches and local Jewish communities about the status and authority of
Jesus influence the Gospels' telling of the story of the Passion. The script
is unaware that "blasphemy" applied to Jesus during his life would have
meant arrogant presumption, but in the post-resurrectional era of the
Gospel writers would involve Christian claims of Jesus' divinity. The
script's naïve use of blasphemy makes the deadly issue a more "religious,"
and hence a more "Jewish" one.

• The script selects elements from among the four different Gospel versions
of the Passion without any obvious method of selection. It chooses, for
example, to follow John's Gospel in having the scourging to Pilate's
stratagem to free Jesus. Mark and Matthew, probably with greater historical accuracy, present the scourging as a normal preliminary to a Roman
crucifixion, while Luke omits it entirely. This choice has inevitable anti-
Jewish consequences, when Pilate in scene 63 must present the tortured
Jesus to the crowd. Similarly, it opts to present a formal Sanhedrin "trial"
of Jesus (held impossibly in the Temple itself instead of the high priest's
residence as all four Gospels indicate). However, the Gospel of John
offers another choice, describing only a "hearing" at dawn (John 18:19).

F. *For these reasons the present script violates many magisterial Catholic documents, including several Vatican instructions.*

As the selected quotations in Appendix 5 show, the Catholic Church insists that when dealing with the Passion of Jesus, "all must take care, lest in catechizing or in preaching the word of God, they teach anything which is not in accord with the truth of the Gospel message or the spirit of Christ" (Vatican Council II, *Nostra Aetate*, 4). The script, regrettably, too often violates this fundamental norm by:

- Utilizing the four distinct Passion narratives haphazardly in ways that increase and sensationalize "Jewish" culpability;
- Utilizing the four distinct Passion narratives without regard for their apologetic and polemical features;
- Failing to incorporate historical studies;
- Adding scenes without any historical or even naïve biblical warrant that increases the guilt of Jewish characters, for example, the egregious scenes 48 and 49;
- Failing to present the theological meaning of the Passion in any significant way.

Viewers without extensive knowledge of Catholic teaching about interpreting the New Testament will surely leave the theater with the overriding impression that the bloodthirsty, vengeful, and money-loving Jews simply had an implacable hatred of Jesus. Catholic leaders informed by the Church's numerous official documents on Catholic-Jewish relations would denounce such an outcome.

G. *The above problems are embedded throughout the script.*
   Substantive revisions of numerous scenes are required to correct them.

We believe that the steps needed to correct these difficulties will require major revisions. The characterizations of the major characters—Jesus,

Pilate, Caiaphas—all require new scripting. If scenes have been filmed of large crowds who display the inhuman qualities called for by the script, these, too, should be replaced.

We realize that such significant alterations will be expensive and time-consuming, but without such revisions the film will inflict serious damage and in all likelihood be repudiated by most Christian and Jewish institutions.

III. GENERAL RECOMMENDATIONS

The Roman nature of Jesus' execution must be stressed. He was executed by the method used by the empire to deal with seditionists. His crime was generating public enthusiasm for the coming "Kingdom/Reign of God," which would by definition transcend and supplant the Roman Empire and all other human governments.

- Pontius Pilate must be presented as the superior of Caiaphas. It must be made clear that Caiaphas served as high priest only with Rome's assent. Caiaphas depended on staying in Pilate's good graces to remain high priest. It is impossible on the basis of the available evidence to discern who took the lead in executing Jesus.
- To make them fully developed dramatic characters the complementary yet distinct motives of Pilate and Caiaphas should be made explicit. Pilate wants to prevent a Passover riot. He orders the crucifixion of one more Jewish messianic preacher to impose order. Caiaphas wants to avoid a popular riot (Mark 14:2) to protect the Temple and his people from the Romans (John 11:47–50). He is not necessarily thrilled that the Roman crucifixion of another Jew may be necessary to do this.
- It must be indicated that everything was done in haste. Jesus was arrested and sentenced quickly and clandestinely because of his popularity among

his Jewish contemporaries (N.B. Mark 14:2). Jesus is to be crucified as a warning before the incendiary Passover period.

- The Jewish "crowd" must be small, perhaps two dozen people. They are underlings of the chief priests, not the Jewish nation. The greater the magnitude and frenzy of this "crowd," the more likely the film will stimulate anti-Semitic sentiments in audiences. Jews hostile to Jesus should be depicted as one group of Jews out of many and be better balanced by other positive Jewish figures who are not disciples of Jesus. Since the Pharisees are notably absent in the Gospels' Passion narratives, if they are presented at all in the deliberations over Jesus' fate, they should be depicted both negatively and positively. The content of conversations between the high priest and the prefect must be carefully constructed.

- Jesus' death must be related to his ministry on behalf of the reign of God. The nature of God's rule, as opposed to the rule of human empires, could be contrasted by recalling pertinent parables. Jesus should be presented as a model of faith, remaining steadfast in his proclamation of the Kingdom no matter what the cost, foreseeing his own suffering as contributing to its establishment (N.B. Mark 14:25 and parallels).

- Overall, the film should present the Passion of Jesus as a reflection of the Jewish plight under the brutal Roman occupation and part of the suffering of the Jewish people of the day.

- The Roman procedure for crucifixion was sadistic and brutal enough. In order to avoid undermining the movie's historical credibility and serious religious content, the script's additional scenes of gratuitous cruelty, unattested in the Gospels themselves, should be eliminated.

APPENDIX I

ROMAN IMPERIAL RULE IN JUDEA

Judea was under "direct" Roman rule from AD 6 to AD. 41, and again from 44 until the first Jewish revolt began in 66. Like modern empires, Rome subcontracted to indigenous elites. In Judea, domestic government radiated from Jerusalem, and was the particular responsibility of the high priest, *who served as an "appointee" of Rome*. He was responsible to Rome for keeping the peace. He also oversaw the governance of the city and the operation of the Temple.

Local Roman government sat in Caesarea Maritima, on the coast. The prefect, who was a Roman, employed roughly 3,000 troops, mostly infantry and a few cavalry. These men were *not* "Roman": they were locals hired from Syria. The prefect and his army came to Jerusalem three times a year, during the Jewish pilgrimage festivals, to facilitate crowd control, since the city could be flooded with upwards of 400,000 pilgrims. Otherwise, a tiny contingent of troops in Rome's employ was quartered at the Antonia tower, near the Temple.

The high priest employed a few hundred Temple guards. These functioned as a sort of domestic police force, both for the city and especially for the Temple area. The Temple precinct in Jesus' lifetime was enormous: the wall around the outer perimeter ran almost 9/10 of a mile. Both the outer wall and the inner wall had huge gates of heavy wood; each inner gate was about a thousand square feet. These were made heavier by their overlay of precious metal. *These gates were closed every evening, and opened every morning*. From sunset to sunrise, the interior of the Temple precinct was inaccessible to people outside. Since the Temple contained many valuable items—contributions, precious metals, sacred objects—the Temple police guarded these gates, and it took a lot of men to move them. People did not move in and out of the Temple at night.

The actual sanctuary of the Temple was a small roofed building at the heart of the complex. It had two chambers. The outer chamber held an altar

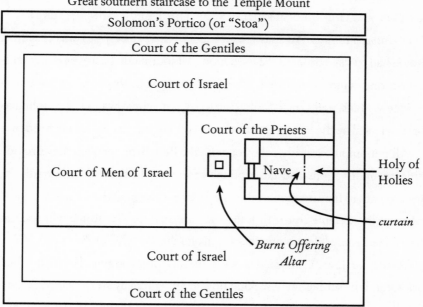

Great southern staircase to the Temple Mount

Solomon's Portico (or "Stoa")

Court of the Gentiles

Court of Israel

Court of Men of Israel

Court of the Priests

Nave

Holy of Holies

curtain

Burnt Offering Altar

Court of Israel

Court of the Gentiles

HEROD'S EXPANDED SECOND TEMPLE
*Although there are various identifications for the courtyards,
the layout of the buildings and walls is fairly well established.*

and a candelabrum. The inner chamber, the "Holy of Holies," was entirely empty. The two chambers were divided by a curtain; the high priest alone went into this part of the Temple, and only on one day a year, Yom Kippur. It was otherwise inaccessible and, of course, to anyone but the high priest, completely invisible.

In the event of any domestic turmoil or trouble, both the high priest and the prefect would have to answer to the emperor. Getting into trouble meant, usually, losing the job. The priests would, naturally, want to shield their own people as much as possible from problems with imperial power; and both the prefect and the high priest had a vested interest in promoting and ensuring domestic calm.

APPENDIX 2

A HISTORICAL RECONSTRUCTION OF THE EXECUTION OF JESUS

Four Gospel Portraits. All four Gospels know that, since Jesus was crucified, Rome had to have ordered the execution. All four name Passover as the holiday during which Jesus died. The Synoptic ("seen-together") tradition— Matthew, Mark, and Luke—hold that Jesus' last supper was a seder; John has the final meal be the last meal before Passover begins, that is, it's *not* a seder.

All four impute priestly collusion with the Roman prefect, but they provide different motivations and descriptions of events. In the Synoptic tradition, Jesus comes to the attention of the priests by overturning the moneychangers' tables in the Temple court. In John, they are anxious that Rome will react to Jesus' mission by "destroying the nation and the Temple" (John 11:48).

In all four Jesus is arrested secretly because he is so popular. "The chief priests and the scribes were seeking how to arrest him by stealth, and kill him, for they said, 'Not during the feast, lest there be a tumult of the people.'" (e.g., Mark 14:2). Matthew, Mark, and Luke show Jesus ensnared by a "crowd": these people are civilians. John depicts a mixed contingent of specifically Roman soldiers and "some officers of the chief priests," that is, the Temple guard. In all four, once Jesus is arrested, he is simply led away to the residence of the high priest.

The Gospels do not explain the sudden wholesale defection of the Jerusalem crowd between nightfall (when Jesus is so popular that he has to be apprehended by stealth) and dawn (when the crowd cries for Barabbas). The Gospels are also not clear on why Barabbas is freed: in the Synoptics, the release of a prisoner is *Pilate's custom* (Matthew 27:15); in John, it's *the people's custom* (John 18:39). The Gospels also show the priests walking in the killing field during the crucifixion, which would have been impossible for them to do on Passover. Serving at the Temple on a high holy day, they certainly could not risk corpse impurity. These difficulties have led most scholars to conclude that these episodes are not historical as depicted, but stem from the apologetic and polemical concerns of the evangelists.

Historical Considerations. Jesus of Nazareth was crucified around AD 30, in Jerusalem, during a Passover holiday when Caiaphas was high priest and Pilate was prefect. The fact that he was killed means that he had enemies. If the priests in Jerusalem had simply wanted him dead, Jesus could have been "privately" murdered, or killed off-stage; but he wasn't. If the priests had wanted him dead but for some reason were constrained from killing him, they could have asked Pilate to kill Jesus, and Pilate could easily have done so by any of the considerable means at his disposal (assassination, murder in prison, and so on).

The fact that Jesus was publicly executed specifically by crucifixion means that *Rome* wanted him dead. The point of such a *public* execution was to communicate a message. Crucifixion implies, further, that Rome was concerned about *sedition*; and that Rome was concerned specifically to disabuse the Jews gathered for Passover of any thought of sedition. Historically, disturbances and riots during the Passover's celebration of freedom from foreign oppression were not uncommon. According to a Jewish historian contemporary with the evangelists, "It is on these festive occasions [i.e., the pilgrimage holidays] that sedition is most apt to break out" [Josephus, *Jewish War*, 1:88].

A Basic Reconstruction. Pilate and Caiaphas colluded in the death of Jesus. Which of the two initiated his arrest is impossible to determine. Jesus' words and deeds on behalf of a coming "Kingdom of God" were enough to convince Pilate that Jesus should be preemptively removed from the scene as a warning to the thousands of Jewish pilgrims in Jerusalem for Passover. Jesus' Kingdom preaching and criticisms of the priestly leadership were enough to persuade Caiaphas that this popular Galilean could incite anti-Roman agitation and so move the Romans to act against the people and destroy the Temple that he was responsible to protect. The high priest was not necessarily personally popular with the people, so he had additional reasons to move carefully in his efforts to maintain the peace.

Caiaphas orchestrated Jesus' nighttime arrest out of sight of the general public; perhaps together with a few priestly colleagues, he questioned him; and then, possibly at dawn, he dispatched Jesus to Pilate for execution. This outcome was likely determined in advance, but the precise content of conversations or disagreements between Pilate and Caiaphas or their subordinates are inaccessible to contemporary historians. Mark 15:25 depicts Jesus being crucified at 9 a.m., before most of Jerusalem would have even been aware of Jesus' arrest, and this is consistent with the need for haste before the Passover and/or the Sabbath.

APPENDIX 3
THE SCRIPT'S PRESENTATION OF THE "CROWD"

The script tells us the following about the crowd—that is, the Jews. The crowd:

- Surrounds Peter, "the UNCOMPOSED ENERGY of their HATEFUL MOCKING and VIOLENT TAUNTS causes him to freeze with fear." Peter is "AWARE of the BLOODTHIRSTY nature of the rising chaos." [scene 31]
- Causes "brouhaha in the Temple," a "CRAZED FRENZY." [scene 33a]
- Is a "MOB of energized people," EXPLODES in jeers and invectives before Pilate: SHOUTS, JEERS, etc. Their noise is deafening. [scene 41]
- It is an "enraged mob," alarming even Pilate by its virulence. The Roman soldiers have to "DRAW THEIR SWORDS and LOCK SHIELDS" in defense. [scene 52]
- It responds to the judgment of Caiaphas and Annas that Jesus be crucified with a RENEWED, DEAFENING ROAR. "Pilate is obviously intimidated

by the crowd's mood." Their shouts, CRUCIFY HIM, CRUCIFY HIM "gain in power." [scene 52]

- The "bloodthirsty roar" of the Pharisees—part of the crowd—evokes a frown from Pilate. [scene 52]

- Echoes the words of Caiaphas to "CRUCIFY HIM! They fill THE PRAETO-RIUM WITH A GREAT DIN: 'CRUCIFY HIM.'" Caiaphas repeats the call for crucifixion. "Another DEAFENING ROAR: 'CRUCIFY HIM'" from the crowd "startles and intimidates Pilate." [scene 63]

- Turns violent when Pilate suggests releasing the innocent Jesus. "The resulting CLAMOR is so violent that PILATE IS SERIOUSLY INTIMI-DATED." [scene 63]

- Is eventually silenced by the "smug and arrogant" Caiaphas, who cries "May his blood be upon us, then, and upon our children." Pandemonium erupts. When the crowd sees the cross, "the CROWD'S BLOODTHIRST redoubles." [scene 65]

- It "breaks into murmurs, then shouts and then a more GENERAL CACOPH-ONY of HOT, PRIMITIVE NOISES, FILLED WITH ANIMAL ANTICIPA-TION" when the thief Gesmas sneers at Jesus. [scene 66]

- Lets out a DEAFENING CHEER when it sees Jesus MOMENTARILY CRUSHED by the weight of the cross. Then Roman Guards "holding the crowd back have a difficult time restraining the IMPATIENT, PREDATORY BLOODTHIRST of the people." [scene 66]

- Is "galvanized" by the scuffle between Roman soldiers protecting Mary and other soldiers. "They are on the verge of breaking through the line of ROMAN SOLDIERS when the ROMANS fall into LOCKSTEP and suddenly vent their own CONTEMPT by turning VIOLENTLY against the jeering crowd." [scene 71]

- IS "A NOISY DEBAUCH FOR THE MOST PART, FUELED BY CRUELTY AND THE ANTICIPATION OF PAINFUL TORMENT AND DEATH." [scene 74C]

- Laughs sadistically in a CACOPHONY of shouts as the cross crashes to the ground [scene 89]; later, it greets Caiaphas' taunt with "derisive laughter." [scene 92]

APPENDIX 4
THE SCRIPT'S PRESENTATION OF PILATE AND CAIAPHAS

- In scene 54, "the crowd is PAYING NO ATTENTION TO PILATE" when he lifts his arms to demand attention. In scene 65, "the MOB BELOW is paying NO ATTENTION TO HIM." Pilate "signals Caiaphas for quiet." In both instances Caiaphas exclaims "SILENCE!" and "the noise immediately quiets down" [scene 54]. In scene 65, Pilate has to catch Caiaphas' eye a second time before he will act to control the mob. "SLOWLY, drawing attention to HIS power, CAIAPHAS raises his hands over his head. SHOUTS of 'QUIET!' 'SILENCE!' The MOB quiets down. CAIAPHAS looks up. Smug. Arrogant." This emotion echoes scene 63 when "CAIAPHAS and ANNAS and the other members of the SANHEDRIN who are present stand separate from the mob, exulting in their sense of power."
- Pilate's depiction has its ironic moments, but they intensify the responsibility of Jewish figures. When Jesus is first brought to him, Pilate asks the Sanhedrin, "Do you always half-kill your prisoners before they are even judged?" [Scene 41] In the same scene, when Caiaphas speaks the words of John 6:53 (which he does not do in John's Gospel), Pilate retorts, "You must all be very eager to attain eternal life...judging by the way you thirst for this body and his blood." The Gospels contain neither of these barbs.
- Pilate tells his wife in scene 50, "If I don't condemn this man, I KNOW Caiaphas will start a rebellion."
- Caiaphas first appears in scene 3, described as "dressed SUMPTUOUSLY" and in "the RICHEST ROBES," just before paying Judas to betray Jesus.

When in scene 22 Judas comes to his home, Caiaphas is "dressed in rich, impressive ceremonial robes." Later, Judas will throw his blood money at Caiaphas, but they bounce off his "opulent robes" [scene 36]. Caiaphas then makes a show of lifting these "opulent robes" over the money on the ground, but he eyes an elder "meaningfully" who collects up the scattered coins after Caiaphas exits.

- When a bruised and battered Jesus is presented to Caiaphas and Annas in scene 31, "ANNAS pretends to look surprised at the sight of Him, and exchanges ironic smiles with CAIAPHAS and others." Later, "CAIAPHAS is filled with secret pleasure" when Nicodemus and other protestors leave the proceedings.

- As Jesus is being escorted from his encounter with Herod [scene 48]:

    ANNAS: All we can do is bring him back to Pilate. We cannot condemn him.

    CAIAPHAS: Not officially, no…

    ANNAS takes this in, scans the faces around them. All of them turn to watch JESUS as he is DRAGGED from the hall. ANNAS turned to a particularly large, BRUTISH MAN among the Temple GUARDS. Their eyes meet, ever so briefly. ANNAS nods. The large GUARD walks towards the GUARDS who are marching Jesus out, mutters a few words to them. Electricity among the conspirators. Fire of hatred.

This cuts to exterior steps near the Temple: "Jesus' ankles are tied with ropes. He is trying to defend himself when the guard drags him down the steps. His head, covered in a bag, repeatedly smashes against a stone" [scene 49].

- When Jesus is scourged, Annas "is MESMERIZED by a DISPLAY…the TORTURERS are now putting on, who, ONE AFTER ANOTHER, select their favorite FLOGGING INSTRUMENT" [scene 54]. As Jesus is reduced to a bloody mess, Caiaphas' eyes are "shiny with breathless excitement. ANNAS, beside him…cannot look, his face TWITCHING" [scene 57].

- Throughout the exchanges between Pilate and the crowd, it is Caiaphas who controls the action. Repeatedly, he shouts out an answer to Pilate and the "mob" simply parrots his words with ever-increasing force.
- After Pilate, drawing on Matthew 27:24, washes his hands and declares that he is innocent of Jesus' blood, it is Caiaphas, not the people, who says triumphantly, "May his blood be upon us, then, and upon our children."
- When Jesus is crucified, Caiaphas and Annas and others of the Sanhedrin ride up on donkeys [scene 77] that had earlier been covered with "colorful wool-saddles" [scene 66]. Their wealth and status is thus reiterated.

APPENDIX 5

SELECTED QUOTATIONS FROM OFFICIAL CATHOLIC DOCUMENTS

Introduction: The Catholic Church, the Bible, and the Jews
Although some Christian communities have adopted the principle that there is no other authority for Christians than the Bible, this has never been the understanding of the Catholic Church. The Catholic perspective is that the Bible is the "Church's book." It is the foundational written authority for Christians. It was assembled within the Church, its New Testament books were composed within first-century churches, and it is interpreted in the Church for each generation. History shows that the Bible has been misused to justify war and violence, racial segregation and slavery, and anti-Semitism. Thus, the Catholic Church encourages all the faithful to study and pray with the Bible, but is also concerned that it be read attentively and wisely.

For Pope John Paul II this need for an informed reading of the Bible has special significance in regard to Jews. "In the Christian world," he stated in 1997, "erroneous and unjust interpretations of the New Testament regarding the Jewish people and their alleged culpability [for the crucifixion] have circulated for too long, engendering feelings of hostility towards this people."

The Pope's concern is exemplified in a recent e-mail received by a member of the ad hoc group. The sender declared: "Matthew 27:25 clearly tells us that 'Then all the people answered, His blood be on us, and on our children.' How strange for Jews or Christians to complain when Jews are merely being given that which they requested!…Contrary to pious-sounding deluded attempts to get Jews (or others) off the hook, these solemn words show a consciousness that the Jewish people recognized their guilt and were even proud of it." This hardly unusual e-mail shows how animosity toward Jews easily arises when the Passion narratives are naïvely read as if they contained verbatim historical transcripts.

The Catholic Church's Biblical concerns in regard to Jews are augmented by an awareness of the long history of Christian teaching of contempt for Jews and Judaism. Cardinal Edward Cassidy, the recently retired Vatican official responsible for Catholic-Jewish relations, summed up this history quite well in a 1998 speech:

> There can be no denial of the fact that from the time of the Emperor Constantine on, Jews were isolated and discriminated against in the Christian world. There were expulsions and forced conversions.
>
> Literature propagated stereotypes, preaching accused the Jews of every age of deicide; the ghetto, which came into being in 1555 with the papal bull, became in Nazi Germany the antechamber of the extermination.

This is why Pope John Paul II prayed for God's forgiveness for the sins of Christians against Jews at both the Basilica of St. Peter and the Western Wall:

> God of our fathers, you chose Abraham and his descendants to bring Your name to the nations: we are deeply saddened by the behavior of those who in the course of history have caused these [Jewish] children of Yours to suffer. And asking Your forgiveness, we wish to commit ourselves to genuine brotherhood with the people of the Covenant.

The following quotations, therefore, should be understood as part of a process of reconciliation and penitence, an effort to be more faithful to the Good News of Jesus Christ.

- Second Vatican Council, *Nostra Aetate* (1965), 4.

  Even though the Jewish authorities and those who followed their lead pressed for the death of Christ, neither all Jews indiscriminately at that time, nor Jews today, can be charged with the crimes committed during his Passion. It is true that the church is the new people of God, yet the Jews should not be spoken of as rejected or accursed as if this followed from Holy Scripture. Consequently, all must take care, lest in catechizing or in preaching the word of God, they teach anything which is not in accord with the truth of the Gospel message or the spirit of Christ.... The church always held and continues to hold that Christ out of infinite love freely underwent suffering and death because of the sins of all, so that all might attain salvation. It is the duty of the church, therefore, in its preaching to proclaim the cross of Christ as the sign of God's universal love and the source of all grace.

- Pontifical Commission for Religious Relations with the Jews, *Guidelines and Suggestions for Implementing the Conciliar Declaration Nostra Aetate,* no. 4 (1974), II.

  With respect to liturgical readings, care will be taken to see that homilies based on them will not distort their meaning, especially when it is a question of passages which seem to show the Jewish people as such in an unfavorable light. Efforts will be made so to instruct the Christian people that they will understand the true interpretation of all the texts and their meaning for the contemporary believer.

  Commissions entrusted with the task of liturgical translation will pay particular attention to the way in which they express those phrases and passages which Christians, if not well informed, might misunderstand because of prejudice.... [T]here should be an overriding preoccupation to bring out explicitly the meaning of a text, while taking scriptural studies into account. (Thus the formula "the Jews," in St. John, sometimes according to the context means "the leaders of the Jews," or "the adversaries of Jesus," terms which express better the thought of the evangelist and avoid appearing to arraign the Jewish people as such. Another example is the use of the words "pharisee" and "pharisaism" which have taken on a largely pejorative meaning.)

- Pontifical Commission for Religious Relations with the Jews, *Notes on the Correct Way to Present Jews and Judaism in Preaching and Teaching in the Roman Catholic Church* (1985)

The urgency and importance of precise, objective and rigorously accurate teaching on Judaism for our faithful follows too from the danger of anti-Semitism which is always ready to reappear under different guises. The question is not merely to uproot from among the faithful the remains of anti-Semitism still to be found here and there, but much rather to arouse in them, through educational work, an exact knowledge of the wholly unique "bond" (*Nostra Aetate,* no. 4) which joins us as a Church to the Jews and to Judaism. [8]

It is noteworthy too that the Pharisees are not mentioned in accounts of the Passion. Gamaliel (Acts 5:34–39) defends the apostles in a meeting of the Sanhedrin. An exclusively negative picture of the Pharisees is likely to be inaccurate and unjust. If in the Gospels...there are all sorts of unfavorable references to the Pharisees, they should be seen against the background of a complex and diversified movement. [19]

The Gospels are the outcome of long and complicated editorial work. The dogmatic constitution *Dei Verbum,* following the Pontifical Biblical Commission's Instruction *Sancta Mater Ecclesia,* distinguished three stages.... Hence, it cannot be ruled out that some references hostile or less than favorable to the Jews have their historical context in conflicts between the nascent Church and the Jewish community. Certain controversies reflect Christian-Jewish relations long after the time of Jesus. To establish this is of capital importance if we wish to bring out the meaning of certain Gospel texts for the Christians of today. All this should be taken into account when preparing catechesis and homilies for the last weeks of Lent and Holy Week. [21,A]

• Pontifical Biblical Commission, *The Interpretation of the Bible in the Church* (1988), IV, A, 3.

Particular attention is necessary, according to the spirit of the Second Vatican Council (*Nostra Aetate*, 4), to avoid absolutely any actualization [contemporary application] of certain texts of the New Testament which could provoke or reinforce unfavorable attitudes to the Jewish people. The tragic events of the past must, on the contrary, impel all to keep increasingly in mind that, according to the New Testament, the Jews remain "beloved" of God, "since the gifts and calling of God are irrevocable" (Rom. 11:28–29).

• Bishops' Committee for Ecumenical and Interreligious Affairs, *God's Mercy Endures Forever: Guidelines on the Presentation of Jews and Judaism in Catholic Preaching* (1988).

Another misunderstanding rejected by the Second Vatican Council was the notion of collective guilt, which charged the Jewish people *as a whole* with responsibility for Jesus' death. From the theory of collective guilt, it followed for some that Jewish suffering over the ages reflected divine retribution on the Jews for an alleged "deicide." While both rabbinic Judaism and early Christianity saw in the destruction of the Jerusalem Temple in AD 70 a sense of divine punishment (see Luke 19:42–44), the theory of collective guilt went well beyond Jesus' poignant expression of his love as a Jew for Jerusalem and the destruction it would face at the hands of Imperial Rome. Collective guilt implied that because "the Jews" had rejected Jesus, God had rejected them. With direct reference to Luke 19:44, the Second Vatican Council reminded Catholics that "nevertheless, now as before, God holds the Jews most dear for the sake of their fathers; he does not repent of the gifts he makes or of the calls he issues," and established as an overriding hermeneutical principle for homilists dealing with such passages that "the Jews should not be represented as rejected by God or accursed, as if this followed from Holy Scripture" (*Nostra Aetate*, no. 4; cf. 1985 *Notes*, VI:33). [7]

Because of the tragic history of the "Christ-killer" charge as providing a rallying cry for anti-Semites over the centuries, a strong and careful homiletic stance is necessary to combat its lingering effects today. Homilists and catechists should seek to provide a proper context for the proclamation of the Passion narratives. [21]

It is necessary to remember that the Passion narratives do not offer eyewitness accounts or a modern transcript of historical events. Rather, the events have had their meaning focused, as it were, through the four theological "lenses" of the Gospels. By comparing what is shared and what distinguishes the various Gospel accounts from each other, the homilist can discern the core from the particular optics of each. One can then better see the significant theological differences between the Passion narratives. These differences also are part of the inspired Word of God. [23]

Certain historical essentials are shared by all four accounts: a growing hostility against Jesus on the part of some Jewish religious leaders (not that the Synoptic Gospels do not mention the Pharisees as being involved in the events leading to Jesus' death, but only the "chief priests, scribers, and elders"); the Last Supper with the disciples; betrayal by Judas; arrest outside the city (an action conducted covertly by the Roman and Temple authorities because of Jesus' popularity among his fellow Jews); interrogation before a high priest (not necessarily a Sanhedrin trial); formal condemnation by Pontius Pilate (cf. the Apostles' and Nicene Creeds, which mention *only* Pilate, even though some Jews were involved); crucifixion by Roman soldiers; affixing the title "King of the Jews" on the cross; death; burial; and resurrection. Many other elements, such as the crowds shouting "His blood be on us and on our children" in Matthew, or the generic use of the term "the Jews" in John, are unique to a given author and must be understood within the context of that author's overall theological scheme. Often, these unique elements reflect the perceived need and emphases of the author's particular community at the end of the first century, *after* the split between Jews and Christians was well under way. [24]

Christian reflection on the Passion should lead to a deep sense of the need for reconciliation with the Jewish community today. [25]

- Bishops' Committee for Ecumenical and Interreligious Affairs,
  Criteria for the Evaluation of Dramatizations of the Passion (1988).

The greatest caution is advised in all cases where "it is a question of passages that seem to show the Jewish people as such in an unfavorable light" (*Guidelines* II). A general principle might, therefore, be suggested that if one cannot show beyond reasonable doubt that the particular Gospel element selected or paraphrased will not be offensive or have the potential for negative influence on the audience for whom the presentation is intended, that element cannot, in good conscience, be used. [C,1,d]

[T]he central criterion for judgment must be what the [1974 Vatican] *Guidelines* called "an overriding preoccupation to bring out explicitly the *meaning* of the [Gospel] text while taking scriptural studies into account" (II, emphasis added). Anything less than this "overriding preoccupation" to avoid caricaturing the Jewish people, which history has all too frequently shown us, will result almost inevitably in a violation of the basic hermeneutic principle of the [Second Vatican] Council in this regard: "the Jews should not be presented as rejected or accursed by God as if this followed from Sacred Scripture" (*Nostra Aetate*) [A,4].

Jews should not be portrayed as avaricious (e.g., in Temple money-changer scenes); bloodthirsty (e.g., in certain depictions of Jesus' appearances before the Temple priesthood or before Pilate); or implacable enemies of Christ (e.g., by changing the small "crowd" at the governor's palace into a teeming mob). Such depictions, with their obvious "collective guilt" implications, eliminate those parts of the Gospels that show that the secrecy surrounding Jesus' "trial" was motivated by the large following he had in Jerusalem and that the Jewish populace, far from wishing his death, would have opposed it had they known and, in fact, mourned his death by Roman execution (cf. Luke 23:27). [B,3,d]

Those constructing a single narrative from the versions of the events in the four Gospels are immediately aware that the texts differ in many details. To take just two examples, the famous phrase, "His Blood be upon us and on our children," exists only in the Matthean text (Matthew 27:24–25), while the question of whether or not there was a full Sanhedrin trial is given widely differing interpretations in each of the Gospel narratives. John, for example, has no Sanhedrin trial scene as such, but only a questioning before the two chief priests at dawn (18:19).

Also in John, it is a Roman cohort, merely accompanied by Temple guards, that arrests Jesus (John 18:3, 12). How is one to choose between the differing versions?

First, it must be understood that the Gospel authors did not intend to write "history" in our modern sense, but rather "sacred history" (i.e., offering "the honest truth about Jesus") (*Notes* IV, 29 A) in light of revelation. To attempt to utilize the four Passion narratives literally by picking one passage from one Gospel and the next from another Gospel, and so forth, is to risk violating the integrity of the texts themselves, just as, for example, it violates the sense of Genesis 1 to reduce the magnificence of its vision of the Creation to a scientific theorem.

A clear and precise hermeneutic and a guiding artistic vision sensitive to historical fact and to the best Biblical scholarship are obviously necessary. Just as obviously, it is not sufficient for the producers of Passion dramatizations to respond to responsible criticism simply by appealing to the notion that "it's in the Bible." One must account for one's selections.

In the above instances, for example, one could take from John's gospel the phrase "the Jews" and mix it with Matthew 27:24–25, clearly implying a "blood guilt" on all Jews of all times in violation of *Nostra Aetate*'s dictum that "what happened in this Passion cannot be blamed on all the Jews then living without distinction nor upon the Jews of today." Hence, if the Matthean phrase is to be used (not here recommended), great care would have to be taken throughout the presentation to ensure that such an interpretation does not prevail. Likewise, the historical and Biblical questions surrounding the notion that there was a formal Sanhedrin trial argue for extreme caution and, perhaps, even abandoning the device. As a dramatic tool, it can too often lead to misunderstanding. [C,1,a-c]

The Role of Pilate. Certain of the Gospels, especially the two latest ones, Matthew and John, seem on the surface to portray Pilate as a vacillating administrator who himself found "no fault" with Jesus and sought, though in a weak way, to free him. Other data from the Gospels and secular sources contemporary with the events portray Pilate as a ruthless tyrant. We know from these latter sources that Pilate ordered hundreds of Jews crucified without proper trial under Roman law, and that in the year 36 Pilate was recalled to Rome to give an account. Luke, similarly, mentions "the Galileans whose blood Pilate mingled with their sacrifices" in the Temple (Luke 13:1–4), thus corroborating the contemporary secular accounts of the unusual cruelty of Pilate's administration. John, as mentioned above, is at pains to show that Jesus' arrest and trial were essentially at Roman hands. Finally, the Gospels agree that Jesus' "crime," in Roman eyes, was that of political sedition, crucifixion being the Roman form of punishment for such charges. The threat to Roman rule is implicit in the charge: "King of the Jews," nailed to the cross at Pilate's order (Matthew 27:37; Mark 15:326; Luke 23:38; John 19:19). Matthew 27:38 and Mark 15:27 identify the "criminals" crucified with Jesus on that day as "insurgents." There is, then, room for more than one dramatic style of portraying the character of Pilate while still being faithful to the Biblical record. Again, it is suggested here that the hermeneutical insight of *Nostra Aetate* and the use of the best available Biblical scholarship cannot be ignored in the creative process and provide the most prudent and secure criterion for contemporary dramatic reconstruction. [C,2,b]

The full texts of these and numerous other church documents can be found on the Web site of the Center for Christian-Jewish Learning at Boston College at www.bc.edu/cjlearning.

LEON WIESELTIER

❖

THE WORSHIP OF BLOOD

There are still some miracles that movies cannot accomplish. If, in the manner of the bleeding images of the old Christian legends, it were possible for Mel Gibson's film itself to bleed, and the blood with which it soaks its wretched hero to burst through the screen and soak its wretched audience, it would have done so. For *The Passion of the Christ* is intoxicated by blood, by its beauty and its sanctity. The bloodthirstiness of Gibson's film is startling, and quickly sickening. The fluid is everywhere. It drips, it runs, it spatters, it jumps. It trickles down the post at which Jesus is flagellated and down the cross upon which he is crucified, and the camera only reluctantly tears itself away from the scarlet scenery. The flagellation scene and the crucifixion scene are frenzies of blood. When Jesus is nailed to the wood, the drops of blood that spring from his wound are filmed in slow motion, with a twisted tenderness. (*Ecce slo-mo.*) It all concludes in the shower of blood that issues from the corpse of Jesus when it is pierced by the Roman soldier's spear.

This is the greatest story ever told as Dario Argento might have told it, in its lurid style and in its contempt for the moral sensitivities of ordinary people. Gibson's subject is torture, and he treats his subject lovingly. There are no lilies in this field. There is only the relentless destruction and dehumanization of a man, who exists here to have his body punished with an almost unimaginable fury. He falls, he rises, he falls, he rises; he bends beneath the blows, but never mentally; his flesh is ripped, his head is stabbed, his eye is beaten shut, his hair is a wig of dried blood, he is a pulp with a cause. He is what the early church fathers, writing with admiration of their martyrs, called an "athlete" of suffering. Jim Caviezel, who plays Jesus, does not act, strictly speaking; he merely rolls his eyes heavenward and accepts more makeup. (He speaks little, as befits a man stupefied by suffering, though his Aramaic, like everybody else's in the film, is grammatically correct and risibly enunciated.)

The only cinematic achievement of *The Passion of the Christ* is that it breaks new ground in the verisimilitude of filmed violence. The notion that there is something spiritually exalting about the viewing of it is quite horrifying. The viewing of *The Passion of the Christ* is a profoundly brutalizing experience. Children must be protected from it. (If I were a Christian, I would not raise a Christian child on this.) Torture has been depicted in film many times before, but almost always in a spirit of protest. This film makes no quarrel with the pain that it excitedly inflicts. It is a repulsive masochistic fantasy, a sacred snuff film, and it leaves you with the feeling that the man who made it hates life.

Gibson is under the impression that he has done nothing more than put God's word into film. No Hollywood insider was ever so inside. "Critics who have a problem with me don't really have a problem with me and this film," he told Diane Sawyer, "they have a problem with the four Gospels." From such a statement it is impossible not to conclude that the man is staggeringly ignorant of his own patrimony. For the Gospels, like all great religious texts, have been interpreted in many different ways, to accommodate the needs and the desires of many different souls; and Gibson's account of these events is, like every other account, a particular construction of them. *The Passion of the Christ* is the expression of certain theological and artistic preferences. It is, more specifically, a noisy contemporary instance of a tradition of interpretation that came into its own in the late medieval centuries, when (in the words of a distinguished historian of Christian art) "the Passion became the chief concern of the Christian soul." In the fourteenth and fifteenth centuries, as a consequence of persecution and war and pestilence, the image of Christ hovering over the world in gilded majesty was replaced by the image of Jesus nailed in the world to the cross. Passion plays were devised for Holy Week. The lacerated Jesus became a commonplace of religious art, in which the Man of Sorrows plaintively displayed his wounds, which were venerated. This Jesus came to be drawn with a brutal realism, which climaxed in the grisly masterpieces of Grünewald. ("The image of the crucified Christ was *the* injured body of the late Middle Ages and the early-modern period," writes Valentin Groebner in *Defaced: The Visual Culture of Violence in the Late Middle Ages*. The fourth chapter of this recently translated book should be required reading—and its accompanying reproductions of late medieval Passion pictures should be required seeing—for all viewers of Gibson's film. It gives the history of its horror.)

The kindest thing that may be said of Mel Gibson is that he is an extremely late medieval. He contemplates the details of pain ecstatically. But this is still too kind, because the morbidity of the Man of Sorrows, even in its most popular versions, was rarely as crude as what Gibson presents. Does Christian dolorousness, a serious reflection upon the fate of Jesus, really require these special effects, this moral and aesthetic barbarity? *The Passion of the Christ* is the work of a religious sensibility of remarkable coarseness. It is by turns grossly physical and grossly magical, childishly literalist, gladly credulous, comically masculine. Gibson's faith is finally pre-theological, the kind of conviction that abhors thought, superstitiously fascinated by Satan and "the other realm," a manic variety of Christian folk religion.

Gibson's literalism is worth examining a little more closely, since it nicely exposes the boorishness of his religious mentality. For he does not seem to understand the difference between words and images. When he claims that he has done nothing more than transpose the text of the Gospel into film, he fails to comprehend the implications of such a transposition. For the Bible is famously, even notoriously, elliptical. Its descriptions of people and places and events are remarkably lacking in details, and basically nonsensory. It is precisely because Scripture leaves so much unsaid that it has provoked so much interpretation: it begs for amplification, for exegesis. Consider some of the verses that served Gibson as the basis for his script. Matthew 27:1: "When the morning came, all the chief priests and elders of the people took counsel against Jesus to put him to death." Was it a bright morning or a gloomy morning? The text does not say. What were the chief priests wearing? The text does not say. With what words, with what arguments, did they take counsel against him? The text does not say. Or Matthew 27:11: "And Jesus stood before the governor, and the governor asked him, Art thou the King of the Jews?" Where did Jesus stand, and where did Pilate stand? The text does not say. What was Pilate wearing? The text does not say. In what tone did Pilate put his question to Jesus? The text does not say.

But all these things that the text does not say a film (or a painting) must show, as Gibson's film has shown them. When the filmmaker comes to present them, the text cannot give him guidance. The visual cues in Scripture are too meager to make a picture. And so he must fill in the details himself—which is to say, he has no alternative but to invent them. For these inventions, he will rely upon his own imagination, or upon the imagination of previous interpreters; upon his own prior assumptions and prior feelings, or upon those of others. And so he cannot convincingly assert that his delineations of the Biblical occurrences have relied only upon the Biblical text. Many years ago, Erich Auerbach authoritatively described the mimetic procedure of the Bible. The style of Scripture, he wrote, is inhospitable to "an externalization of phenomena in terms perceptible to the senses." In these stories, "certain parts [are] brought into high relief, others [are] left obscure." There are gaps and obscurities and silences everywhere. For this reason, the visualization of biblical narratives is the work of the reader. In this regard the "realism" of the Bible differs in kind from the realism of many other narrative forms and genres. Of all the texts that may be adapted for the screen, then, the text of the Bible is the least helpful. Of all the films that have been adapted from a text, films about the Bible may least plausibly claim to be accurate, or faithful to their source, or works of verisimilitude. The problem with Gibson's literalist rendering of the Passion is not that it is wrong. The problem is that there is no way to know if it is right or wrong, because literalism in this instance is simply not possible. Nobody knows what these fateful scenes looked like and sounded like; nobody.

It will be objected that I see only pious pornography in *The Passion of the Christ* because I am not a believer in the Christ. This is certainly so. I do not agree that Jesus is my savior or anybody else's. I confess that I smiled when the credits to *The Passion of the Christ* listed "stunts." So I am not at all the person for whom Gibson made this monotonous movie. But I do not see how a belief in Jesus strengthens the case for such a film. Quite the contrary. Belief, a theory of meaning, a philosophical convenience, is rarely far away from cruelty. Torture has always been attended by explanations that vindicate it, and justify it, and even hallow it. These explanations, which are really extenuations, have been articulated in religious and in secular terms. Their purpose is to redescribe an act of inhumanity so that it no longer offends, so that it comes to seem necessary, so that it edifies. My victim of torture is your martyr.

There is a small chapter in *The City of God* in which Augustine denounces torture—"a thing, indeed, to be bewailed, and, if that were possible, watered with fountains of tears"—and then complacently accepts the necessity of it. (He asks only that we "condemn human life as miserable.") Augustine is speaking not of the duties of the martyr, but of the duties of the wise judge. Introduce God into the grim situation, and you will find fountains of tears shed not only over the success of some individuals in making the ultimate sacrifice, but also over the failure of other individuals to do the same. This is true of all the religious traditions. There is an ideal of holy suicide in all of them. It is important that we know how such extreme deeds were understood by the men and the women who performed them, but we have no obligation to concur in their understanding of what they did. Religious belief may actually interfere with a lucid analysis of religious life. Anyway, is the sanctification of murder really what this country needs now?

There is another problem with the insistence that a movie such as *The Passion of the Christ* can be intelligible only to a believer. When a non-Christian such as myself reads the Gospels, he is filled with a deep and genuine pity for the man who endured this savagery, and for his mother. (Jesus' mother is infinitely more affecting than his father.) In its meticulous representation of Jesus' excruciations, Gibson's film is designed to inspire such pity. The spectacle of this man's doom should be unbearable to a good heart. Yet pity is precisely what *The Passion of the Christ* cannot inspire, because the faith upon which it is based vitiates the sympathetic emotions. Why feel pity, if this suffering is a blessing? Why mourn, if his reward for his torment, and the world's reward, is ordained? If Jesus is not exactly human, then it is not exactly dehumanization that we are watching, and that we are deploring.

Such prior reassurance, the ancient assuagement of theodicy, is found in all the religions when they come to the terrors of mortality; but the confidence in the outcome of Jesus' anguish is especially flamboyant. Gibson's film undoes itself in this way most completely in the crucifixion scene. Just as the hammer is about to drive the nail into Jesus' hand (the hammer is held by the director's own hand, he proudly wishes you to know), the film flashes back to the Last Supper, where the camera catches Jesus' lovely gesticulating hands as he teaches that the bread is his body; and when the cross is raised, another flashback shows him instructing his disciples that his blood is the new covenant. So this *passion* is not a tragedy; it is a gift. The film ends three days later, when a ray of golden light penetrates the tomb as the stone is rolled away, and the shroud lies empty on the slab, and Jesus is alive again. As he rises to leave, the hole in his hand passes before our eyes. And the sight of the wound is about as moving as the sound of a doctrine. For we know by now that no atrocity has really been committed. All that has taken place is the temporarily discomfiting fulfillment of a divine plan for the redemption of the world. The ending is happy, which has the effect of making the viewer, or at least this viewer, feel like he has been duped. His sympathy was based on a misunderstanding. He had assumed that what was done to this man was outrageous, but he was wrong. He should have been rooting all along, with Gibson, for the whips and the nails.

The Passion of the Christ is an unwitting incitement to secularism, because it leaves you desperate to escape its standpoint, to find another way of regarding the bloodletting that you have just observed. This is unfair to, well, Christianity, since Christianity is not a cult of Gibsonesque gore. But there is a religion toward which Gibson's movie is even more unfair than it is to its own. In its representation of its Jewish characters, *The Passion of the Christ* is without any doubt an anti-Semitic movie, and anybody who says otherwise knows nothing, or chooses to know nothing, about the visual history of anti-Semitism, in art and in film. What is so shocking about Gibson's Jews is how unreconstructed they are in their stereotypical appearances and actions. These are not merely anti-Semitic images; these are classically anti-Semitic images. In this regard, Gibson is most certainly a traditionalist.

Now that Gibson has made the mistake of allowing people to see *The Passion of the Christ*—the film was much more interesting before it was released—it is plain that the controversy about its inclusion of Matthew 27:25, the infamous cry of the Jews that "his blood be on us and our children," the imprecation that served through the centuries as the warrant for the Christian assault on the Jews, was a fake, a cynical game. When Jewish groups objected to this passage in the script, Gibson expediently deleted the English translation of it.

I say expediently, because decency would have prevented him from including it, from shooting it, at all. But he may as well have kept it in, because it is entirely of a piece with the Jews whom he has invented. The figure of Caiaphas, played with disgusting relish by an actor named Mattia Sbragia, is straight out of Oberammergau. Like his fellow priests, he has a graying rabbinical beard and speaks with a gravelly sneer and moves cunningly beneath a *tallit*-like shawl streaked with threads the color of money. He is gold and cold. All he does is demand an execution. He and his sinister colleagues manipulate the ethically delicate Pilate into acquiescing to the crucifixion. (You would think that Rome was a colony of Judea.) Meanwhile the Jewish mob is regularly braying for blood. It is the Romans who torture Jesus, but it is the Jews who conspire to make them do so. The Romans are brutish, but the Jews are evil.

Gibson pleads that these are nothing but the elements of the Gospel narratives, but the Gospels are not clear and reliable historical documents. His notion of authenticity has no time for history. Historiographically speaking, after all, there is no such thing as gospel truth; and so his portrayal of the Jews is based on nothing more than his own imagination of what they looked like and sounded like. And Gibson's imagination has offered no resistance to the iconographical inheritance of Western anti-Semitism. Again, these things are not passively received. They are willingly accepted. Gibson created this movie; it was not revealed to him. Like his picture of Jesus, his picture of the Jews is the consequence of certain religious and cinematic decisions for which he must be held accountable. He has chosen to give millions of people the impression that Jews are culpable for the death of Jesus. In making this choice, which defies not only the scruples of scholars but also the teaching of the Catholic Church, Gibson has provided a fine illustration of the cafeteria Catholicism of the right. And the American media, which flourish by confusing gullibility with curiosity, go merrily along. A few weeks ago the cover of *Newsweek* asked, over a close-up of Caviezel crowned with thorns, WHO REALLY KILLED JESUS? The article inside the magazine exon-erated us, so we are safe. But is this really the question facing America? Up next: Should his blood be upon us and our children or shouldn't it? We'll be back right after this message. Don't go away.

No, go away. And take this low moment with you—but not until a little attention is paid to some of the praise that has been offered for this pernicious film. The apologetics for *The Passion of the Christ* must represent an intellec-tual nadir in contemporary American conservatism. Thoughtful people have been uttering thoughtless words. "Heartbreaking," declared Michael Novak after a screening, as if he had just walked out of *Waterloo Bridge*. "A medita-tion," he lazily called it in *The Weekly Standard*. It is hard to think of any-thing more unlike a meditation than *The Passion of the Christ*. But the discus-sion of the film was immediately and ferociously politicized, as conservatives conflated the defense of Gibson's religion with the defense of religion. If you turned away from Gibson's Jesus, you turned away from Jesus. The Via Dolorosa became the slippery slope. To criticize the film was to be godless. To suggest that it is not an accurate record of Jerusalem in the first century was to be anti-Christian. To worry that it is anti-Semitic was to be liberal. (The vigilance about anti-Semitism upon which conservatives like to con-gratulate themselves suddenly vanished.) Come to think of it, Pilate is the liberal in Gibson's film. And Gibson shrewdly encouraged this view of his slasher movie as the bulwark of a civilization: He made cultural warfare into a marketing strategy. Is the film violent? Of course it is, but this is God's vio-lence. This violence is good for America.

The success of Gibson's film is one of the most discouraging develop-ments in recent American life. I do not believe that the many thousands of people who are flocking to it are anti-Semitic, even if it will leave them tem-porarily well disposed, or temporarily indifferent, toward the hoariest libel against the Jews. They are buying their tickets, I suppose, as some sort of protest against what they regard as the hegemony of the secular in American

life. They are so angry about the indecency of so much of American entertainment that they are blind to the indecency of Gibson's entertainment.
They are so worried about the uncontrollable materialism in their society
that they do not notice the uncontrollable materialism in Gibson's strain of
Christianity. (In his obsession with the body, Gibson is a loyal son of Hollywood.) They, I mean traditionalist Catholics and evangelical Protestants,
feel so oppressed in their land that they are glad to ignore the oppressive-
ness—and the complicity with a history of oppression—in this film. *The
Passion of the Christ*, in other words, is just another measure of how low our
society has sunk in its disputation about its values. It is another illustration of
the vituperation, the demagoguery, the polarization, the race for the intellec-
tual bottom, that now characterizes political and cultural debate in the United
States. American conservatism truly is precarious, and also ruthless, if it
must resort to *The Passion of the Christ* to fortify itself.

Gibson's Jewish defenders have been especially disgraceful. "Jewish
organizations must not attempt to take responsibility for deciding what
Christians can and cannot believe," wrote Michael Medved in *The Christian
Science Monitor*, as if the Jewish criticism of Gibson's film is anything other
than the behavior of American citizens freely expressing an opinion. "If we
are empowered to edit their doctrine," David Klinghoffer asked ominously in
the *Forward*, "then why are they not empowered to edit ours?" reminding his
readers that once upon a time the Christians censored the Talmud. Is Gibson
now doctrine? Is criticism now censorship? And where is the Sanhedrin on
the Upper West Side that is poring over Christian texts with a black marker?
Then there was the argument for timidity. "Jewish denunciations of the
movie only increase the likelihood that those who hate us will seize on the
movie as an excuse for more hatred," Medved declared. I wonder if he feels
the same way about Jewish denunciations of Islamic anti-Semitism. In a
journal of the American Enterprise Institute, he warned that "sadly, the battle over the *The Passion* may indeed provoke more hatred of the Jews." Yet

the hatred of the Jews is not simply a response to the Jewish response to the hatred of the Jews. Anti-Semitism is not anti-anti-anti-Semitism. It is an old and independent and vital tradition of fear and hallucination, a non-Jewish disorder that has nothing to do with the Jews, as *The Passion of the Christ* demonstrates.

But the loathing of Jews in Mel Gibson's film is really not its worst degradation. *Kim le bi-deraba mine,* as Yeshua might have said: Its loathing of Jews is subsumed in its loathing of spirituality, in its loathing of existence. If there is a kingdom of heaven, *The Passion of the Christ* is shutting it in men's faces.

STEPHEN PROTHERO

❖

JESUS NATION, CATHOLIC CHRIST*

Don't look now, but here comes the Catholic Jesus. In February 1804, Thomas Jefferson sat in the White House, cutting verses out of two Bibles and pasting them together into an abridged New Testament that cast Jesus as a rational ethicist. Two hundred years later to the month, Mel Gibson was furiously cutting and pasting a cinematic testament to his own ultra-conservative Catholic Christ. Jesus may be "the same yesterday, and today, and forever" (Hebrews 13:8) but, at least in the United States, everyone can write his own gospel.

Since the Evangelical century of the 1800s, Protestants have dominated American religion, and over time they have gravitated toward a Mister Rogers Jesus, a neighborly fellow whom they could know, love, and imitate. The country's megachurches got that way in part because they stopped preaching fire and brimstone and started singing "What a Friend We Have in Jesus." Their parishioners are sinners in the hands of an amiable God. Their Jesus is a loving friend.

*Portions of this essay appeared previously in *The New York Times Magazine*, *The Wall Street Journal*, and Slate.com.

Gibson's Christ is by all accounts a very different character. If the mind is the seat of Jefferson's Jesus and the heart the seat of the Evangelical Friend, Gibson's hero is his body. He came to earth neither to deliver moral maxims nor to exude empathy, but to spew blood. The drama of the Gospel according to Gibson derives from our thirst for that blood, intensifies as we drive in the nails, and does not stop until asphyxiation staunches the flow. This is not a therapeutic, "I'm O.K., you're O.K." Christianity. In fact, *The Passion of the Christ* seems hell-bent on crashing head-on into a parking lot full of American Protestant assumptions. Its leading man is the crucified Christ of devotional Catholics who for centuries have approached their redeemer through the Eucharist, gratefully imbibing his body and blood. And in scene after gory scene Gibson is shoving that Christ in our faces, thrusting the Man of Sorrows of medieval Passion plays and Renaissance altarpieces into the American conversation about Jesus (and in Latin and Aramaic, no less).

THE AMERICAN JESUS

This national conversation began in earnest after the Revolutionary War, when Evangelical Protestants first pledged their allegiance to the Second Person of the Trinity rather than to the First. After liberating themselves from the tyranny of George III, these pious patriots were in no mood to bow down before another distant king, especially since, according to the reigning Puritan theology, God the Father had capriciously predestined each one to either heaven or hell. So they reinvented Christianity as a Jesus-loving rather than a God-fearing faith, transfiguring Jesus in sermons and songs from an abstract theological sign into a living, breathing human being.

Later Protestants liberated Jesus not only from Calvinism but also from the creeds and then even from the Bible, freeing him up to be, in the words of the apostle Paul, "all things to all men" (1 Corinthians 9:22): male and female, black and white, gay and straight, a socialist and a capitalist, a pacifist and a warrior, a civil rights activist and a Ku Klux Klansman. Over the American centuries, this American Jesus has stood not on some unchanging rock of ages but on the shifting sands of economic circumstances, political calculations, and cultural trends. Part Proteus, part Paul, he became during the Victorian period a sentimental Savior beloved by women and adored by children. During the Progressive Era of Teddy Roosevelt's Rough Riders, he flexed his muscles and carried a big stick. During the counterculture of the 1960s and 1970s, he grew his hair long and strummed his guitar for peace.

Though this American discussion about Jesus has been dominated by Christians, non-Christians have joined in too, asserting their right to interpret in their own way one of the core symbols of Christianity (and of the United States). Between the Civil War and the 1930s, virtually every major Reform rabbi in the United States wrote a book or pamphlet reclaiming Jesus as a Jew. Echoing Jefferson, these rabbis drew a sharp distinction between the true religion *of* Jesus and the false religion *about* him, and then used the former to attack the latter. While other Americans loved Jesus because of Christianity, these Americans loved him despite it. The man from Nazareth, they argued, was a faithful son of the synagogue who scrupulously observed the Law and died with the Shema ("Hear, O Israel: the Lord our God is one Lord") on his lips.

Buddhists and Hindus have also remade Jesus in their own image. In *The Good Heart: A Buddhist Perspective on the Teachings of Jesus* (1996), the Dalai Lama recognized him as "either a fully enlightened being or a bodhisattva of very high spiritual realization."[1] Swami Yogananda, the author of *Autobiography of a Yogi* (1946) and the founder of a Hindu organization called the Self-

1. Dalai Lama, *The Good Heart: A Buddhist Perspective on the Teachings of Jesus* (Boston: Wisdom Publications, 1996), p. 83.

Realization Fellowship, flattered the Galilean (and himself) when he called Jesus a "spiritual giant" and a secret practitioner of Kriya Yoga.[2]

Gradually, the American Jesus slipped the bonds not only of Christianity but also of religion itself, morphing in the 1920s into a celebrity and more recently into a national icon beloved by politicians and pop stars alike. Today, presidential candidates tap him as their favorite political philosopher, and on the radio the likes of Mick Jagger and Bono sing his praises too. There are now more books on Jesus (roughly 17,000) in the Library of Congress than on any other historical figure. And Jesus is a fixture as well in the rough and tumble of popular culture, celebrated in novels and movies, theme parks and hot-air balloons, night lights and tattoos. Polls reveal that Americans of all faiths now view Jesus "overwhelmingly in a favorable light" and that he has "a strong hold even on those with no religious training." Amazingly, nearly half of the country's non-Christians believe that Jesus was born from a virgin and raised from the dead. In a best-selling novel from 1925, Bruce Barton described Jesus as *The Man Nobody Knows*. Today he is the man nobody hates.[3]

THE CATHOLIC CHRIST

Catholic contributions to this messy midrash on Jesus have been sporadic and muted. Catholics, who now constitute roughly one-quarter of the U.S.

2. Paramahansa Yogananda, *The Divine Romance* (Los Angeles: Self-Realization Fellowship, 1986), p. 336.

3. George Gallup, Jr., and George O'Connell, *Who Do Americans Say That I Am?* (Philadelphia: Westminster Press, 1986), pp. 69, 83; Humphrey Taylor, "Large Majority of People Believe They Will Go to Heaven; Only One in Fifty Thinks They Will Go to Hell" (Harris Poll #41, August 12, 1998), Harrisinteractive, http://www.harrisinteractive.com/harris_poll/index.asp?PID=167.

population, have weighed in occasionally on their Savior (via prints of the Sacred Heart of Jesus, for example, and the occasional life of Christ by a popular priest). But few have participated in the quests for the historical Jesus that have bedeviled American Protestants and Jews. Few have written christological novels to rival *In His Steps: "What Would Jesus Do?"* (1897) by the Congregationalist minister Charles Sheldon, or *The Nazarene* (1939) by the Yiddish writer Sholem Asch. When the *National Catholic Reporter* held a turn-of-the-millennium art contest for the best depiction of "Jesus 2000," a non-Catholic won.

Catholics inhabit a cosmos overflowing with sacred power, supercharged with the spiritual potencies of saints and sacraments, angels and demons, popes and priests. By contrast, Protestants have since the sixteenth century sought to strip away those accretions of popery, banishing the saints and slashing the sacraments from seven to two (baptism and the Eucharist), or, in the case of the Quakers, to zero. Whereas Catholics based their faith on Scripture and tradition, Protestants relied on the Bible alone. But as textual criticism and Darwinism chipped away at the Bible's authority after the Civil War, *sola scriptura* gave way among many American Protestants to *solus Jesus*: Jesus alone. To be a Christian was no longer to attend the mass or even to read the Bible, but to have a personal relationship with Jesus. To be an American, it seemed, was to contemplate, as Matthew 8:27 puts it, "what manner of man" Jesus might be.

American Catholics have never quite gotten what the fuss is all about. They access God through the saints, Scriptures, and sacraments of the Church; their spiritual drama is not a one-man show. Still, they have not entirely neglected the Jesus wars. During the Roaring Twenties, an era as besotted with Jesus (and celebrity) as our own, *Life of Christ* (1923) by the Italian Catholic Giovanni Papini, spent three years near the top of the U.S. best-seller list, captivating readers with its purple prose and perfervid faith. *The New Republic* described Papini as "an engine without a governor, with boilers always at the bursting point," adding that in this book "he is careening madly down the main highway of orthodoxy at a rate of a hundred thousand per edition." Protestant critics took Papini to task for creating an "uncritical" and "naïve" book that "neither debates nor searches." But for the author (and, one suspects, for many readers) that was just the point. His page-turner was intended to edify and entertain, not to enlighten.[4]

Gibson and Papini have much in common. Both are outlanders who found their largest audiences in the United States. Both are traditionalist Catholics who came to intense faith relatively late in life (Papini as a convert from skepticism, Gibson as a prodigal son). Each plumps for his Savior with the glee, and at times with the bigotry, of a man of fresh faith. And each seems to be, as *The New Republic* described Papini, "a wild and gusty soul, violent, infinitely unstable and insatiably ambitious."[5] Unlike Gibson's *Passion of the Christ*, which confines itself to the last twelve hours of Jesus' life, Papini's volume covers the whole story. But the book tends inexorably toward the trial and the cross, where "hook-nosed" Jews mutate into serpents ("Pharisaical vipers") and uncontrollable violence rains down.[6] Papini's Jesus is indisputably divine, but he is trapped nonetheless in the tomb of the flesh. The book's symbols are easy enough to unpack: the thorns point to Jesus' suffering with us, the wounds to his sacrifice for our sins, and the blood to his "real presence" in the Eucharist. This is Gibson's Jesus too: a Suffering Servant who takes the lash with us, exhales his last breath for us, and comes to us in the liturgies of the one true Church.

There is one crucial difference, however, between Papini and Gibson.

4. C.E.A., "Papini Finito," *The New Republic* (August 6, 1924), p. 304; Carl D. Gage, "What Think You of Papini's Christ," *Methodist Review* 106 (November 1923), p. 938.

5. C.E.A., "Papini Finito," *The New Republic* (August 6, 1924), p. 304.

6. Giovanni Papini, *Life of Christ*, trans. Dorothy Canfield Fisher (New York: Harcourt, Brace and Company, 1923), pp. 319, 339.

Whereas Papini hated Protestants, Gibson has courted them like he wooed Helen Hunt in *What Women Want*. "America," Papini once fumed, "is the land of millionaire uncles, the fatherland of trusts, of skyscrapers, of the phonograph, of the electric streetcar, of lynch law, of the insupportable Washington, the boresome Emerson, the degenerate Walt Whitman, the sickening Longfellow, the angelic Wilson, the philanthropic Morgan, the undesirable Edison, and other men of like quality."[7] And for those sins, God in His wisdom visited on the nation the curse of Protestantism. Who knows what Gibson is thinking? Nevertheless, he has said nothing to rile born-again Americans. In fact, he has played the Evangelical himself, emphasizing at nearly a year of prayer summits before the movie's opening his own adult reawakening to the Christian faith. In response, Evangelicals have embraced him as a brother even as Catholic writers have raised concerns.

HAIL MARY

One of the puzzles about this film is why born-again Christians have given such a big thumbs-up to what is so unapologetically a Catholic movie. *The Passion of the Christ* draws on all sorts of extra-biblical genres, including the macho brutality of the action-adventure movie (blood, gore, repeat) and the supernatural horror of the Gothic tradition of Edgar Allan Poe and Stephen King. In fact, all the hallmarks of the latter genre—underground dungeon, shackles and chains, sadistic torturers, innocent maiden, stone-heavy architecture, and supernatural terror—are in this film in spades. The movie is also deeply indebted to muscular Christianity and its manly redeemer—to martial hymns such as "Onward Christian Soldiers" and vigorous preachers such as the baseball evangelist Billy Sunday, who once

7. "Preparing for Papini," *Literary Digest* 80.4 (January 26, 1924), p. 32.

called his virile Savior "the greatest scrapper who ever lived."[8] Jesus doesn't do too much fighting here, and Gibson chooses not to flash back to the cleansing of the Temple (a stock scene for the macho Jesus crowd), but Caviezel portrays Jesus as a man with a mission, a manly man who defies the religious and political authorities, and who impresses the ladies along the way. (Virtually every female shown along the Via Dolorosa is weeping uncontrollably over Jesus' fate.)

Still, *The Passion*, which begins with an epigraph from Isaiah 53:5 ("He was wounded for our transgressions...and with His stripes we are healed"), is most plainly an artifact of devotional Catholicism. From medieval Passion plays, which survive in the popular extravaganza still staged every ten years by the townspeople of Oberammergau in the Bavarian Alps, Gibson borrowed his blood-and-guts sacramentalism and the tradition of cranking up Jewish culpability for dramatic effect. (Oberammergau, Adolf Hitler once remarked, portrays "the whole muck and mire of Jewry."[9]) Gibson also borrowed from Oberammergau and its European and American imitators the tradition of the *tableaux vivants*: "living pictures" in which motionless actors attempt to reproduce on the stage pious Renaissance sculptures and paintings. The movie proper—before the denouement of the resurrection—ends with a cinematic *tableau vivant* in which the Virgin Mary and her dead son are frozen in the form of Michelangelo's *Pietà*. An earlier moment (not in the Gospels, by the way), in which the Roman centurion who has become a believer is baptized by the liquid spurting from Jesus' lanced side, recalls a 1555 altarpiece by Lucas Cranach the Younger (which depicts blood spraying from Jesus' abdomen onto Cranach himself). And the movie as a whole

8. Quoted in William G. McLoughlin, *Billy Sunday Was His Real Name* (Chicago: University of Chicago Press, 1955), p. 179.

9. Quoted in James S. Shapiro, *Oberammergau: The Troubling Story of the World's Most Famous Passion Play* (New York: Pantheon Books, 2000), p. 168.

seems inspired by the gruesome and gangrenous *Crucifixion* of the Northern Renaissance painter Matthias Grünewald (1515).

Gibson's sermon on the screen is also inspired by Catholic meditations on the fourteen Stations of the Cross and the Five Wounds of Christ, by the mystical writings of the anti-Semitic Bavarian nun Anne Catherine Emmerich, and above all by Marian devotions. The intense Mariology in the film has gone largely unremarked upon, perhaps because Evangelical defenders and liberal critics of the film don't like it or (more likely) because they don't get it. But the Virgin Mary appears in virtually every scene in the movie, and in keeping with traditional Catholic theology we witness its horrors not so much through our own eyes as through the mediation of hers. As Jesus ascends the Via Dolorosa to Golgotha, Mary walks with him, like Christian pilgrims have for centuries (and still do). At one point, however, the brutality overtakes her, and it seems for a moment that, like us, she has finally seen enough. Gibson cuts quickly to Jesus' childhood: Mary's boy has fallen, and she runs to him in a panic, soothing him (and herself) with kind words, a gentle touch. Cut back now to the alley off the Via Dolorosa and again to Mary, who is running as before to her son. And as she touches him and sends him yet again on his way, she reassures us that, like her, we can summon the resolve to accompany Jesus to the cross, to see his divinely ordained mission through to the bitter end.

There are centuries of Catholic devotion to the Blessed Virgin Mary packed into this scene, this movie. And the Romanian actress Maia Morgenstern evokes them masterfully. Whereas James Caviezel's Jesus is a one-dimensional victim (in fact, he may be the least developed lead in any Jesus movie ever), Morgenstern's Mary is a wonderfully complex character. True, she does not have many lines. But like the great silent film heroines of the twenties, she does not need them. In a scene that Gibson stole from Emmerich's *Dolorous Passion of Our Lord Jesus Christ* (1833), she stoops to sop onto fresh linens the pools of sacred blood let loose by the Romans' sadistic scourging of her son. In so doing, she carries the weight not only of the anguish of all bereaved mothers everywhere, but also of the sacred secret that her son is (with her help) making all things new. And so she functions in the film, as she does in popular Catholic piety, not simply as a mediator between God and his faithful, but also as the co-redeemer of our fallen world.

LIONS AND LAMBS

Among the things being made new in post-*Passion* America is the long-standing anatagonism between Evangelicals and Catholics. Evangelicals have been in the forefront of anti-Catholic nativism since a Protestant mob burned a convent to the ground in Charlestown, Massachusetts, in 1834. It was Evangelicals who instigated the deadly anti-Catholic Bible riots in Philadelphia in 1844, Evangelicals who revived the Ku Klux Klan in the 1920s, and Evangelicals who as recently as John Kennedy's run for the presidency continued to claim that the United States is not just a Christian country but a Protestant one. For the time being, however, the Evangelical lion is lying down with the Catholic lamb, vindicating those who have discerned a trend in American religion toward a two-party system in which the key divide is not between Protestants and Catholics but between conservatives and liberals.

The importance of this rapprochement should not be underestimated, and it demands some sort of explanation. Why did Evangelicals put their grass-roots organizations at the beck and call of the producer formerly known as Mad Max, buying tickets by the millions to an R-rated film? Why did they embrace so enthusiastically a man who has given the spiritual equivalent of the middle finger to their warm and fuzzy Jesus? Why are they bowing down before a cinematic Christ who owes as much to medieval Passion plays and Hollywood horror movies as he does to the Gospels, who runs so hard against the American Protestant grain?

The ongoing culture wars no doubt have something to do with the Evangelicals' decision to close ranks with Gibson, who must be commended for so adroitly spinning the debate over his depiction of Jews into an apocalyptic battle between secular humanists and true believers. The Evangelicals' "amen" to the movie may also demonstrate that conservative Protestants have bought more into Hollywood's culture of violence than they would like to admit. (Witness "Halloween Hell Night" at your local nondenominational church.) Or that, while anti-Semitism is still alive in the United States, anti-Catholicism is finished (good news, that, for John Kerry).

When it comes to the backstory of the American Jesus, however, the decision by conservative Protestants to break bread with a traditionalist Catholic director may be telling us that the Buddy Christ is on the way out. Calling on the authority of the apostle Paul, who once boasted that he gloried only in the cross, a group calling itself the Alliance of Confessing Evangelicals has taken American Protestants (Evangelicals included) to the woodshed for preaching a "self-esteem gospel" and a "health and wealth gospel" rather than the tough truths of the creeds. And Gerald McDermott, a professor of religion at Roanoke College, has complained that American Protestants are reducing Jesus "to no more than the Dalai Lama without the aura, an admirable sort of guy."[10]

Evangelicals less concerned about the fine points of atonement theology may be growing tired of the sentimental Savior too. During the second half of the twentieth century, the Protestant pendulum swung back toward the feminized faith that Billy Sunday once derided as "flabby-cheeked, brittle-boned, weak-kneed, thin-skinned, pliable, plastic, spineless, effeminate, sissified, three-carat Christianity."[11] Now, at the start of the twenty-first, it seems to be swinging in the other direction.

10. "The Cambridge Declaration of the Alliance of Confessing Evangelicals" (April 20, 1996), http://www.bible-researcher.com/cambridge1.html; Gerald McDermott, interview with the author, February 2004.

11. Quoted in Betty A. DeBerg, *Ungodly Women: Gender and the First Wave of American Fundamentalism* (Minneapolis: Fortress Press, 1990), p. 89.

The last hundred years have been the most brutal in world history. Until now, however, American Protestants have largely averted their eyes from the realities of twentieth-century mass death: the wars, the genocides, the bomb. Protestants have long preferred an empty cross to the Catholics' crucifix, and the most successful megachurches in the United States have banished even that sanitized symbol from their spiffy sanctuaries. Though U.S. Evangelicals have by no means rejected the theology of the vicarious atonement (which sees Jesus' sacrifice on the cross as a debt paid for the sins of the world), they have preferred to reflect on the meaning of the crucifixion rather than brood over the fact of it. But on September 11, and via the subsequent wars in Afghanistan and Iraq, mass death came home forcefully to citizens of all religious persuasions. So it should not be surprising that Americans are beginning to frown at the happy-face Jesus who has been helping them feel good about themselves at least since Victorians gave up mourning clothes for funeral flowers. Warner Sallman's "Head of Christ," a high school yearbook-style portrait of a dreamy Christ with perfectly coiffed hair and unblemished skin, may be the most reproduced religious image ever, but today it is decidedly on the way out. Too Caucasian for U.S. blacks, Asians, and Latinos, Sallman's metrosexual Messiah is also too prissy for patriotic Americans who want their Savior to muscle up and charge into battle.

It is unlikely that Evangelicals will immediately dump this amiable Jesus for Gibson's medieval Man of Sorrows. Jerry Falwell is not likely to start meditating on the Five Wounds of Christ; Franklin Graham probably will not begin ruminating on the Stations of the Cross. Complacent optimism runs too deep in the national psyche to be scared away by Gibson's Munchish scream. Still, the popular success of this movie (to say nothing of the runaway popularity of the macho *Left Behind* novels, which have sold over 60 million copies since their debut in 1995), seems to indicate that, in twenty-first-centuryAmerica, there is something unseemly about keeping your sunny side up, at least while the war on terrorism is on.

"I'LL BE BACK"

In *The Kingdom of God in America* (1937), the neo-orthodox theologian H. Richard Niebuhr famously summed up liberal Protestantism like this: "a God without wrath brought men without sin into a kingdom without judgment through the ministrations of a Christ without a cross."[12] Gibson, who has declared publicly that his Episcopal wife will probably go to hell,[13] shares Niebuhr's disdain for the facile pieties of liberal religion, and in *The Passion* he has forcefully reintroduced wrath, sin, judgment, and the cross into America's visual religious lexicon. As a result, a culture (and an industry) so enamored of the beautiful is meditating on the ugly and the grotesque. And at least for a time, Americans seem willing to set aside the sentimental sensibilities of therapeutic spirituality, to stare sin and evil in the face.

Cecil B. DeMille, who directed the original Jesus blockbuster *The King of Kings* (1927), once bragged that only the Bible had introduced Jesus to more people than had his epic. Soon Mel Gibson may be telling us the same. In all likelihood, millions of Americans will now conjure up James Caviezel's morgue Messiah when they bow their heads to pray. Readers who find this prospect unappealing or appalling can take refuge, however, in the wisdom of Ecclesiastes—that this too shall pass.

In the United States, believers and nonbelievers alike now routinely apply the "What Would Jesus Do?" test to matters as disparate as homelessness, vegetarianism, SUVs, and gay marriage. New Jesus controversies arise every few years, most recently over a burial box inscribed "James, son of Joseph, brother of Jesus." And new Jesus movies come to the cineplex nearly as regularly. Arnold Schwarzenegger's vow in *The Terminator*—"I'll be back"—is the perennial promise of the American Jesus, who over the course of the next

12. H. Richard Niebuhr, *The Kingdom of God in America* (New York: Harper, 1959), p. 193.

13. Peter J. Boyer, "The Jesus War: Mel Gibson's Obsession," *The New Yorker* (September 15, 2003), p. 71.

few decades will surely continue to reincarnate himself in novels and television shows, pop songs and Broadway plays.

Ironically, the success of Gibson's dolorous deity may be sowing the seeds of its own supersession. Given a box-office take of hundreds of millions (not counting the vigorish from $62.95 "soldier for Christ" medals and other officially licensed Jesus tchotchkes available through the movie's Web site), *The Passion* is sure to inspire a spate of Jesus movies to come, leaving observers of American culture to wonder just what Jesus would make of all of this. What would Jesus think of Gibson's latest Passion? Of Ron Howard's recently announced decision to direct a movie on *The Da Vinci Code*? Of a Jesus nation that has turned the Son of God into a national icon, pasting him on billboards and bumper stickers and cashing in on his brand name at every turn? That is anyone's guess. Perhaps he is sitting on his throne at the right hand of the Father, shaking his finger at us all—at Gibson for making a sado-masochistic and anti-Jewish movie, at his Melomaniacs for flocking to it like lost sheep, and at critics for keeping the whole bloody mess alive by endlessly kvetching about it.

But perhaps Jesus has more of a sense of humor than Gibson's grim ghost of a Christ. A few years ago, the Roman Catholic magazine *Liguorian* ran on its cover an image of a guffawing Jesus, his head tilted back, roaring with laughter. To many critics, this image is a prime example of the cultural captivity of Jesus, his capitulation to the banality of American culture. Surely H. Richard Niebuhr and his neo-orthodox brethren would have seen it that way. Yet Christianity is no doubt about the resurrection as well as the crucifixion, pleasure as well as pain, happiness as well as heartache. And as the Harvard Divinity School professor Harvey Cox observed, grim joylessness is not a necessary prerequisite for religious revolutionaries. If Jesus came to die on the cross, he also came, as John 10:10 has it, so that we "might have life, and have it more abundantly." And at least at the wedding in Cana, such a life meant an abundant supply of intoxicating beverages.

At times, laughter, or, at least bemusement, seems to be the best response to the vagaries of religious experience in the United States. What would Jesus think of the "Holy Land Experience"™ theme park, run by messianic Jews not far from Disney World in Orlando, Florida? Of the 258,000 cubic feet of hot air that allow the "Jesus balloon" to lift off each Easter over northern California, preaching the Risen Christ to citizens below? Of the sixty-seven-foot, white-robed Jesus statue that lords over The Great Passion Play™ held every summer in Eureka Springs, Arkansas? Is Jesus venting his righteous anger at our many efforts to collapse Christ into culture, the sacred into the secular? Perhaps. But maybe, as Professor Cox has argued, he is a jester after all. Maybe our trickster has bought a ticket and is taking a ride. Maybe, as the *Liguorian* had it, he is tossing his head back and roaring with laughter.

❖

STUDIO SCRIPT NOTES ON "THE PASSION"

Dear Mel,

We love, love the script! The ending works great. You'll be getting a call from us to start negotiations for the book rights.

- Love the Jesus character. So likable. He can't seem to catch a break! We identify with him because of it. One thing: I think we need to clearly state "the rules." Why doesn't he use his superpowers to save himself! Our creative people suggest that you could simply cut away to two spectators:

  SPECTATOR ONE
  Why doesn't he use his superpowers to save himself?

  SPECTATOR TWO
  He can only use his powers to help others, never himself.

- Does it matter which garden? Gethsemane is hard to say, and Eden is a much more recognizable garden. Just thinking out loud.

- Our creative people suggest a clock visual fading in and out in certain scenes, like the Last Supper bit: "Thursday, 7:45 p.m.," or "Good Friday, 5:14 p.m."
- Love the repetition of "Is it I?" Could be very funny. On the eighth inquiry, could Jesus just give a little look of exasperation into the camera? Breaks the frame, but could be a riot.
- Also, could he change water into wine in Last Supper scene? Would be a great moment, and it's legit. History compression is a movie tradition and could really brighten up the scene. Great trailer moment, too.
- Love the flaying.
- Could the rabbis be Hispanic? There's lots of hot Latino actors now, could give us a little zing at the box office. Research says there's some historical justification for it.
- Possible title change: "Lethal Passion." Kinda works. The more I say it out loud, the more I like it.
- Is there someplace where Jesus could be using an iBook? You know, now that I say it, it sounds ridiculous. Strike that. But think about it. Maybe we start a shot in Heaven with Jesus thoughtfully closing the top?
- Love the idea of Monica Bellucci as Mary Magdalene (yow!). Our creative people suggest a name change to Heather. Could skew our audience a little younger.
- Love Judas. Such a great villan. Our creative people suggest that he's a little complicated. Couldn't he be one thing? Just bad? Gives the move much more of a motor. Also, thirty pieces of silver is not going to get anyone excited. I think it'd be very simple to make him a "new millionaire." Bring in the cash on a tray. Great dilemma that the audience can identify with.
- Minor spelling error: on page 18, in the description of the bystanders, there should be a space between the words "Jew" and "boy."
- Merchandising issue: it seems the Cross image has been done to death and is public domain—we can't own it. Could the Crucifixion scene involve

something else? A Toyota would be wrong, but maybe there's a shape we can copyright, like a wagon wheel?

• I'm assuming "The dialogue is in Aramaic" is a typo for "American." If not, call me on my cell, or I'm at home all weekend.

By the way, I'm sending a group of staffers on a cruise to the North Pole, coincidentally around the time of your picture's release. Would love to invite your dad!

See you at the movies!

Yours,

Stan

ACKNOWLEDGEMENTS & PERMISSIONS

❖

Meacham, Jon, "Who Really Killed Jesus?" A prior version of this essay was originally published as "Who Killed Jesus?" in Newsweek, February 16, 2004, © 2004 Newsweek, Inc. All rights reserved. Reprinted by permission.

Kulman, Linda and Jay Tolson, "The Other Jesus: How a Jewish Reformer Lost his Jewish Identity," © 2004 John J. Tolson and Linda Kulman. A prior version of this essay was originally published as "The Real Jesus" in the March 8, 2004 issue of U.S. News & World Report. Copyright 2004 U.S. News & World Report, L.P. Reprinted with permission.

Fredriksen, Paula, "Gospel Truths: Hollywood, History, and Christianity," © 2004 Paula Fredriksen

Cunningham, Philip, "Much Will Be Required of the Person Entrusted with Much: Assembling A Passion Drama from the Four Gospels," © 2004 Philip A. Cunningham

Frizzel, Lawrence, "The Death of Jesus and the Death of the Temple," © 2004 Lawrence Frizzel

Witherington, Ben, "Numb Struck: An Evangelical Reflects on Gibson's *Passion*," © 2004 Ben Witherington

Martin, James, "The Last Station: A Catholic Reflection on The Passion," © 2004 James Martin

Wallis, Jim, "The *Passion* and The Message," © 2004 Jim Wallis

Thistlewaite, Susan, "Mel Makes a War Movie," © 2004 Susan Thistlewaite

Boys, Mary, "Seeing Different Movies, Talking Past Each Other," © 2004 Mary C. Boys

Reinhartz, Adele, "Jesus of Hollywood," © 2004 Adele Reinhartz. Portions of this essay were originally published in The New Republic. Copyright 2004 The New Republic, LLC. Reprinted with permission.

Korn, Eugene and John Pawlikowski, "Commitment to Community: Interfaith Dialogue and Faithful Witness," © 2004 Eugene Korn and John Pawlikowski

Levine, Amy-Jill, "'First Take the Log Out of Your Own Eye: Different Viewpoints, Different Movies," © 2004 Amy-Jill Levine

Caldwell, Deborah, "Selling 'PASSION,'" © 2004 Deborah Caldwell

Ad Hoc Scholars Committee Report. Printed with the consent of the Ad Hoc Scholars Group.

Wieseltier, Leon, "The Worship of Blood," © 2004 Leon Wieseltier. Portions of this essay were originally published in The New Republic. Copyright 2004 The New Republic, LLC. Reprinted with permission.

Prothero, Stephen, "Jesus Nation, Catholic Christ," © 2004 Stephen Prothero. Portions of this essay were originally published in The Wall Street Journal, The New York Times Magazine, and Slate.com.

Martin, Steve, "Studio Script Notes on *The Passion*," Reprinted by permission of International Creative Management, Inc. Copyright © 2004 by Steve Martin. First appeared in *The New Yorker*.